MW00387601

On the German
Art of War

The Art of War

Series Editor, David T. Zabecki

On the German Art of War

TRUPPENFÜHRUNG

edited and translated by

Bruce Condell
David T. Zabecki

Foreword by James S. Corum

LYNNE
RIENNER
PUBLISHERS

BOULDER
LONDON

Published in the United States of America in 2001 by
Lynne Rienner Publishers, Inc.
1800 30th Street, Boulder, Colorado 80301

and in the United Kingdom by
Lynne Rienner Publishers, Inc.
3 Henrietta Street, Covent Garden, London WC2E 8LU

© 2001 by Lynne Rienner Publishers, Inc. All rights reserved

ISBN 1-55587-996-9

Printed and bound in the United States of America

This English translation of Truppenführung
is dedicated to the memory of
Colonel General Ludwig Beck (1880–1944),
soldier, scholar, German patriot,
and victim of the Third Reich

CONTENTS

FOREWORD

James S. Corum

There are several key elements to success on the battlefield: equipment, leadership, training, and doctrine. Of these elements, equipment (weaponry) and leadership receive by far the most attention from military historians. Training, although very important, is rarely discussed in detail. The element of doctrine is granted somewhat more attention than training, but not nearly as much as its real importance requires. This has long been a serious problem in the study of military operations.

World War II is dramatic proof of the importance of operational and tactical doctrine in war. During the first half of World War II the German Army rampaged across Europe, through Poland, France, Norway, the Low Countries, the Balkans, North Africa and deep into Russia in an unprecedented string of operational successes. In the second half of the World War as the *Wehrmacht* was pushed back on all fronts and eventually defeated, the German Army repeatedly demonstrated great tactical and operational competence in fighting enemies who outnumbered it. Despite the evil nature of the regime that it served, it must be admitted that the German Army of World War II was, man for man, one of the most effective fighting forces ever seen.

The possession of a superior tactical/operational doctrine was one of the things that made the German Army such a formidable and effective force during World War II. The campaign of 1940 and the defeat of France in six weeks provide a study in the importance of doctrine. For years after the 1940 campaign the German victory was explained by Germany's employment of masses of tanks, motorized forces and aircraft against an enemy bound to the Maginot Line and a defensive strategy. However, we know now that in terms of numbers of troops and weapons, the *Wehrmacht* in 1940 held few advantages. Indeed, it was often at a disadvantage against the Allied forces. The British-French coalition in 1940 had about as many divisions as the Germans. The French army had a considerable advantage in numbers and quality of tanks and a two-to-one advantage in artillery. In the air, the *Luftwaffe* had only a slight margin of superiority against the British and French in terms of the number and quality of aircraft available.

In short, the forces in 1940 were fairly evenly matched and the Germans did not have the clear margin of force superiority they enjoyed in 1914 when the French and British stopped the German offensive at the Marne.

What explains the German battlefield success in 1940 and in the first half of the war was a superior doctrine. The Germans had an effective and realistic doctrine of employing combined arms and maneuver warfare that gave them a tremendous advantage over their foes who, in the case of the British and French, had an operational doctrine more suitable for the conditions of 1918 rather than 1940. From France to North Africa to Russia the Germans demonstrated the value of an effective doctrine against more numerous, well-trained and well-equipped enemies. After learning some hard lessons on the battlefield, the British, Russians, and Americans modified their own tactical/operational doctrine which, not surprisingly, looked a great deal like the German doctrine. From 1942 on, the German advantage was eroded as the Allies used effective tactics and operational doctrine to beat down and overwhelm the *Wehrmacht.*

German Army *Regulation 300, Truppenführung,* written in 1933, is one of the most important expressions of doctrine in military history. *Truppenführung* served as the primary guidelines for tactics and the conduct of operations for the German Army from its publication until the end of World War II. It is, on the whole, a remarkable document. It is a very effective presentation of the concepts of modern maneuver warfare worked out by the German army in the years after World War I. Yet, while outlining the concepts of maneuver warfare that would find their ultimate expression in the *Blitzkrieg* campaigns of 1939–1942, there is almost as much weight in the regulation devoted to the conduct of defensive operations. The opening chapter that describes the characteristics and requirements of good military leadership can stand alone as a classic document on officership.

As the editors/translators point out, *Truppenführung* is not really a revolutionary document. It stands firmly in the tradition of Clausewitz, Moltke, and Seeckt as an expression of the German way of war. It is essentially a synthesis of the best operational and tactical thought in the German tradition. *Truppenführung* effectively incorporated weapons introduced in World War I, such as tanks, trucks, armored cars, and aircraft, into the German tradition of maneuver warfare and tactical flexibility.

As the editors also point out, some sections of *Truppenführung* were superseded shortly after its publications by developments in weapons and tactics. *Truppenführung* mentioned tanks and tank brigades but did not discuss *Panzer* divisions, which weren't developed until 1935 in Germany. However, the *Panzer* division was more than just a tank force. It owed its effectiveness in battle to its employment as a balanced, combined arms unit. The employment of combined arms was one of the core principles of *Truppenführung* and German doctrine.

One of the strengths of German doctrine was the process by which it was created and adapted. German doctrine was less a product of individual genius than of extensive debate and discussion within the General Staff and a policy of testing doctrinal concepts against the experience of war and exercises. Doctrine was not sacrosanct, and the General Staff and army leadership had no problem discarding and adapting parts of *Truppenführung* when necessary. For example, when *Truppenführung* was written the concept of mixing cavalry and motorized troops in cavalry divisions was standard practice in the doctrine of all the major powers. However, in late 1932 and into 1933 the German Army tested the doctrinal concept of combining cavalry and motorized troops in a series of divisional exercises. The concept of the combined cavalry/motorized force, which looked great on paper, turned out to be a flop in reality. Horse-mounted troops could simply not keep up with motorized troops and the problems of logistics and coordination between such different forces were too much to overcome. At this point the cavalry enthusiastically embraced motorization and began the conversion to motorized/mechanized divisions. The cavalry operations described in *Truppenführung* were rendered obsolete. It is illustrative that the Germans would test and discard tactics and operational concepts found wanting while the French army, at that time regarded as the best in the world, failed to test doctrine in realistic conditions. The French Army employed several of the cavalry/motorized divisions in 1940 that the Germans had found deficient in 1932.

David Zabecki and Bruce Condell have performed a sterling service to the study of military history by providing a full and readable translation of *Truppenführung*. They have done much more than just translate an important military document. In their opening essay and in their extensive notes, Zabecki and Condell provide a first-rate scholarly commentary that sets *Truppenführung* into the context of the German military tradition and its role as the primary doctrine of the German army in World War II. The editors guide the reader through the strengths and weaknesses of *Truppenführung* and of the German approach to war. As they rightly point out, while the German military leadership excelled at the tactical and operational level of war, they demonstrated a poor grasp of strategy. Apparently, there were some parts of Clausewitz that the German General Staff just didn't get in the years after the death of Count von Moltke.

For the U.S. military, *Truppenführung* has been a very influential document since its publication. Much of the U.S. Army doctrine published in 1941 was taken directly from *Truppenführung*. Much of the post–World War II army doctrine was heavily influenced by the German experience of

World War II and the German tradition of maneuver warfare. Adapting the
German tradition also played a central role in the development and publication of the U.S. Army's *AirLand Battle* operational doctrine developed in
the 1970s and 1980s.

Doctrine is just as important as an element of battlefield success today
as it was in 1940. The rapid and decisive victory of the U.S. and coalition
forces against the large and well-equipped Iraqi Army in the 1991 Gulf War
cannot simply be attributed to superior weapons. The AirLand Battle doctrine of the U.S. military, a doctrine largely based on the German military
tradition, had a lot to do with the lopsided battlefield victory. For fifteen
years the U.S. Army had trained hard and prepared to fight the Soviet
Union with a highly flexible maneuver warfare doctrine. Rather than fighting the Soviets, the U.S. force used its maneuver warfare doctrine against
an Iraqi army in strong defensive positions, trained for the defense and following a rigid defensive doctrine. The U.S. plan, based on combined arms
and rapid maneuver, worked impressively well with surprisingly few losses
as the Iraqi army was annihilated in a four-day campaign.

If one wants to do more than a cursory examination of a historical subject, one should try to go to the most important original documents. Yet, all
too often, some of the most important documents are not easily available.
Indeed, it's hard to find *Truppenführung* in the original German. This
excellent and scholarly translation of *Truppenführung* is an important step
in developing a better historical picture of the German army in modern history for a broad audience that wishes to study military history and operations in some depth but does not know fluent German. Condell and
Zabecki's work in this book ranks with Dan Hughes's excellent translation
of Moltke's writings as a major contribution to the field.

In many respects, like much of Clausewitz's *On War, Truppenführung*
is a historical period piece. However, there is much about the nature of
operations, of leadership, and even of combat tactics in this book that is as
valid today as it was when it was written almost 70 years ago. The importance of operational doctrine as a component of battlefield success has not
lessened in 70 years; it may have even increased. Although weapons and
technology have dramatically changed, the nature of operations and the
operational level of war have not changed. Fog and friction are still present
on the battlefield, despite various new technologies. Commanders still have
to make life-and-death decisions and carry out the mission in times of
stress and confusion. There is still a tension between firepower and maneuver, and both are employed to gain the victory. The goal of the commander
is still to destroy the enemy armed forces. Combined arms are still the
foundation of tactics and the commander who can most effectively employ
all of his forces will win.

This translation offers some important insights into the nature of operations and tactics, and I would strongly recommend this book to military officers and NCOs.

James S. Corum
Professor of Comparative Military Studies,
USAF School of Advanced Airpower Studies
Lt. Col. US Army Reserve

ACKNOWLEDGMENTS

We wish to express our sincere thanks to Dr. and Mrs. Ekkhardt Guth and to Wolfram Berger for their support in preparing the first series of rough drafts in English, to Dr. Bernard Graf and Marlies Schweigler for their meticulous corrections and textual suggestions, and to Nicole Condell for her indispensable help and unlimited patience in preparing the text. Thanks also go to Ernst Hofmann, a veteran of Monte Cassino who served in the *Luftwaffe* 3rd Parachute Division, and to Colonel G. F. Baath, a former signals reconnaissance officer in the *Deutsche Afrika Korps*, for their most helpful comments and encouragement. Finally, we wish to thank Robert Citino for vetting the English text and the appendixes, and for offering many helpful historical insights.

Bruce Condell
David T. Zabecki

Nothing could be more dangerous than to follow sudden inspirations, however intelligent or brilliant they may appear, without pursuing them to the logical conclusions, or to indulge in wishful thinking, however sincere our purposes. We need officers capable of following systematically the path of logical argument to its conclusion, with disciplined intellect, strong enough in character and nerve to execute what the intellect dictates.

—General Ludwig Beck
From a speech on the
125th anniversary of the
Kriegsakademie,
10 October 1935

EDITORS' INTRODUCTION

Armies are reflections of the societies from which they are drawn. Americans, with their material abundance and penchant for technical solutions, have produced armies that tend to rely upon sophisticated weaponry and what is unquestionably the best and most lavish logistical system in military history. Likewise, the German armies of the last 150 years have mirrored the German national traits of organization and discipline. In several key respects, however, the German Army that reinvented itself from the ashes of World War I, and came very close to winning World War II in the face of overwhelming odds, was very different from the society from which it came.

To a certain degree, there is a level of validity to many of the commonly believed characteristics of the German society and character. These include an almost unquestioning acceptance of authority, social rigidity, and an intense preoccupation with record keeping, paperwork and all forms of bureaucratic procedure. Nowhere are these characteristics so prominent as in the German civil service. And while the U.S. Army tends to reproduce faithfully most of the worst features of the U.S. civil service, the German Army was remarkably free of such afflictions.

The post–World War I German Army, therefore, was very successful in retaining and reinforcing within its own social framework those features of the broader German society that would most contribute to the success of combat operations—while at the same time eliminating those features that would tend to hinder effective operations. Despite the popular stereotypes, reinforced by countless Hollywood movies and television programs, the common German soldier of World War II was anything but stupid and unimaginative, and his officers and NCOs were neither machinelike nor inflexible autocrats.

The keys to understanding the psychology, philosophy, and social values of the German Army that entered World War II are to be found in the pages of the manual titled *Truppenführung (Unit Command)*. The manual was published as the German Army's *Heeresdienstvorschrift 300* in 1933 (Part 1) and 1934 (Part 2).[1] It is as important to the understanding of

German military operations as *Field Manual 100-5 Operations*, or *Field Service Regulations* are for American and British operations respectively. In many ways *Truppenführung* was a modern version of Sun Tzu's *The Art of War*. According to Professor Williamson Murray, "It remains the most influential doctrinal manual ever written." And, "It also represents one of the most thoughtful examinations of the conduct of operations and leadership ever written."[2]

The German Army fought World War I with a set of field service regulations issued in 1905. Although that body of doctrine drew heavily from the ideas of Major General Carl von Clausewitz and Field Marshal Helmuth von Moltke the Elder, the 1905 manual bore the clear and heavy imprint of General Alfred von Schlieffen, Chief of the Great General Staff from 1891 to 1906. Despite the great credibility Clausewitz's theories enjoy to this day, many in the pre-1945 German Army either rejected or ignored some of his most important concepts, including the inherently superior strength of the defense and the relationship between war and politics. One Clausewitzian concept almost universally accepted was the idea of the battle of annihilation (*Vernichtungsschlacht*).

Because of Germany's geographic position in Europe, German military planners generally believed they had to be able to fight a two-front war. To do this successfully, they would have to fight and defeat their enemies one after the other in quick succession, rather than simultaneously. That meant short and violent wars, decided by completely destroying an enemy—or each in turn—through a single decisive battle. Schlieffen became the apostle of the annihilation principle (*Vernichtungsprinzip*). Some historians think he took the concept far beyond what Clausewitz intended, others believe he was only faithfully echoing The Philosopher of War. Either way, the annihilation principle was the bedrock German warfighting doctrine in 1914. World War I, however, never worked out the way the Germans had planned it.

Despite the traditional image of gridlock, stagnation, and trench warfare in World War I, the period between 1914 and 1918 saw the birth of most of the tactical concepts we currently associate with modern warfare. On the defense from 1915 to 1917, the Germans pioneered and mastered the concepts of flexible defense, defense-in-depth, and reverse-slope defense. On the offense in 1918, they perfected the techniques of fluid, nonlinear infiltration tactics supported by neutralizing artillery fire. After the end of World War I, when General Hans von Seeckt became the head of the Germany Army, the *Reichswehr* studied and analyzed the developments of the Great War very carefully.

The most important product of the Seeckt Reforms was the new manual for tactical doctrine. *H.Dv.487, Führung und Gefecht der verbundenen Waffen* (*Command and Combat of the Combined Arms*—universally called "*Das FuG*"). Published as Part 1 in 1921 and Part 2 in 1923, it truly was a remarkable piece of work. Unlike the post–World War I doctrinal manuals of almost every other country, *Das FuG* completely disregarded positional, or trench warfare (*Stellungskrieg*). Instead, it focused on mobile warfare (*Bewegungskrieg*) while at the same time adopting many of the tactical techniques developed between 1914 and 1918. *Das FuG* also restored the emphasis to the annihilation principle that had faded during the war.[3] Other Schlieffen concepts embedded in *Das FuG* included the primacy of the offensive; encirclement combined with frontal action as the path to the best results; and defense as a purely temporary prelude to the offense.[4]

Truppenführung, which was written primarily by Generals Ludwig Beck, Werner von Fritsch, and Otto von Stulpnaegel, updated the basic concepts in *Das FuG* to bring them into line with the rapidly emerging potentials of motorized warfare, aviation, and electronic communications. The underlying mobile and offensive focus of *Das FuG* remained unchanged,[5] and entire paragraphs and sections were carried over into *Truppenführung.*[6] One very significant addition to the new manual, however, was the Introduction section, with its fifteen highly philosophical paragraphs that set the manual's tone.

The idea of winning a war through a single decisive battle is a purely tactical notion. It is the very antithesis of operational art and the operational level of war, for which sequential operations and cumulative effects are the keys. Although the U.S. military and NATO recognized the concept of the operational level of war only in the mid-1980s, operational thinking has been evolving slowly but steadily since the time of Napoleon. Without using the specific term, Clausewitz in *On War* clearly identified a level of war between the tactical and strategic. The Soviets get the credit for much of the theoretical work on the operational level prior to World War II, but *Truppenführung* clearly delineated Clausewitz's concepts of the tactical and operational levels.[7]

Author Shimon Naveh called *Truppenführung* "The best evidence confirming the existence of operational cognition prior to the year 1938."[8] Despite this recognition, *Truppenführung*'s focus was almost exclusively tactical. With the rejection of sequential operations—which they equated with war of attrition (*Materialschlacht*)—German military doctrine remained firmly tied to the tactical level. Thus, many historians have argued that what passed for operational art in the German Army was really little more than tactics on a very large scale.

One of the most important concepts of the post–World War I German military system was that of *Auftragstaktik*. The term can be translated loosely to "mission-type orders," but there is no real English equivalent that adequately conveys the full meaning. *Auftragstaktik* is based on the principle that a commander should tell his subordinates what to do and when to do it by, but not necessarily tell them how to do it. In accomplishing their missions, subordinate commanders are given a wide degree of latitude and are expected to exercise great initiative.

Prior to World War I, the German Army operated under a principle known as *Weisungsführung* (leadership by directive), which was similar to *Auftragstaktik*, but only entrusted commanders down to the army level—or sometimes the corps—with broad discretionary powers in the execution of their missions. *Auftragstaktik*, which was a post–World War I creation of *Das FuG* and carried forward into *Truppenführung*, extended that principle down to the lowest squad leader and even, when necessary, to the individual soldier. Writing in his 1925 *Observations of the Chief of the Army Command*, von Seeckt noted:

> The principal thing now is to increase the responsibilities of the individual man, particularly his independence of action, and thereby to increase the efficiency of the entire army. . . . The limitations imposed by exterior circumstances causes us to give the mind more freedom of activity, with the profitable result of increasing the ability of the individual.[9]

For *Auftragstaktik* to work, a subordinate leader or even a common soldier given a mission must fully understand his commander's intent—and in most cases, the intent of the next higher commander. This, of course, implies that the subordinate leader must understand "why." If he doesn't understand, he has the obligation to ask. Conversely, the superior leader issuing the order has the obligation to explain. Such a process does not fit the popular stereotype of military organizations in general, nor especially is it characteristic of German society. Thus we find in *Truppenführung* passages that would still be considered radical in many of the world's armies today:

> 2. The conduct of war is subject to continual development. New weapons dictate ever changing forms. Their appearance must be anticipated and their influence duly evaluated. Then they must be placed into service quickly. . . .
> 4. Lessons in the conduct of war cannot be compiled exhaustively in the form of regulations. The principles enunciated must be applied in accordance with the situation. . . .
> 6. The command of an army and its subordinate units requires leaders capable of judgement, with clear vision and foresight, and the ability to make independent and decisive decisions, and to carry them out unwaveringly and positively. . . .
> 15. Every man, from the youngest soldier upward, must be required at all times and in all situations to commit his whole mental, spiritual, and physical strength. Only in this way will the full force of a unit be brought to bear in a decisive action.

Although traditional German deference to higher authority and preference for well-defined procedures are the very antithesis of *Auftragstaktik*, the German Army made it work to a degree unsurpassed by any other army in history. Oddly enough, the term itself never appears in print in *Truppenführung,* but the concept is clearly embedded throughout the manual. See, for example, Paragraphs 6, 9, 10, 15, 36, 37, 73, 74, 75, and 76.

Paragraph 15 was especially significant. When von Seeckt formed the 100,000-man *Reichswehr*, he envisioned a dual-purpose force. Initially it was to serve as a small, professional, high-quality army, an *Eliteheer*. But it also could serve as a cadre army, a force to provide the leadership corps of a greatly expanded army of the future. Thus, Seeckt also was designing a *Führerheer*—an army of leaders. By adding Paragraph 15, the authors of *Truppenführung* were putting all the members of the *Reichswehr* on notice. On 1 October 1934, shortly after the publication of Part 2, Hitler ordered the secret expansion of the *Reichswehr* to three times its size. Conscription was reintroduced in March 1935, establishing an objective base strength of thirty-eight divisions and approximately 600,000 men.[10] By October 1943 the German officer corps stood at 246,453, a sixty-four-fold expansion in ten years.[11]

The rapid expansion of the officer corps naturally created some institutional stress and social tensions, but the German Army handled them relatively well. Like the British military and society before 1914, the rigid class structure of German society had placed solid barriers between the officers and the enlisted men of the World War I German Army. Facing defeat in 1918 after four years of war, those social barriers became the fault lines that split the German Army, as the country itself went through political and social revolution. After the war, the Seeckt Reforms set out to eliminate from the army many of those barriers, in order to form a more cohesive fighting force based on trust, mutual respect, and genuine feelings of comradeship—regardless of social background or the level of one's military responsibilities and authority. Thus, in *Truppenführung* we find passages such as:

> 7. An officer is in every sense a leader and a teacher. In addition to his knowledge of men and his sense of justice, he must be distinguished by superior knowledge and experience, by moral excellence, by self-discipline, and by high courage. . . .
> 12. Leaders must live with their troops and share with them their dangers and deprivations, their joys and sorrows. Only thus can they acquire a first-hand knowledge of the combat capabilities and needs of their soldiers.

First *Das FuG* and then *Truppenführung* were largely successful in redefining the German Army's social landscape. Writing after World War II in his classic book, *Panzer Battles*, Major General F. W. von Mellenthin noted:

> In Venice, while dining at a hotel, I surprised the Italians by having my driver at the same table. While normally officers and other ranks took their meals separately, it was a matter of course for us to eat together like this when an officer and a private were all on their own. In contrast to 1918 the inner knowledge that officers and enlisted men belonged together was never shaken, and even in 1945 there were no signs of rot in the German Army.[12]

Chapter XIV, Armored Combat Vehicles, and Chapter XV, Air Forces, are among the most interesting in *Truppenführung*. Both chapters were updated and carried over from *Das FuG,* which was written right after the Versailles Treaty specifically restricted Germany from possessing such arms. In the brief introduction to *Das FuG*, von Seeckt justified their inclusion.

> These Regulations are based on the strength, armament, and equipment of an army suitable for a first class modern military power, and not on the present German Army of 100,000 men, as organized in accordance with the treaty of peace. Only by keeping alive the memory of the combat arms of which we are now deprived (air service, heavy artillery, tanks, etc.) will we be able to find ways and means of sustaining combat against an enemy with modern equipment. The lack of these arms must not lead to hesitation in the attack.

Even *Truppenführung,* which came out several years before the formation of the first *Panzer* division and the official formation of the *Luftwaffe,* noted, "This manual assumes strength, arms, and equipment in an army with unlimited resources." The first three German *Panzer* divisions were formed in the fall of 1935, but they were not fully operational until the Great Fall Maneuver of September 1937.[13] Until then, future General Staff officers attending the War Academy (*Kriegsakademie*) were still using a notional *Panzer* division structure in their exercises. (See Appendix B.) On 1 October 1934, Hitler ordered the secret creation of the *Luftwaffe*. When Hitler publicly announced the existence of the *Luftwaffe* on 11 March 1935, the Germans already had 1,888 aircraft of all types in service. After recalling reserve pilots and ground crew from the German national airlines, Luft Hansa, the German Air Force grew to 20,000 officers and men within a matter of weeks.

Truppenführung was written in anticipation of emerging weapons technology. In Paragraph 783, for example, the manual notes the expected introduction of air-to-air radio communications between combat aircraft.

Portions of the manual, however, clearly were outdated by 1939. The Germans did start to update *Truppenführung*. In January 1938 the *Kriegsakademie* circulated a draft of an updated manual to be called *Kriegsführung (War Command)*. The new manual would have been the first German attempt to integrate the operations of all three services in a single comprehensive statement of doctrine. When World War II started, however, work on *Kriegsführung* came to a halt, and the manual was never completed.[14] As interesting as it might be to contemplate what the final version of *Kriegsführung* might have looked like, *Truppenführung* was the manual the German Army fought with through 1945.

The popular notions about the German Army focus on their reputation as the masters of offensive maneuver. They were, however, skillful and tenacious defenders when the situation required. As already noted, the Germans in World War I developed most of the concepts we associate with defense on the modern battlefield. And as Naveh noted, *Truppenführung* "reflected a balanced approach to offensive and defensive, seeing both as essential and complementary forms of operational maneuver."[15] World War II German commanders, especially Field Marshal Walther Model, executed masterful defenses again and again. The principles laid out in Paragraphs 564 and 566 read almost like a script for the 1944 battle of the Hürtgen Forest, where the outnumbered and under-equipped defenders inflicted almost 25,000 casualties on the U.S. Army in a three-month period.

German tactical thinking did not stagnate with the publication of the manual, of course. In *Panzer Battles,* von Mellenthin noted an intense struggle within the German General Staff in the 1935 to 1937 period over the use of armor. Beck, then the Chief of the General Staff, apparently wanted to follow French doctrine and tie the tanks down to close support of the infantry. Werner von Fritsch and Heinz Guderian were among those who opposed that idea.[16] Guderian's own postwar memoirs tend to paint Beck—who by then was dead and not able to defend himself—as a narrow-minded defeatist with no operational comprehension.[17] And, *Truppenführung*'s Paragraph 339 does seem to indicate infantry and armor actions that are coordinated but not combined. The true combination of infantry and armor in the German Army, however, did not take place until after the 1940 France Campaign, when Colonel Hermann Balck recommended the formation of combined infantry-armor teams.[18] As Professor Robert Citino points out, Beck became the Chief of the General Staff in 1933 (then called the *Truppenamt*), and the first *Panzer* divisions were formed in 1935. Thus, Guderian's claim to have waged a "long, drawn-out fight" with Beck over the creation of the *Panzer* divisions can only be sheer exaggeration at best.[19]

Artillery was an area in which *Truppenführung* anticipated future developments, but with somewhat less success. The manual mentions heavy and long-range flat-firing artillery (Paragraphs 417, 605), although in 1934 the German Army had no such guns. Because of the devastating effect of German artillery in World War I, Article 164 of the Versailles Treaty limited the *Reichswehr* to a total of 288 artillery tubes, none larger than 105mm.[20] *Truppenführung* incorporated many of the artillery lessons of World War I, such as using gas for counterbattery fire to neutralize the enemy guns (Paragraph 358). On the other hand, the manual rejected predicted (as opposed to observed) artillery fire (Paragraph 338), although Colonel Georg Bruchmüller demonstrated its effectiveness beyond all doubt during the German offensives of 1918. In 1944 and 1945, the U.S. Army proved with a vengeance the effectiveness of these fire direction techniques in mobile warfare.

Truppenführung anticipated the advent of self-propelled guns (Paragraph 339), but German artillery never developed to anywhere near its full potential. It remained a constant tactical weakness that cost the Germans dearly on the battlefield. The *Panzer* divisions of World War II had self-propelled guns, but as late as 1944 the infantry divisions remained woefully under-gunned, and the bulk of their artillery was horse-drawn. Relying heavily on the combination of tactical air power and tanks, the formula worked well enough for the Germans in Poland and France. It worked far less well in the vast expanses of Russia, where the *Luftwaffe* could not be overhead, everywhere, all the time. The Soviet Army, meanwhile, started World War II with 67,000 tubes, and ended the war with some 90 artillery divisions and several artillery corps. Back on the western front in 1944 and 1945, the Germans did not have the artillery to fall back on for fire support after the Allies achieved first air superiority, and then air supremacy.[21]

Combat intelligence was a weak area for the Germans. Although *Truppenführung* did stress the importance of intelligence in the decision making process, it also stressed that uncertainty was the rule in combat. Commanders seldom would be justified in waiting for complete or perfect intelligence. Commanders and staffs, then, were to consider the enemy's most dangerous course of action (Paragraph 62). By contrast, American and NATO military staffs today consider both the enemy's most dangerous and most likely courses of action in their decision making process.[22] In focusing entirely on the enemy's most dangerous course of action, German commanders and staffs tended to ignore his most probable course of action. Since the latter threat is far more difficult to estimate than the former, the role of intelligence diminished in the German decision-making process.[23]

Logistics was yet another major blind area in German military thinking. Because sustainment requirements increase with time, weaknesses in an army's logistical system cause far greater problems at the operational level of war than at the tactical. Although the Germans were masters of using railway systems for large-scale troop movements, most other elements of their logistics system were not robust. This hurt the Germans severely in both World Wars. Two of *Truppenführung's* twenty-three chapters deal with logistics matters, but many of those who managed these functions on a divisional staff were not even soldiers; rather, they were military civil servants (*Wehrmachtsbeamten*). Captain Harlan N. Hartness attended the *Kriegsakademie* from 1935 to 1937 as an American exchange officer. In his after action report to the U.S. Army he noted that the instructor-to-student ratio at the school was 1:20 for tactics, but only 1:120 for supply and 1:240 for transportation.[24]

Truppenführung was not a perfect body of doctrine by any means. It paid little attention to the political and strategic levels of war, largely ignoring Clausewitz's critical analysis of those dimensions. This level of thinking was almost completely absent in the German military systems of World Wars I and II.[25] And they paid the price accordingly. The German officer education system, however, simply was not designed to produce senior commanders like George C. Marshall, Dwight D. Eisenhower, Alan F. Brooke, or Colin Powell. Thus, Germany produced excellent and even brilliant field commanders like Erwin Rommel, who had very little understanding of broader strategy. Erich von Manstein and Albert Kesselring were the notable exceptions among the World War II field commanders; and Beck's personal writings indicate that he understood very clearly the relationship between policy and war as Clausewitz defined it.[26]

Despite its shortcomings, *Truppenführung* was a doctrinal manual far ahead of its time. Its purpose was not to give German military leaders a "cookbook" on how to win battles, but rather it was designed to give them a set of intellectual tools to be applied to complex and ever-unique warfighting situations. As James Corum points out, the very word *doctrine* (*Doktrin*) is not at all common in the German language; and when used it does not imply the sense of the "proper way to do things," as Americans tend to apply it to tactics.[27] Commenting on the *Kriegsakademie* training philosophy for future General Staff officers, Captain Hartness wrote:

> The solution arrived at may not be the perfect or the best one, but if it is a workable solution, capable of execution with the means at hand, it is a solution which will stand the test of combat and such is given equal credit with other solutions, which in more or less detail may appear better. The decision, the reaching of a workable solution is the objective. Seldom in war is the paper perfect solution achieved.[28]

Following one year behind Hartness as a student exchange officer, Captain (later Lieutenant General) Albert C. Wedemeyer put it even more succinctly: "Better a faulty plan or decision permeated with boldness, daring, and decisiveness, than a perfect plan enmeshed in uncertainty."[29]

Although *Truppenführung* was already ten years old by the middle of World War II, it still contained many of the seeds of the battlefield innovations of some of Germany's greatest commanders. Many people believe, for example, that the exceptionally successful expedient of using the 88mm antiaircraft gun against tanks was devised by Rommel while fighting the British in North Africa. It certainly took the British by surprise. Yet a good seven years earlier, the manual clearly stated:

> 812. The use of antiaircraft weapons in ground operations reduces their effectiveness in their primary role and should be limited to exceptional situations. This use is justified only for defensive fire against combat vehicles at close ranges.

Truppenführung was not a manual on military staff operations and procedures. The German Army had the best organized and most highly trained staffs in both world wars. And although Annexes 8 and 9 of *Truppenführung* deal briefly with the formats for combat reports and the maintenance of situation maps and war diaries, the primary reference for such procedures was an entirely separate manual; *H.Dv.92, Handbuch für den Generalstabsdienst im Kriege (Handbook for General Staff Service in War)*. It was the equivalent of the U.S. Army's *FM 101-5, Staff Organization and Procedures.*

Truppenführung and *Das FuG* were not the German Army's only warfighting manuals, of course. They were what we today would call the "capstone" doctrinal manuals. Immediately after the publication of *Das FuG* in 1921, the German Army issued a series of far more detailed tactical manuals, geared toward the operations of specific arms and smaller units. These manuals included: *Ausbildungsvorschrift für die Infantrie (Infantry Training Regulations); Ausbildungsvorschrift für die Artillerie (Artillery Training Regulations): Feldbefestigungsvorschriften (Regulations for Field Fortifications);Der Nachrichtendienst im Reichsheer (The Signal Service in the National Army):* and *Ausbildung der Schützengruppe (Training of the Rifle Squad)*. Many of those manuals had more than one volume. *Ausbildungsvorschrift für die Infantrie* alone ran five volumes.[30]

Truppenführung was widely influential, both in its own time and long after World War II. Translated into English by U.S. Army Intelligence in the late 1930s, *Truppenführung* greatly influenced the 1940 and 1944 editions of *FM 100-5*. The 1940 edition was organized in a very similar manner (see Appendix D), and its writers even lifted entire sentences from *Truppenführung*.[31] Although many of the basic concepts in the two manuals are the same, however, *FM 100-5* often fell far short of the true spirit of *Truppenführung*.

In the years immediately following World War II, the Americans continued to pay serious attention to German military thought. In the early 1950s, the Historical Office of the U.S. Army in Europe (USAREUR) commissioned former Chief of the General Staff, General Franz Halder, and a group of other former German generals and General Staff officers to analyze the 1949 edition of *FM 100-5*. Halder's committee produced a detailed, paragraph-by-paragraph analysis that ran 155 typewritten pages. The first three chapters of the report were a general appraisal of *FM 100-5*. Although Halder and his team were supposed to be talking about the American manual, they were really expanding on and providing insight into the thinking that underlay *Truppenführung*. Those three chapters (reproduced in Appendix E) highlight the key differences between German and U.S. military thinking.

Thought about large-scale and conventional military operations atrophied in the West during the years of the Cold War, with its long nuclear shadow, and the Vietnam period of low-intensity and unconventional warfare. Following the shock of the defeat in Vietnam, classical military thought entered a period of renaissance in the U.S. military.[32] Many of the classical German concepts—both those in *Truppenführung* and those that *Truppenführung* ignored—found their way into the editions of *FM 100-5* that appeared in 1984, 1986, and 1993. These included Clausewitz's concepts of the political dimension and the operational level of war, and the notion of the decisive point and the center of gravity (*Schwerpunkt*). They also included the *Truppenführung* concepts of the commander's intent (*Absicht*), initiative and independently thinking leaders, and mission orders. Instructional material used at the U.S. Army Command and General Staff College during the period even used the word *Auftragstaktik*. Many U.S. commanders, however, remain far more comfortable talking about *Auftragstaktik* than practicing it.

Although the Germans declassified Part 1 of *Truppenführung* as early as November 1935, the Americans did not declassify their English translation of Part 1 until February 1957. Known as *Report No. 14,507*, it is available in typewritten form in some U.S. military history libraries. The translation of Part 2 was still classified for some inexplicable reason as late as the end of year 2000. Since many of the tactical and operational concepts in *Truppenführung* did not exist in the pre–World War II English-speaking military world, they were misconstrued in the original translations. The original translations also were very uneven and appear to have been the work of multiple translators.

In this new translation, the objective has been to use language and terms that today's reader would understand, without superimposing concepts that did not exist 65 years ago. One problem has been the fact that some of the terms used in *Truppenführung* changed slightly between the time of the manual's publication and World War II. One of the best examples is the German term for an infantry mortar. *Truppenführung* throughout uses the term *Minenwerfer*, which was the term used in World War I when trench mortars were primarily combat engineer (pioneer infantry) weapons. By the time *Truppenführung* was written, mortars were clearly infantry weapons, but the old term was still in use. By World War II, the designation for the weapon had shifted to *Granatenwerfer*.

Interestingly, *Truppenführung* uses the concept of the center of gravity much differently than Clausewitz defined it. As the term *Schwerpunkt* is used in the German original in Paragraphs 323 and 389, it means the point of main effort. As it is used in Paragraph 358, it means the decision point. To Clausewitz, however, the *Schwerpunkt* and the decision point (*Entscheidungsstelle*) were two different things.[33] The 1986 edition of *FM 100-5* also used the two concepts interchangeably. The 1993 edition corrected the error by stating clearly; "Decisive points are not centers of gravity; they are keys to getting at centers of gravity."[34]

German and English are related tongues, but they employ very different notions of style and expression. As author Richard Simpkin once noted, when translating from German to English, "one has to dissect out the underlying thought and express it in a radically different way."[35] In carrying out this translation, we used the principle of dynamic equivalence rather than a word-for-word translation.

Throughout this translation we have kept the paragraph and the subparagraph breaks as they were in the original manual. The original manual also had twelve sets of annexes. For the most part these annexes contained organizational and distribution system schematics, and equipment technical data tables. Much of this information, such as in the tank, aircraft, and communications equipment tables, was already obsolete by 1939. In the interest of space, we have not translated and reproduced these annexes, with the exception of Annex 8 and Annex 9, mentioned above. Wherever the main text makes a direct reference to an annex, an accompanying footnote will explain and summarize the relevant information.

Truppenführung provided the doctrinal foundation for the victories of Hitler's armies in the first half of World War II. In one of history's greatest ironies, the manual's principal author was one of the most important military figures in the opposition to Hitler. In 1938 Beck resigned as Chief of the General Staff, in protest against Hitler's plans for a war of aggression. A key leader in the July 1944 bomb plot against Hitler's life, Beck was arrested immediately after the failed coup. He committed suicide before he could be brought to trial.

Notes

1. Abbreviated as *H.Dv.300*.

2. Williamson Murray, "Leading the Troops: A German Manual of 1933," *Marine Corps Gazette*, September 1999, p. 95.

3. Robert Citino, *Path to Blitzkrieg* (Lynne Rienner: 1999), p. 10.

4. Jehuda L. Wallach, *The Dogma of the Battle of Annihilation: The Theories of Clausewitz and Schlieffen and Their Impact on the German Conduct of Two World Wars* (Greenwood Press: 1986), pp. 219–234.

5. From 1936 to 1938, Captain (later Lieutenant General) Albert C. Wedemeyer attended the German *Kriegsakademie* as an American exchange officer. He reported that during the two year course of instruction, his class was given less than ten defensive tactical problems, out of a total of more than seventy. None of the exercise problems involved position or trench warfare. Albert C. Wedemeyer, *Report No. 15,999, German General Staff School,* 4 August 1938, p. 140 (National Archives and Records Administration, Record Group 165, Box 1113), hereafter *Wedemeyer Report.*

6. James S. Corum, *The Roots of Blitzkrieg: Hans von Seeckt and German Military Reform* (University Press of Kansas: 1992), p. 199.

7. Murray, p. 95.

8. Shimon Naveh, *In Pursuit of Military Excellence: The Evolution of Operational Theory* (Frank Cass: 1997), p. 116.

9. Cited in Citino, p. 57.

10. Herbert Rosinski, *The German Army* (Preager: 1966), pp. 220–227.

11. Jürgen Förster, "The Dynamics of Volksgemeinschaft: Effectiveness of the German Military Establishment in the Second World War," in *Military Effectiveness, Volume III, The Second World War,* edited by Allan R. Millet and Williamson Murray (Allen & Unwin: 1988), pp. 207–208.

12. F.W. von Mellenthin, *Panzer Battles* (University of Oklahoma Press: 1956), p. 46.

13. Citino, pp. 236–239.

14. Wallach, p. 212.

15. Naveh, p. 117.

16. von Mellenthin, p. xvi.

17. Heinz Guderian, *Panzer Leader* (Easton Press: 1990), pp. 32–33.

18. von Mellenthin, pp. 19–20.

19. Citino, p. 231.

20. David T. Zabecki, *Steel Wind: Colonel Georg Bruchmüller and the Birth of Modern Artillery* (Praeger: 1994), p. 106.

21. Zabecki, pp. 108–110, 129–133.

22. Department of the Army, *FM 101-5, Staff Organization and Operations* (U.S. Government Printing Office: 1997), p. 5–6.

23. Geoffrey P. Megargee, *Inside Hitler's High Command* (University Press of Kansas: 2000), pp. 108-109. Also, *Wedemeyer Report*, p. 78.

24. Harlan N. Hartness, *Report No. 15,260, Report on German General Staff School, Staff Methods, and Tactical Doctrine,* 3 May 1937, p. 7 (National Archives and Records Administration, Record Group 165, Box 1113), hereafter *Hartness Report.*

25. Murray, p. 95.

26. Ludwig Beck, *Studien*, edited by Hans Speidel (Koehler Verlag: 1955), pp. 60–63.

27. Corum, p. xv.

28. *Hartness Report,* p. 149.

29. *Wedemeyer Report*, p. 18.

30. Citino, pp. 11–12, 23.

31. Martin van Creveld, *Fighting Power: German and U.S. Army Performance, 1939-1945* (Greenwood: 1982), p. 131.

32. The U.S. Army's "rediscovery" of Clausewitz was spurred largely by the late Colonel Harry G. Summers, Jr., and his widely influential book, *On Strategy: The Vietnam War in Context.*

33. Carl von Clausewitz, *On War,* edited and translated by Michael Howard and Peter Paret (Princeton University Press: 1976), Book VIII, Chapter 4, pp. 595–597.

34. Department of the Army, *FM 100-5, Operations* (U.S. Government Printing Office: 1993), pp. 6–8.

35. Richard Simpkin, *Race to the Swift: Thoughts on Twenty-First Century Warfare* (Brassey's: 1985), p. 229.

Truppenführung,
Part I: 1933

Chief of the Army High Command
Reference: TA Nr. 3000/33 T 4   17 October 1933

Truppenführung (*Unit Command*) contains the basic principles for command, field service, and joint operations in war.

This manual assumes strength, arms, and equipment in an army with unlimited resources.

As far as this doctrine is applied to the training and deployment of units, consideration must be given to the limits set by peacetime conditions, by law, and by international treaty.

Any amendment of or addition to this manual must be authorized by me.

Freiherr von Hammerstein-Equord

INTRODUCTION

1. War is an art, a free and creative activity founded on scientific principles. It makes the very highest demands on the human personality.

2. The conduct of war is subject to continual development. New weapons dictate ever-changing forms. Their appearance must be anticipated and their influence evaluated. Then they must be placed into service quickly.

3. Combat situations are of an unlimited variety. They change frequently and suddenly and can seldom be assessed in advance. Incalculable elements often have a decisive influence. One's own will is pitted against the independent will of the enemy.* Friction (*Reibung*)† and errors are daily occurrences.

4. Lessons in the conduct of war cannot be exhaustively compiled in the form of regulations. The principles enunciated must be applied in accordance with the situation.

Simple actions, logically carried out, will lead most surely to the objective.

5. War subjects the individual to the most severe tests of his spiritual and physical endurance. For this reason, character counts more in war than does intellect.†† Many who distinguish themselves on the battlefield remain unnoticed in peacetime.

6. The command of an army and its subordinate units requires leaders capable of judgement, with clear vision and foresight, and the ability to make independent and decisive decisions and carry them out unwaveringly

---

*In *On War*, Book 1, Chapter 1, Clausewitz noted, "War is thus an act of force to compel our enemy to do our will."

†Clausewitz introduced the concept of friction on military operations in *On War*, Book 1, Chapter 7. "Friction is the only concept that more or less corresponds to the factors that distinguish real war from war on paper."

††In explaining the selection criteria for the *Kriegsakademie*, Hartness wrote, "And here let me emphasize that strength of character, will, is the attribute most highly valued" [*Hartness Report*, p. 3].

and positively. Such leaders must be impervious to the changes in the fortunes of war and possess full awareness of the high degree of responsibility placed on their shoulders.

7. An officer is in every sense a leader and a teacher. In addition to his knowledge of men and his sense of justice, he must be distinguished by superior knowledge and experience, by moral excellence, by self-discipline, and by high courage.

8. The example and personal bearing of officers and other soldiers who are responsible for leadership has a decisive effect on the troops. The officer, who in the face of the enemy displays coolness, decisiveness, and courage, carries his troops with him. He also must win their affections and earn their trust through his understanding of their feelings, their way of thinking, and through his selfless care for them.

Mutual trust is the surest foundation for discipline in times of need and danger.

9. Every leader in every situation must exert himself totally and not avoid responsibility. Willingness to accept responsibility is the most important quality of a leader. It should not, however, be based upon individualism without consideration of the whole, nor used as a justification for failure to carry out orders where seeming to know better may affect obedience. Independence of spirit must not become arbitrariness. By contrast, independence of action within acceptable boundaries is the key to great success.

10. The decisive factor, despite technology and weaponry, is the value of the individual soldier. The wider his experience in combat, the greater his importance.

The emptiness of the battlefield (*die Leere des Gefechtfleld*) requires soldiers who can think and act independently, who can make calculated, decisive, and daring use of every situation, and who understand that victory depends on each individual.

Training, physical fitness, selflessness, determination, self-confidence, and daring equip a man to master the most difficult situations.

11. The caliber of a leader and of the men determines the combat power (*Kampfkraft*) of a unit, which is augmented by the quantity, care, and maintenance of their weapons and equipment.

Superior combat power can compensate for inferior numbers. The greater this quality, the greater the force and mobility in war.

Superior leadership and superior unit readiness are guaranteed conditions for victory.

12. Leaders must live with their troops and share in their dangers and deprivations, their joys and sorrows. Only thus can they acquire a first-hand knowledge of the combat capabilities and needs of their soldiers.

The individual is a part of the whole and is not only responsible for himself alone, but also for his comrades. He who is capable of more than the others, who can achieve more, must guide and lead the inexperienced and the weak.

Out of such a foundation grows genuine comradeship, which is as important between the leaders and the men as it is among the men themselves.

13. Units that are only superficially held together, not bonded by long training and discipline, easily fail in moments of grave danger and under the pressure of unexpected events. From the very beginning of a war, therefore, great importance must be attached to creating and maintaining inner strength and to the discipline and training of units.

It is the duty of every officer to act immediately and with any means at his disposal—even the most severe—against a breakdown in discipline or acts of mutiny, looting, panic, or other negative influences.

Discipline is the backbone of an army, and its maintenance is in the best interests of all.

14. The readiness and strength of units must be capable of meeting the highest demands in decisive moments. The commander who needlessly tires his unit jeopardizes success and is responsible for the consequences.

The forces deployed in battle must be committed in proportion to the objective. Orders that are impossible to execute will reduce confidence in the leadership and damage morale.

15. Every man, from the youngest soldier upward, must be required at all times and in all situations to commit his whole mental, spiritual, and physical strength. Only in this way will the full force of a unit be brought to bear in decisive action. Only thus will men develop, who will in the hour of danger maintain their courage and decisiveness and carry their weaker comrades with them to achieve deeds of daring.

The first criterion in war remains decisive action. Everyone, from the highest commander down to the youngest soldier, must constantly be aware that inaction and neglect incriminate him more severely than any error in the choice of means.*

---

*Emphasis in the original.

I

ORDER OF BATTLE
AND TASK ORGANIZATION

16. The order of battle (*Kriegsgliederung*)* establishes the structure for the command and control of a field army. It is established and can only be changed by the Army High Command (*Heeresleitung*).

17. The field army consists of armies, cavalry units, air units, and army troops.†

18. An army consists of infantry divisions,†† usually grouped under corps commands. Corps have corps troop units, and armies have army troop units.

Two or more armies may be organized into army groups.

19. Army-level cavalry units generally are organized in cavalry divisions.§

Multiple cavalry divisions can be grouped together as a cavalry corps—to which corps troop units are added.

---

*The German Army was organized on the unit principle (*Einheitsprinzip*). As far as practicable, the component elements were standardized units, capable of being attached or detached as required, without the loss of tactical integrity and without administrative and supply problems. [*Wedemeyer Report*, p. 141]

†The Germans had two different words for army. *Heer* meant the German Army itself. *Armee* meant the level of field command above corps. The Field Army (*Feldheer*) meant that portion of the German Army that conducted combat operations, as distinct from the Replacement Army (*Ersatzheer*) that provide the training and support base from home territory (*Heimat*). Henceforth in this translation, Army will be used for *Heer*, and army will be used for *Armee*.

††[Original footnote] "All operating principles for the infantry divisions apply for other arms when conducted as infantry and when no other specific principles have been published."

§A cavalry division had three brigades of two regiments each, a mounted reconnaissance regiment, a motorized reconnaissance battalion, an antitank battalion, a combat engineer battalion, a signal battalion, and an artillery battalion. [*Truppenführung*, Annex 1]

Cavalry brigades and larger cavalry units generally are attached only to army groups and armies.*

20. Air Force units consist of air strike forces (reconnaissance squadrons, fighter squadrons, and bomber squadrons) and air defense units.

Air Force units may be attached to army groups, armies, or army and cavalry corps,† and in exceptional situations to infantry and cavalry divisions.

21. Army troop units consist of:

Special purpose staffs, cyclists, motorcycle units, machine-gun units, mortar units, antitank units, motorized reconnaissance battalions, artillery (including observation battalions and balloon units), armored units, chemical units, engineer units, signal units, special troops, and rear area units.

22. Infantry and cavalry divisions are the smallest units capable of independent operations by reason of their organic composition. They have the means to carry out missions independently and to support themselves.

23. Army and corps troop units are organized similar to Army troops. The supply services of the corps are only as large as necessary to supply the corps troop units.

24. Task organization (*Truppeneinteilung*) is made on the basis of operational and tactical missions—advance guard (*Vorhut*), rear guard (*Nachhut*), flank guard (*Seitendeckung*), march columns (*Marschkolonnen*), and battle groupings (*Gefechtsgruppen*).†† Unit integrity should be maintained as far as possible.

25. Command is divided into higher and lower command. Higher command encompasses all units down to infantry and cavalry divisions. Lower command includes all smaller units.§

26. The title of troop commander (*Truppenführer*) applies to any officer in permanent or temporary independent command of a combined arms unit (*gemischter Verband*).

---

*Earlier German doctrine limited the attachment of these units to Army General Headquarters (*Heeresleitung*) and army groups. [*Das Fug*, Paragraph 2]

†The two types of German corps were army corps and cavalry corps. For the most part, this translation will use simply corps for army corps.

††The concept of a combined arms task force (*Kampfgruppe*) did not really crystallize until World War II.

§The Germans had two different terms for a unit. *Verband* referred to battalion-sized units and larger. *Einheit* referred to companies, batteries, and smaller units. A command headquarters at division level or above was called a *Kommandobehörde*.

II

COMMAND

---

27. Great success requires boldness and daring, but good judgement must take precedence.

28. One can never be strong enough at the decisive point. The commander who tries to be secure everywhere, or who wastes his forces on secondary missions, acts contrary to this basic rule.[*]

The weaker force can become the stronger at the decisive point through speed, mobility, great march capability, and the use of darkness, terrain, surprise, and deception.

29. Space and time must be correctly calculated. Favorable situations must be quickly recognized and decisively exploited. Every advantage over the enemy increases one's own freedom of action.

30. Rapidity of action can be facilitated or hindered by the route and by terrain conditions. The season, the weather, and the condition of the troops are also important influences.

31. The duration of operational and tactical engagements cannot always be estimated in advance. Even successful combat often develops slowly. Frequently the success of a day's fighting can only be determined on the following day.

32. Surprise is a decisive factor in success. Actions based on surprise are only successful if the enemy is given no time to take effective counter measures.[†]

The enemy also will attempt surprise. This must be taken into account.

33. Knowledge of the enemy's methods of leadership and combat can

---

[*]In *On War*, Book 3, Chapter 11, Clausewitz noted, "The best strategy is *to be very strong*, first in general, then at the decisive point. Apart from the effort needed to create military strength, which does not always emanate from the general, there is no higher and simpler law of strategy than that of *keeping one's forces concentrated*. No force should ever be detached from the main body unless the need is definite and *urgent*."

[†]In *On War*, Book 3, Chapter 9, Clausewitz noted, "The two factors that produce surprise are secrecy and speed."

influence one's own decision and support mission execution, but should not lead to preconceptions.

34. Account must be taken of conditions that facilitate the conduct of war in one's own country, but make it more difficult in enemy territory.

35. In periods of strenuous combat, heavy demands exhaust units quickly. They must promptly be provided with replacement officers, men, horses, weapons, and any necessary equipment.

36. **The mission and the situation define the course of action** (*Grundlage für die Führung*).

The mission dictates the objective. The responsible commander must not lose sight of it. A mission that consists of multiple tasks can easily distract attention from the main objective.

Uncertainty always will be present. It rarely is possible to obtain exact information on the enemy situation. Clarification of the enemy situation is an obvious necessity, but waiting for information in a tense situation is seldom the sign of strong leadership—more often of weakness.*

37. The mission (*Auftrag*) and the situation (*Lage*) lead to the decision (*Entschluss*) of the course of action. If the assigned mission no longer suffices as the basis for action, or if it is overtaken by events, the course of action must take these circumstances into account. An officer who changes a mission or does not carry it out must report his actions immediately, and he assumes responsibility for the consequences. He always must act within the overall framework of the situation.

The course of action must designate a clear objective that will be pursued with all determination. It must be executed with the full will of the commander. Victory often is won by the stronger will.

Once a course of action has been initiated it must not be abandoned without overriding reason. In the changing situations of combat, however, inflexibly clinging to a course of action can lead to failure. The art of leadership consists of the timely recognition of circumstances and of the moment when a new decision is required.[†]

The commander must allow his subordinates freedom of action, so long as it does not adversely affect his overall intent (*Absicht*). He may not,

---

*Wedemeyer noted: "Better a faulty plan or decision permeated with boldness, daring, and decisiveness, than a perfect plan enmeshed in uncertainty." [*Wedemeyer Report*, p. 18]

[†]Prior to World War I, it was standard practice in the Germany Army for higher commanders to assign missions solely for the purpose of developing a situation, and then change assigned missions accordingly in mid-action. Based on World War I experience, changes in assigned missions became the exception. [*Hartness Report*, p. 27]

however, surrender to his subordinates decisions for which he alone is responsible.

38. An engagement (*Gefecht*)—which when it involves larger units is called a battle (*Schlacht*)—is the forceful armed struggle arising from an encounter with the enemy.

39. The attack is launched on the enemy in order to defeat him. The attacker has the initiative. Superior fighting qualities of leaders and units provide the best advantage in an attack. Numerical superiority does not always guarantee victory.

In special situations the objective of an attack may be limited.

The possibility that an attack might fail should never justify limitations on the leadership effort with which it is executed.*

40. Pursuit (*Verfolgung*) guarantees the culmination of victory.† The purpose is to annihilate the enemy†† when such action was not possible in the preceding engagement. Only a relentless pursuit, one that does not allow the enemy the chance to regroup and make a stand, will prevent additional friendly casualties in follow-on actions.

41. The defense waits for the enemy. The aim is to prescribe the terrain of battle.

The defense is adopted when one's own inferiority leaves no other choice, or for other reasons when it seems advantageous.

Its purpose is to break up the enemy's attack. In such cases the attack is met on selected terrain, which is held to the end.

The commander may set a time limit on the defense.

A decisive victory can only be achieved through judicious resumption of the offense.

A delaying action has the objective of inflicting the highest possible loss on the enemy, while at the same time avoiding decisive engagement. To accomplish this it is necessary to disengage from the enemy at the appropriate time, and to trade space for time.

42. An engagement is broken off to terminate a battle, or to yield a

---

*"The German sees the solution of his tactical problem in the attack, for it is through the attack that the unclarified situation can be best clarified, and a basis reached upon which the commander can best estimate his future action. It may be said almost without danger of contradiction that in a nebulous situation the average German commander will attack." [*Hartness Report*, p. 27]

†Clausewitz discussed the culminating point of victory in Book 7, Chapter 22 of *On War*.

††Many post–World War II military historians have criticized German doctrine as focusing too exclusively on attempting to annihilate the enemy with a single decisive battle. While such an approach generally works at the tactical level, it is the antithesis of sequencing, which is the heart of the operational level of war.

position so as to continue the engagement from a more favorable position. In the latter case, a delaying action often is employed.

43. The withdrawal is employed to avoid further combat. The fight must be broken off and security must be provided for the withdrawing units.

44. The changing situation of combat often requires transition from one type of engagement to another.

The transition from attack to defense can occur when holding a position that has been taken, or when necessary, under enemy pressure. Units are reorganized and disposable forces are withdrawn from the line.

In the transition from the defensive to the attack, strong forces must be assembled at the decisive points in a timely manner.

45. Decision is avoided in a delaying action. The objective is to gain time, to keep the enemy occupied, and to confuse him.

Deception can be achieved through feint attacks (*Scheingefechte*).

46. The width of battle zone depends on the intent, on the disposition of adjacent support, and on the terrain. It is influenced by the breadth and conduct of the enemy and on whether or not one or both flanks are open. The width of zones and sectors is different. Greater width can be allowed in favorable terrain, especially if it had been fortified. It also can be used through the employment of battle groups. Great width can bring the effect of weapons into full play at an early stage, but it also can bring one's own forces to a premature standstill. Too great a width produces the danger of penetration. If the width is too small, especially if there is not enough depth, there is a danger of being outflanked or enveloped. An attack having width superior to the enemy's can result in great success.

Organization in depth ensures the commander's freedom of movement in uncertain situations. Initially, it is always appropriate in the face of a quicker or more mobile opponent. The follow-through of a battle usually requires depth of formation at the decisive point.

The commander must distribute his forces before contact with the enemy, and in battle distribute them according to the width and depth required by the situation.

47. During the course of a battle the commander influences the action most directly by the increase and concentration of fire and the commitment of his reserve.

Keeping ammunition supplies mobile will allow him, at the decisive point and at the decisive moment, to increase his firepower to the maximum and to continue to influence the course of the fighting, even if the reserve is already committed.

Assessing the strength of the reserve, constituting the reserve, and committing the reserve requires careful consideration. Mobility increases the opportunities for its commitment.

Allowing units already committed to the battle to weaken, while protecting the reserve, often leads to failure and increases the danger of defeat in detail. There are instances where it is better not to retain a reserve. Combined arms units are particularly effective as reserves because they are capable of independent action. One should avoid dispersing such units or any piecemeal commitment of the reserve.

The position of the reserve depends on its intended use and on the terrain. The reserve must be committed in a timely manner. Usually it is positioned behind a wing. The distance and interval from the wing increase with the strength of the reserve.

Holding back the reserve protects it and makes it easier to commit in different directions. Holding the reserve farther forward accelerates its commitment. The surer the commander becomes about its commitment and the more imminent this becomes, the farther forward he brings it. An operational reserve must be held well back as long as its commitment is not required.

By committing his reserve, the commander plays his last card regarding the shock elements at his disposal. He must not be led into doing this too early. On the other hand, he must not hesitate if committing the reserve means achieving a decision or if the battlefield situation requires it.

Once the reserve is committed, the rapid formation of a new reserve is critically important.

Communications, Dispatches, Reports, and Situation Maps

48. Communications and reports concerning the enemy provide one of the most important bases for the estimate of the situation, for the commander's decision, and for its execution.

The initial elements of intelligence about the enemy usually are obtained from general knowledge of enemy methods or from special information sources. Knowledge of the enemy takes on a more solid form through aerial and ground reconnaissance, through establishing contact with the enemy and keeping him under constant observation, and through information secured by special means. Apart from accurate information and reports, one also must reckon with incomplete and inaccurate information. Drawing on the entirety of information from different sources, the commander will be able to reach the appropriate conclusions. Apparently unimportant details take on significance in the context of other information.

Every report and even the best information may be of no value if it arrives too late at the headquarters for which it is destined.

49. Every commander has a duty within his area of operations to report continually on the enemy situation and to reconnoiter the terrain day and night. When contact with the enemy has been established, it must be maintained.

All commanders have a duty to inform their higher commander as quickly and fully as possible on the situation and to pass on all important information.

50. In higher commands, and if necessary in the lower commands, one officer must be responsible for analyzing the results of reconnaissance and other elements of information.

Information and reports must be evaluated factually, avoiding any temptation to read into them what might appear favorable or advantageous.

51. The person reporting must express himself clearly and factually. He must distinguish between what he himself has seen, what another has noticed or said, and what is surmised. The source of the information must be cited. Suppositions must be justified.

52. Exact figures and the exact time and place are very important.

Often it is useful to know where the enemy has not been encountered. It also is valuable to confirm earlier reports or to note that circumstances have not changed within a given period.

Important details about the condition of the terrain must be included automatically with any reports about the enemy.

53. The content and reliability of reports are far more important than the number of reports. Reports must present the events in a matter of fact manner. Exaggerated reports are detrimental, and in certain situations they can be fatal. Colored reports undermine trust and make commanders uncertain.

The first contact with the enemy must always be reported, unless there is an order to the contrary. Moreover, a decision must be made on every occasion whether to report an enemy action at once or whether to report it at all. Unnecessary reports weaken the effectiveness of the reporting system, overload the channels of communication, and complicate the actions of the commander.

Important reports related to the enemy may require verification.

54. Combat itself provides the most reliable point of reference for estimating the enemy.

Battlefield reports are essential for the conduct of a battle.

During the battle there must be constant reporting on the enemy, the friendly situation, the terrain, and the ammunition supply. The communication of impressions, suggestions for exploiting favorable opportunities, and the state of the terrain facilitate the decision making process. Experience shows that timely reports during lulls in the battle, and reports at night are especially valuable for higher headquarters.

At the close of a battle, reports should be sent without delay detailing the opposing forces, the conduct of the enemy, the condition of the enemy units, the friendly situation, ammunition levels, and other key elements of information.

55. In pressing situations, reports must be made directly to the senior headquarters as well as the immediate next higher headquarters. Units immediately threatened by the enemy must report this at once, regardless of other necessary reports. If a report is submitted simultaneously to different headquarters, that fact must be noted in each dispatch.

56. Adjacent elements must communicate important observations on the enemy and changes in their own situation.

57. A report often provides a full version of short messages. Short messages sent immediately after the engagement do not eliminate the requirement for a combat report. The report must be made as soon as possible after the action. The contents of the report will be in chronological order. For this reason, frequent notation of the time should be made during the battle.

Orders and messages that have been sent during the actions being described are copied verbatim into the report or attached as annexes.

58. Every command post must establish situation maps and keep them constantly updated. These maps should show the enemy situation, the friendly situation, and that of adjacent units. This information facilitates the commander's tasks and his decision making process. Lower echelon commanders also act accordingly.

Estimate of the Situation and the Decision

59. Every decision is preceded by an estimate of the situation. This process requires rapid mental effort, simple and logical consideration, and a clear focus on only the essentials.

60. Orders received from higher headquarters are the basis and starting point. They must be analyzed to determine the mission and how best to execute it.

Knowledge and correct assessment of the terrain have a very strong influence on the tactical considerations and the courses of action.

61. The assessment of the friendly situation establishes the positions of the various units of the force, which are immediately or later available for commitment, the availability of additional forces, the support of adjacent units, and whether these units will require reinforcement.

Previous action, the condition of the troops, the state of equipment, and the ammunition supply all must be taken into consideration.

62. The estimate of the enemy situation follows the same procedure. Based on all available information, an assessment must be made of the enemy's ability to prevent the friendly intent. Essential to this process is the evaluation of how we would act in the enemy's place. Such an assessment must not lead to prejudgement. A thorough assessment must be made of those enemy actions that would most seriously counter one's own actions. This assumes no special reason to conclude that the enemy will act differently.

Normally, the areas or lines the enemy can reach, the indicators of his strength and deployment, and the direction he can advance all should be estimated in detail.

In larger commands consideration must be taken of the enemy road and rail network, as well as the actions of the enemy air force, air defense units, and communications units.

The character of the enemy commander and his troops also serves as a reference for estimating the actions of the enemy, especially if experience exists from previous battles.

63. A sound decision must be the logical outcome of the estimate process.

The decision may not always correspond to the actual situation presented. In such situations the commander most likely to succeed is the one who makes the quickest and most skillful use of any further development of the situation, without allowing himself to be distracted from his original decision, except for compelling reasons.

Orders

64. An order (*Befehl*) translates a decision into action.

65. Clear orders are an important condition for the smooth cooperation of all commanders. Verbal agreements can be unreliable.

66. The written order is the basic means by which the senior commander controls his units. It is sent to subordinate units in the form of a printed or carbon copy, typewritten or handwritten, or transmitted by technical means. Often it is dictated over the telephone. In every case, the most appropriate and secure method should be used.

In the case of simple or short orders, the commander may transmit the order verbally. Later, however, the text must be committed to writing.

67. Subordinate-level commanders usually issue verbal orders. They issue orders in writing when oral or telephone transmission is not possible for technical reasons, or is inadequate, or may be intercepted.

68. The more urgent the situation, the shorter must be the order. Verbal

orders, where the circumstances allow, must be given based on the actual terrain and not simply on the basis of map inspection. This is especially true for subordinate commanders in the front line.

69. An order transmitted by technical means must be verified or authenticated. Such an order should be repeated to the sender.

In the case of important orders, it is better to use two or more means of transmission.

70. The time required for the arrival of an order is often underestimated.

In some cases it may be necessary for the issuing commander to verify the receipt and execution of the order.

71. Issuing too many orders, especially during a battle when messages may be lost, creates the serious risk of loss of independence of subordinate commanders.

72. In accordance with special procedures (Chapter XVII), secret orders must be encoded, except those that relate to the immediate coordination of various arms. Orders also must be transmitted by wire when a danger of interception exists.

In special situations, written orders also should be partially or totally encoded.

73. An order should contain all that a subordinate needs to know to be able to execute his mission—and nothing more. Accordingly, the order must be short, clear, specific, and complete. It must be understandable by the recipient and conform to his situation. The commander who issues the order must always put himself in the position of the recipient.

74. The language of orders must be simple and understandable. Clarity that eliminates any doubt is more important than correct format. Clarity must not be sacrificed for brevity.

Meaningless expressions and figures of speech that lead to partial measures should be avoided at all costs. Exaggerations make dull reading.

75. Orders may only be valid as long they relate to the situation and conditions. Nonetheless, it often is necessary to issue orders when the situation is obscure or uncertain.

76. If changes in the situation are anticipated before an order can be executed, the order should not go into detail. This is especially important in larger operations, when orders must be issued for several days in advance. The general intent is stated and the end to be achieved must especially be emphasized. The general intent must be stated for the execution of impending operations, but the method of execution is left to the subordinate commanders. Otherwise, the order becomes a directive.

77. In order to maintain secrecy, careful consideration must be given to how far and to whom the intent of the operation is revealed.

In special operations, commanders occasionally are informed by special written instructions or in person by liaison officers sent from head-quarters.

In larger operations there should be no hesitation in giving a thorough analysis of the intent and detailed mission orders for the battle to ensure coordination in the common objective. When the battle starts, there should be no doubt in any commander regarding the intent of the senior command-er.

As far as the situation permits, the commander will explain his intent verbally to his subordinate commanders. He may not, however, become dependent on his subordinates. Decisions and orders are his responsibilities alone.

78. Written orders that direct the assignment of different elements to the common objective should be divided into numbered paragraphs.

The important information must be put first. Matters relating to each unit or element are placed in separate paragraphs under separate numbers.

79. Operations orders coordinate the actions of combat units and give the necessary instructions for the combat and service trains. Orders are designated according to the name of the issuing headquarters (e.g., army, corps, divisional, regimental order, etc.), or if more practical, according to the task organization (e.g., advance guard, outpost order) or according to individual arms (e.g., artillery order).

80. The following sequence should be used for operations orders (*Operationsbefehle*):

Information about the enemy and about adjacent units, as far as they are important to the recipient.

The intent of the commander, so far this information is necessary for the accomplishment of the mission.

Missions for the elements of the entire command.

Orders for the light motorized columns, the field trains, the baggage trains, the combat echelon, and the other rear units, as far as this is important for those units.

The position of the command post and the procedures for communications to and from the commander.

The exact elements to be included in the operations order depend on the particular situation.

Information about the enemy also should include the commander's estimate of the enemy's intent.

Estimates and assumptions must be indicated as such. The reasoning behind specifically ordered measures will only be included in the order in exceptional situations. Detailed instructions covering all possible situations, particularly those that are matters of standard training, do not belong in an order.

81. A warning order (*Vorbefehl*) is often issued prior to the main order.

The warning order should contain the most current information on the situation. This allows subordinate commanders to make the most immediate preparations. A warning order also can be used to place units in rest status earlier, or to extend their rest period.

Warning orders are especially effective when units can be informed verbally by telephone or radio.

82. Often, the urgency of a situation requires the issue of simple extracts of orders. These fragmentary orders (*Einzelbefehl*) are extracts of the main order and must contain everything that the recipient needs to know for the execution of the mission.

Through the use of fragmentary orders, not all units will necessarily be informed of the overall picture. In larger operations the complete operations order usually follows. In other situations individual commanders should be informed of the most important elements of the overall situation as soon as possible.

83. The unit task organization is detailed separately from the main body of the operations order, and listed by branch in the following sequence:

Infantry, cavalry, horse and motorized reconnaissance battalions, artillery, armor, chemical troops, engineers, signal, horsed or motorized transport, medical and veterinary troops, other troops (air forces and air defense units).

If the march sequence is already fixed in the order, the units will be so designated in the task organization. The corresponding unit organization (main body, advance guard, rear guard, etc.) will contain the notation, "according to march sequence." Likewise in a retrograde movement, units must be specified in march sequence.

84. The ending of an order should indicate the issuing authority and the manner of distribution.

The time the order is completed or the hour of transmission must be indicated.

Commanders and their key staff should only be called together for an orders brief when required by the situation.

85. In most cases, the higher headquarters operations order with its annexes is not passed in complete form to subordinate units. Subordinate commanders issue their own orders based on the order of the higher headquarters, including all necessary information and instructions.

The divisional operations order generally forms the basis for orders to the subordinate units.

86. Orders for a withdrawal or retreat should be communicated in a secure manner to the next lower commanders only.

87. Operations orders must avoid all forms of stereotyping. Task organizing units might be necessary in some situations, but in combat the

commander should deploy his units based on the standard organization tables whenever possible.

The situation dictates whether an operations order is issued as a complete order or as a fragmentary order. The form of the order must ensure the coordination of all elements.

88. Special instructions (*besondere Anordnungen*) to supplement the operations order contain information not necessarily required by the entire command. They detail the missions and tasks of the individual arms, the resupply of ammunition, motor transport maintenance and supply, medical and veterinary service, food supply, the supply of weapons material and equipment, and sometimes the actions of the field supply and baggage trains. In order to ensure speed and brevity in the orders process, it may be necessary to include such information in the main operations order.

In all other situations, all necessary orders issued by the commander to the supply services will be issued as special orders.

Special instructions go only to the element concerned. If these elements do not receive the basic operations order, then the information relevant to them must be contained in the special order.*

89. Corps and divisional orders of the day (*Tagesbefehle*) concern internal functions, personnel actions, promotions, decorations, etc.

Staff orders (*Stabsbefehle*) regulate the internal functions of the staffs.

Transmission of Orders and Reports: Communications Between the Commander and His Units

90. Depending upon distance and circumstances, orders and reports will be transmitted by technical signal means, individuals, dispatch riders, carrier pigeons, or messenger dogs.

Technical means of signal communications should be used when rapid transmission can be accomplished without compromising security. Such transmissions also may require the employment of other means. Long orders and messages can be transmitted more rapidly and safely from one officer to another by telephone.

91. Senior commanders, and occasionally subordinate commanders, can deploy forward message centers to areas with the heaviest signal traffic. These centers conserve manpower and facilitate the transmission of

---

*The basic operations order and the supply special order contained different elements of logistics information. The former told the combat units what they needed to know to coordinate with the support units; the latter gave the support units their instructions for supplying and sustaining the combat units. [*Hartness Report*, p. 22]

orders and reports. The forward message center must be located easily, secured against enemy action, and have solid connectivity with the commander. All subordinate units must know its position.

In larger commands, correctly located message centers can save manpower and time. They must be equipped with the necessary means of signal communications and must be strong enough to defend against small enemy forces. Each center is commanded by a specially selected officer who evaluates incoming messages and decides upon time and type of transmission according to importance. In certain situations, multiple messages can be summarized efficiently in a single outgoing report.

See Paragraphs 161 and 168 concerning message centers for reconnaissance.

92. Communications between aircraft and ground troops is accomplished by pyrotechnic and signal devices, dropped messages, pickup stations, and by radio (Paragraphs 138 and 139).

93. Senior commanders have the resources on their staffs for the transmission of orders. Orders liaison officers also can be attached temporarily or permanently to the headquarters staffs of combined units.

The host unit is responsible for the rations and billeting of liaison officers.

94. Consideration for frontline strength requires that the number of liaison personnel be limited. Those attached to staffs must return immediately to their units upon the completion of their duties.

95. Motor vehicles, motorcycles, and bicycles may be used where adequate and secure routes are available.

Riders and runners should be used on open roads, rough terrain, and especially on the battlefield.

In larger commands aircraft can be used over long distances.

96. Subordinate commanders should be summoned to the headquarters to receive the orders brief only during the advance to the battlefield. This procedure will not be used during actual combat.

97. When verbally transmitting an order or a report, the messenger must repeat the wording to the individual issuing the report. The messenger carrying a written report should know its key contents as far as the situation permits. As a rule, officers carrying orders should know the tactical situation.

98. Important orders and reports must be sent by officer, if possible.

For especially important messages, or when the routes are not secure, multiple copies should be sent by different routes. Under such conditions, or if the route is long, officers should be protected by escorts, mounted troops, or armored vehicles.

99. The sender must consider where his message can reach the receiver and should indicate to the messenger to whom the order or the message is

to be delivered, and the route that should be followed. If necessary a sketch of the route will be provided. Especially dangerous sectors of the route should be indicated. If necessary, the latest time by which the message must be delivered will be designated. Messengers also must be instructed on what to do at the end of their mission.

100. Upon meeting superiors, mounted messengers maintain their speed. They report to senior officers the destination of the message. When riding past a march column, they report to the commander as well as to the leader of the advance (or rear) guard. When passing security elements, they report to the nearest commander. When danger is imminent, they call out the contents of the message to the commanders and the units. They must be trained to ask, without inhibition, for the location of the commander to whom the message or the order is directed. Bicyclists conduct themselves similarly to mounted messengers. Reports cannot always be obtained from motorcyclists when they are moving.

Senior commanders and the commanders of reconnaissance battalions are authorized to read passing messages, but they must not delay messages. They must note on the message that they have read its contents.

Every commander is obliged to show the way to messengers. All troops must to give way for them. Every element must assist in the transmission of messages and orders, even by providing transportation facilities if necessary.

101. The number of crosses placed on a message or its container indicates the speed to be maintained by a mounted messenger.

$$X = 1 \text{ kilometer in 7 to 8 minutes}$$

$$XX = 1 \text{ kilometer in 5 to 6 minutes.}$$

102. If necessary, the speed for bicycle and motorcycle messengers will be given in kilometers per hour.*

103. It may become necessary to establish relay messenger posts for the rapid movement of orders and messages over greater distances where technical means of signal communication cannot guarantee secure transmission.

Relay messengers can be runners, mounted troopers, bicyclists, or motorcyclists. This work is tiring. Runners and mounted messengers should be used only when bicyclists and motorcyclists are not available or cannot be employed because of the terrain.

---

*Standard speeds were 15 to 20 kilometers per hour for bicycle messengers, and 30 to 40 kilometers per hour for motorcycle messengers. [*Wedemeyer Report*, p. 62]

104. The distance between the relay messenger posts is a function of the purpose of the relay messenger line, its total distance, and the condition of the roads and the terrain. The strength of each post is determined by its required duration, the volume of message traffic, and the local security requirements.

105. Carrier pigeons and messenger dogs will be used for communications with the most forward units when other methods fail.

106. The higher headquarters is responsible for establishing communications with the lower, and for the construction and maintenance of the circuit.

Communications between adjacent elements will be established and maintained from left to right, unless otherwise ordered. This does not, however, relieve a unit on the right from the responsibility of establishing contact with the left if communications for some reason have not been established.

107. In larger commands the headquarters may send liaison officers to attached units and to adjacent units, for either a fixed period or permanently. These officers provide situation updates and inform the units to which they are sent of the intent of the higher headquarters. Liaison officers require clear perception, independent judgement, and great military tact. Without creating friction, they must ascertain the intent and orders of the commander to whom they are attached. Prior to sending their reports, they must verify their own understanding of the subordinate commander's situation. They must indicate to him any difference of opinion and subsequently report their assessments to their own headquarters. They will return to their own headquarters only when their mission is accomplished, or when they must report in person. The assignment of a liaison officer does not relieve a commander from the responsibility to keep his own superior commander continuously informed.

108. Communications between the arms is covered in Chapter VI.

The Position of the Commander and His Staff

109. The personal influence of the commander on his troops is vitally important. He must position himself close to the combat units.

110. The selection of the command post of the corps commander is based on the requirement for continuous communications with the divisions and with the rear. The corps commander cannot rely on technical connections alone.

Great distance, despite perfect technical means of signal communications, lengthens the command and reporting chain, increases the vulnerability of the connection, and can lead to the delayed arrival or loss of information and orders. Moreover, the greater the distance, the more difficult it is for the commander to manage the battle and to understand the nature of the terrain.

On the other hand, the high volume of communications traffic to and from the divisions and other subordinate commands requires that the corps command post remain in constant operation. Its change of location must be made quickly, even over long distances.

Before moving into a new position, the technical communications connections must be established.

Personal communications with his divisions is especially important for the commander of a cavalry corps. Whenever the corps commander is not accompanying one of his divisions, he generally follows closely behind.

111. The division commander's place is with his troops.

112. During an advance, the division commander with his immediate staff should position themselves well forward.

When advancing with several march columns, the commander of an infantry division, unless he is moving between columns, generally moves with the column along whose route the signal trunk line will be laid, or where available communications means can be used. Depending on the situation, the commander of a cavalry division remains with the main march column or moves between the march columns.

The division commander advances by bounds. Horses and motor vehicles must always be at his disposal. The remainder of the staff follows within the march column (Paragraph 288) until it is ordered forward. Reports must reach the division commander quickly and at all times.

113. If contact with the enemy is imminent, the division commander remains with the advance guard of the march column which, based on his estimate, will play the key role. It is there that he can most quickly exert his influence.

Personal observation is best upon contact with the enemy. The division commander, therefore, must position himself on the battlefield at the decisive point, and as early as possible. His position must be located and reached easily.

114. At the commencement of the attack, the divisional command post should be in a very advanced position, but it also should be chosen in such a way that lateral and rearward communications are effectively screened from enemy fire. Observation of the battlefield, either directly from the command post or from a closely located position, and the capability of establishing a forward airstrip nearby are key considerations.

In the defense, a greater width of the front usually requires a divisional command post positioned farther to the rear.

As far as is possible, the division commander should consider the recommendations of the communications officer for the positioning of the command post and for the time required to establish it. Frequent relocations of the command post must be avoided. A move should be made only after the new command post is set up and the signal connections are established. The notification to reposition must be given to the communications officer in sufficient time. Provision must be made for the forwarding of orders and messages that may arrive at the previous command post.

115. During pursuit operations, the commander must move with the forward elements. His presence in the front line will inspire his units.

116. If at the end of a battle fighting continues in the rearward areas, the division commander should move to the area of new resistance, having first assured himself that his orders for follow-on operations are being executed. During difficult situations, he remains with his units. Subordinate commanders should always remain with their units.

117. The command post of the senior commander and the access routes to it must be recognizable by day and night. The command post flag facilitates its identification, but it should not be visible to the enemy.

Defense must be established against air and ground surprise attacks from any direction. Security considerations may require that the combat units provide the security for the forward command post.

118. The correct composition of the staff and the appropriate assignment of tasks are very important planning factors. The senior staffs must operate at their fully authorized strengths.

Sure and quiet leadership in the command post is maintained by diligent adherence to duty. Every effort must be made to relieve the commander of the burden of unnecessary detail.

119. When the commander temporarily leaves the command post, the chief of staff acts as his deputy.

III

RECONNAISSANCE

120. Reconnaissance (*Aufklärung*) should produce a picture of the enemy situation as rapidly, completely, and reliably as possible. The results are the most important basis for the commander's decisions and the deployment of the force.

121. Reconnaissance, both air and ground, can be either tactical or operational. It can be augmented by special means (Paragraphs 184 to 189).

122. Operational reconnaissance (*operative Aufklärung*) provides the basis for the operational decisions.

Tactical reconnaissance (*taktische Aufklärung*) provides the basis for the command and deployment of units. Combat reconnaissance (*Gefechtsaufklärung*) begins after initial contact with the enemy and provides information for the control of the battle. All arms participate in this process.

123. The forces deployed for reconnaissance missions should not be greater than the mission requirement.

Reconnaissance forces must be deployed in the primary direction in sufficient time, especially if superior enemy reconnaissance forces are anticipated. Only the absolute minimum force will be committed to secondary directions.

Short duration missions should be the objective. Based on the situation, it may be necessary to withhold reconnaissance forces, to extend their mission, or to commit them in a new direction.

124. Reconnaissance superiority facilitates friendly missions and restricts those of the enemy.

Chapter XV covers the establishment of air superiority.

The establishment of reconnaissance superiority on the ground is facilitated by aggressive action toward enemy reconnaissance. Accordingly, all reconnaissance forces down to the level of patrols must act within the limits of their mission and the situation.

If friendly reconnaissance elements are forced to break through the enemy reconnaissance screen in order to accomplish their missions, they must assemble their forces quickly to push through with surprise. If the enemy has superiority, friendly reconnaissance may be accomplished through the use of skillful evasive measures.

Army cavalry units are effective in collecting information, even in the face of stronger enemy forces. Independent motorized reconnaissance battalions committed to such a mission must be reinforced in a timely manner by additional motorized forces.

Occasionally, the conditions necessary for superiority in the reconnaissance zone can be created by the rapid and surprise occupation of key terrain. Motorized forces are especially suitable for such an action because of their speed.

125. Good ground reconnaissance also contributes to good security. Conversely, the actions of a security unit produce a certain amount of reconnaissance. Reconnaissance and security on the ground complement one another and cannot be separated. Reconnaissance units must be able to orient themselves against the enemy and move freely over the ground. Security forces, on the other hand, are positioned locally by the units requiring security.

In an exceptional situation it may become necessary to assign a reconnaissance unit simultaneous missions of reconnaissance and security. Its priority of tasks must be specified in its orders. If the unit has sufficient strength available, it will assign forces for each task.

126. Reconnaissance involves many tasks simultaneously. These include reconnaissance of the terrain and its passability; the condition of roads, railways, and bridges; obstacle possibilities; observation points; concealment; and positions for signal installations.

Even in the absence of specific orders, all reconnaissance forces must combine observation of the enemy with reconnaissance of the terrain as far as the situation permits.

Aerial photographic reconnaissance (Paragraph 130) supports and extends ground reconnaissance.

Reconnaissance Methods and Coordination

127. Aircraft assigned to reconnaissance squadrons conduct aerial reconnaissance.

Prior to the initiation of combat reconnaissance, the primary means of ground tactical reconnaissance are the patrols of the motorized and mounted reconnaissance units.

128. The advantages of aerial reconnaissance come from the speed of the aircraft; the ability to overfly enemy security forces, obstacles, and positions; and the resulting ability to acquire a broad overview of the enemy situation. The type of terrain does not affect aircraft. Under favor-

able conditions a reconnaissance pilot can quickly secure and report a picture of the enemy situation.

Aerial reconnaissance, however, can only provide a snapshot of the immediate situation. Continuous observation of the same area is usually impossible. Weather, terrain cover, and enemy actions induce further restrictions.

129. The simplest method of aerial reconnaissance is visual. The results depend on the flight altitude—determined by the mission and enemy defenses—and by general observation conditions and enemy camouflage.*

Daytime flights are the most common. The timing of such flights should be irregular.

Nighttime aerial reconnaissance becomes increasingly necessary as the enemy attempts to evade daytime aerial reconnaissance by security measures and night movements. Night aerial reconnaissance is conducted visually at low level, often assisted by various means of illumination. It cannot replace daytime flights completely, because night flights require good landmarks such as roads, railroads, and rivers. This limits night flights to pre-planned missions.

Reconnaissance flights in the early hours of the day or late at night can detect the completion or the commencement of enemy night movements.

130. Photographic reconnaissance complements and confirms visual reconnaissance. The higher the aircraft must fly, the more necessary photographs become. Aerial photographs can provide information on the enemy, the effects of friendly fires, and the effectiveness of friendly camouflage. Photographic reconnaissance has very limited value for acquiring targets of opportunity during a battle.

Photographic reconnaissance also can be used for terrain reconnaissance and for artillery survey.

Aerial photographs can be taken as a strip mosaic or as a single photo. Good aerial photographs require bright daylight and their development takes time. The results of a combat aerial reconnaissance, which provides a limited number of photos, can be reported in one to two hours. The evaluation of the greater numbers of photographs of an tactical aerial reconnaissance requires from two to five hours. An operational aerial reconnaissance produces a large number of photographs and can take ten hours or more. The photo-interpretation section at the airfield conducts the evaluation.

---

*In average visibility and in the absence of camouflage efforts, the following types of targets could be detected from the various altitudes: combined arms march column, 3,000 to 4,000 meters; infantry squads, 1,200 to 1,500 meters; individuals and specific weapons, 600 meters; artillery firing battery, 600 meters; railroad train with a steam engine producing smoke, 7,000 meters; railroad train with an electric engine, 4,500 meters. [*Wedemeyer Report*, p. 123]

Mobile photo laboratory vehicles also can be brought to an advanced landing field or can be positioned close to a command post.

131. Ground reconnaissance normally cannot observe the enemy situation in depth. Aerial reconnaissance often identifies the most lucrative direction of action for ground reconnaissance. On the other hand, only ground reconnaissance can determine definitely whether or not the terrain is occupied by the enemy. Ground reconnaissance forces can provide information about enemy deployments through the interrogation of prisoners, the inspection of enemy dead, and other methods. Only ground forces can maintain continuous contact with the enemy; report on his activity, strength, composition, and combat effectiveness; and determine if chemicals contaminate the terrain. Ground reconnaissance forces also can produce results when air operations are not possible or are severely restricted by bad weather.

132. Motorized reconnaissance units can produce results quickly and at great distances. They will not always be able to identify details. Their operations normally are limited to daylight hours. They can, however, conduct their approach marches during darkness. Their speed is the greatest when using roads. They must remain independent of the slower moving reconnaissance forces.

The effectiveness of a motorized reconnaissance unit depends upon the capabilities of its vehicles, refueling capabilities, route and road conditions, terrain and weather, time of day, and especially on the availability of their own communications assets.

133. Mounted reconnaissance units have the advantage of high mobility over all types of terrain, plus the capability to conduct split operations over great distances. They are less restricted by weather, terrain, or supply than motorized reconnaissance units. Their speed and march duration are limited. They have the capability to observe the enemy from covered positions, and to form a fine-meshed net of observation. They are most valuable when detailed observation is required.

134. Commanders of ground reconnaissance units, down to the level of patrols, must perform to the highest standards. The personality of the commander is decisive. Imagination, flexibility, an understanding of the mission, determination, good driving or riding skills on all types of terrain, skill in the use of terrain (especially at night), coolness, and rapid and independent action are all essential requirements.

All commanders are responsible for maintaining contact with the enemy, once gained—as long as the mission does not dictate otherwise. Lost contact must be reestablished immediately.

135. Different methods of reconnaissance supplement one another. The shortcomings of one method are compensated for by the strengths of the

others.

136. The deployment of reconnaissance elements depends on the situation; the commander's intent; the reconnaissance units available; and enemy countermeasures based on the terrain, the route, and road net. Additional factors include the time of year and the weather. These variables produce so many possibilities that a universal technique for all situations cannot be established.

All reconnaissance elements must be deployed on a uniform basis. Only in such a manner can they work together effectively and develop as complete a picture of the enemy as possible.

The deployment of reconnaissance elements must be based on all available information. This is the only sure means of avoiding the inefficient use of these resources.

The size of a reconnaissance force does not guarantee the quality of the results. It is decisively important that every reconnaissance element knows where to send its reports; the commander's intent and his priority intelligence requirements; the situation; and the mission of adjacent reconnaissance elements and those previously sent out.

137. The missions given to reconnaissance element commanders must be defined precisely, unambiguously, and in order of priority.

138. Communications connectivity between aerial and ground reconnaissance elements is the responsibility of the senior commander of both elements. That commander also establishes any special markings or signals. Communications are coordinated through him. Direct communications between a reconnaissance pilot and a ground reconnaissance element will be the exception, because of the difficulty of fixing in advance the time, position, and communications means. In most cases, the coordination necessary for direct communications can only be made before the start of a new mission.

In the absence of an air commander on the staff, the air liaison officer coordinates communications between the senior commander and the aerial reconnaissance element. Because of the great the distance to the advanced landing fields, his function increases in importance whenever a forward airstrip must be established near the command post. Such a landing strip must be adequately staffed and supplied.

The aerial reconnaissance unit commander must be given the planned routes of the ground reconnaissance elements; the routes of march of the main body; and the planned locations of the advanced landing fields. He passes this information to his pilots, along with the locations of all friendly troops. Recognition means also must be established between friendly air and ground elements.

As the situation requires, senior commanders may hold individual aircraft for their own immediate use.

139. Reconnaissance pilots and ground reconnaissance elements communicate via lights and signal devices, and through message drops and pickup stations. Radio may be used if suitable radio sets are available and compatible.

Reconnaissance pilots normally cannot alert ground reconnaissance elements to the presence of the enemy's most forward elements. Such units are difficult to identify from the air.

140. The senior commander coordinates communications between motorized and mounted reconnaissance elements. Communications also should be established independently at every opportunity. Radio is the preferred means for the most forward elements. Upon meeting, reconnaissance elements should exchange all key information. Paragraph 100 covers the exchange of report information.

141. The rapid and secure transmission of reconnaissance results to the senior commander must be controlled tightly.

Reconnaissance pilots generally submit their reports at the airfield or at the advanced landing strip. The reports are transmitted by telephone, motor vehicle, or in exceptional situations, by radio. In special cases the observer reports personally. The critical elements of the reconnaissance report should be transmitted in advance of the complete report. The final reconnaissance report must be written and presented in a clear, short, concise, but complete form. Reports directly from the aircraft will be made by radio or by message drop.

In the absence of existing communications lines, reports by reconnaissance elements will be submitted by radio or by motorized messenger. Mounted reconnaissance elements use mounted messengers in emergencies. Mounted patrols normally report by mounted messengers—although bicyclists and motorcyclists may be attached. Existing communications facilities should be used whenever possible. High-priority mounted patrols may be augmented with a radio transmitter or signal lamps.

Combat reconnaissance reports generally are valuable only when the information can be transformed into action as rapidly as possible.

142. Lengthy radio transmissions within the zone of reconnaissance must be controlled tightly by the senior headquarters in order to limit the risk of interception. When radio silence is imposed, alternate communications means must be established.

Conduct of Reconnaissance

143. Operational reconnaissance encompasses the surveillance of the enemy's concentration. It includes his movements by rail, his advance or withdrawal, the loading or unloading of army-level elements, the construc-

tion of field or permanent fortifications, and enemy air unit concentrations. The early detection of large enemy motorized units, especially those on open flanks, is critically important.

144. Special air units conduct operational aerial reconnaissance.

Operational aerial reconnaissance generally employs photographic means at altitudes between 5,000 and 8,000 meters. The depth of this reconnaissance can extend to the maximum range of the aircraft.

If immediate contact with the enemy is not anticipated, the army's tactical aerial reconnaissance squadrons can be committed to operational reconnaissance missions along with the special squadrons. The aircraft of the squadrons attached to an army for tactical reconnaissance generally have less range, speed, and rate of climb than those in the special reconnaissance squadrons.

145. Independent motorized reconnaissance battalions and cavalry units are used for operational ground reconnaissance. Cavalry is used generally for operational reconnaissance on open flanks and in directions that will correspond to subsequent combat operations.

146. The principles of operational reconnaissance are generally the same as those of tactical reconnaissance.

Because the missions assigned to operational aerial reconnaissance are generally limited to the observation of important routes and railroads, it is seldom necessary to assign reconnaissance zones to these units.

In most cases, independent motorized reconnaissance battalions and cavalry units are given only a direction and an objective. If necessary, they may be assigned boundaries on one or both flanks.

147. Tactical reconnaissance involves the detailed identification of the enemy's assembly areas; his approach movements; his organization for combat; the width, depth, and direction of his deployment; his supply elements; his reserves; his air capabilities (especially new airfields); and his air defense assets.

The timely reporting of enemy motorized forces is very important.

The depth of tactical reconnaissance depends upon the situation and the capabilities of the reconnaissance elements.

The deployment of tactical reconnaissance elements, especially the determination of their main direction of effort, should be based upon the results of the operational reconnaissance—provided this causes no unnecessary delays. If operational reconnaissance results are not available, tactical reconnaissance elements should be deployed farther toward the enemy.

The closer the enemy, the more the detailed the reconnaissance must be.

148. The reconnaissance squadrons attached to the command conduct tactical aerial reconnaissance.

The motorized and mounted reconnaissance battalions of the army and the cavalry and infantry divisions conduct ground tactical reconnaissance.

149. The army commander and the corps or cavalry corps commanders deploy the reconnaissance battalions immediately under their command and ensure their coordination with the reconnaissance forces of subordinate units.

The cavalry division commander may deploy his motorized and mounted reconnaissance battalions in column, or he may deploy his mounted battalion to the front, and the motorized battalion from one wing (*Flügel*) against the enemy flank (*Flanke*).* Motorized cavalry reconnaissance units should be utilized to the fullest so the mounted units can maintain their cohesion for combat.

150. Tactical aerial reconnaissance is flown usually at altitudes of between 2,000 to 5,000 meters.

Normally, reconnaissance zones will be assigned to aerial reconnaissance units. Named areas and lines of interest are included within the boundaries of adjacent elements. Overlapping zones may be assigned. There is no direct correlation between aerial boundaries and boundaries assigned to ground forces. Units on the friendly wing conduct reconnaissance against the enemy flank.

151. In addition to the primary mission, the orders for the commander of an aerial reconnaissance unit may include instructions regarding communications with and transmission of information to the senior commander and to the reconnaissance units; special message deliveries; the routes of the main body and the reconnaissance elements, including their arrival and departure times; and details on the advanced landing fields. The flight echelon commander distributes the orders to the aircrew and briefs them. He selects the crews and aircraft for the operation and the time of the mission. Specific flight planning is the responsibility of the aircrews.

152. Reconnaissance pilots normally operate individually and during times when the best results can be expected. They do not engage enemy aircraft. Reconnaissance and fighter aircraft may be deployed simultaneously.

153. Reconnaissance missions are long and tiring. Aircrews generally will fly only one sortie per day. Subject to crew availability and rest, the

---

*The distinction between a wing and a flank has fallen out of use as a modern military concept. The wing referred to the extreme right or left of the front of a deployed military force. The flank was actually the right or left side of that force. The wing of a unit did not necessarily have depth, the unit's flank usually had depth. Because a flank is so vulnerable to attack, every effort was made to tie it to the flank of another unit, or anchor it on a piece of terrain, such as a river. The distinction between a wing and a flank began to disappear as tactics became less linear and more mobile.

aircraft can operate several short missions per day. Limited availability may restrict aircraft to high priority missions. In such cases, other reconnaissance means should be used for lower priority missions.

154. For tactical ground reconnaissance, units normally are assigned sectors of responsibility. They generally are assigned only one reconnaissance objective in order to ensure their independence or to facilitate any necessary shifts in their direction. Under such conditions, boundaries can be established between adjacent reconnaissance units.

The width of a reconnaissance zone is a function of the situation, the type and strength of the reconnaissance unit, the road net, and the terrain. If a wide area is to be reconnoitered, gaps often will occur between adjacent units.

Roads should not be used for boundaries or for lateral limits of reconnaissance zones. Main routes should lie in the middle of sectors.

155. Reconnaissance units should avoid all unnecessary engagement with the enemy, except those required to drive the enemy off or to force the reconnaissance through (Paragraph 124). If reconnaissance units are committed to security missions in exceptional situations, they must be reinforced adequately. All commanders are responsible to ensure that reconnaissance effectiveness does not suffer from such missions.

156. The orders issued to a reconnaissance unit specify its exact mission. They also include the time of departure; information on adjacent reconnaissance elements; sectors or direction; the reconnaissance objective; the daily phase line patrols much reach; instructions for the transmission of reports; and the location of intermediate objectives that must be reported when reached. Additional elements of information include required reporting times; instructions for communicating with aerial reconnaissance elements; and the departure time, route of march, and objective of the main body.

It may be necessary to include instructions concerning contact with the enemy and with the local civilian population.

Patrols receive similar orders.

157. Motorized units advance by bounds when contact with the enemy is imminent. Cover, the form of the terrain, and the road net all influence the length of the bounds. The bounds are shortened as the distance to the enemy decreases. The security measures for an advance by bounds depends on the situation.

All elements of a motorized reconnaissance unit will use existing roads for as long as possible. In enemy territory alternate routes of return should be used. Towns and points along roads that are important for freedom of movement must be secured.

To secure a rest position at night, motorized forces can pull back from the enemy, but they must send out patrols as security elements. Towns on major routes are not usually suitable for bivouac.

158. The width of the reconnaissance zone for a motorized reconnaissance battalion generally will not exceed 50 kilometers.

The depth to which a battalion is deployed must include provisions for a secure refueling site. When planning the march, a fuel reserve should be provided for unanticipated contingencies.

The operating range of armored vehicles without refueling is 200 to 250 kilometers.

159. Reconnaissance patrols may be composed of armored vehicles, machine-gun motor vehicles; and armed motorcyclists. All may be required based on the mission, enemy activity, the civilian population, the road distance, and the probable method of sending reports back. Stronger patrols are committed to the most important routes and against the most important areas. The commander of the motorized reconnaissance battalion normally sends out the patrols.

160. Patrol orders include the route of march and the objectives. Patrols normally cannot be used for additional close-in security of the battalion or of their parent unit. Patrols advance by bounds from observation point to observation point. The forward distance of a patrol is a function of the situation, the terrain, and the range of available communications means. As a rule, patrols will not be pushed out farther than one hour's travelling distance.

161. The motorized reconnaissance battalion serves as the reconnaissance reserve for patrols and the report collection point. It also provides general support for the reconnaissance elements. The deployment of intermediate elements will ensure rearward communications when patrols are deployed to greater distances in front of the battalion.

Contact with the enemy, once established, must be maintained. If necessary, this will be accomplished by the commitment of additional reconnaissance vehicles. Armed motorcyclists can be used to reinforce the reconnaissance net.

162. If the motorized reconnaissance battalion can no longer be deployed as the enemy closes, the unit should be withdrawn. The commander then assigns the close reconnaissance mission to the mounted reconnaissance battalion in sufficient time so no breaks occur in the reconnaissance and contact with the enemy is maintained. For limited periods, elements of the motorized reconnaissance battalion can be attached to the mounted battalion for support.

When the motorized reconnaissance battalion is withdrawn from the front, it should reconnoiter the flanks and rear of the enemy or screen gaps between elements. It also can be held in reserve behind the front.

163. Mounted reconnaissance battalions must be deployed early to establish the necessary distance in front of the main body and to have suffi-

cient time to execute their mission. They establish a reserve for their reconnaissance patrols and a collection point for reports. They advance by bounds and generally avoid the main routes, but keeping them under observation. This is especially true if they lack antitank weapons. The more difficult the terrain and the closer the enemy, the shorter the bounds by which they advance.

164. Cavalry mounted reconnaissance elements are constituted based on the situation and terrain. Their strength varies between one platoon and two troops.* In special situations a cavalry regiment† can be assigned a reconnaissance mission. Bicycle troops can be provided with radio communications. Heavy machine guns, motorcycles, and antitank weapons can be attached as the situation requires. In some cases artillery can be attached as well. For the most part, however, the attachment of less mobile elements should not reduce the mobility of mounted reconnaissance forces. For similar reasons baggage vehicles can be left temporarily in the rear. In such cases it might be necessary to substitute locally requisitioned vehicles that can be abandoned if the situation requires.

165. The frontal width assigned to a cavalry division for reconnaissance will generally not exceed 50 kilometers. This is the practical limit that such a unit can cover without gaps. The number of mounted reconnaissance detachments depends on the width of the division zone. If it exceeds 50 kilometers, the division must attempt to maintain a reconnaissance without gaps in the most important direction.

166. Mounted reconnaissance battalions are assigned reconnaissance zones corresponding to the road net. The zone assigned to a troop generally will not exceed 10 kilometers. Troops deployed in secondary directions and platoons and independent officer patrols deployed in their own sectors will normally be assigned only a direction and reconnaissance objective. It is seldom possible to conduct such lateral reconnaissance without gaps.

167. The cavalry division commander must maintain firm control of his mounted reconnaissance battalion. Its distance in front of the main body of the division depends on his intent and the situation. It seldom will be more than 30 to 40 kilometers. At the level of platoons and independent officer patrols, the maximum range of the radio sets is a key planning factor.

Mounted reconnaissance battalions generally receive daily mission orders. When missions can be assigned for several days at a time, the units

---

*A German cavalry squadron (*Schwadron*) was the equivalent of an American troop.

†A standard cavalry regiment had four cavalry troops (squadrons), a machine-gun and mortar troop, and an antitank troop. A cavalry division's reconnaissance regiment had six troops.

should execute the subsequent day's task only if they receive no order to the contrary by a fixed time.

During the night mounted reconnaissance units rest off the main routes, which they observe and block as the situation requires.

168. If multiple mounted reconnaissance elements are deployed, a message collection center can be established in a forward area. It will be indispensable should the cavalry division change its direction of advance.

169. The deployment of the divisional reconnaissance battalion* depends on the commander's intent, the situation, and the width and the depth of its reconnaissance area.

The division commander assigns reconnaissance missions and directions based on the corps operations order. He determines the battalion's distance to the front of the division, which generally is less than that of the mounted reconnaissance battalion of a cavalry division. The division commander also assigns any special tasks. In exceptional situations, the reconnaissance battalion of a division advancing in single column may be attached to the advance guard. In such cases the advance guard commander will assign the tasks and designate the distance to the front of the advance guard. These tasks are always based on the intent of the division commander. The fragmentation of the divisional reconnaissance battalion and its assignment to individual march columns should be avoided.

The fact that other reconnaissance elements may be operating to the division's front does not relieve the commander from the responsibility for conducting his own reconnaissance. If no other reconnaissance element is operating to the front of the divisional reconnaissance battalion, the division commander can set its objective farther forward. Communications with the division and the transmission of messages and orders, however, must be maintained.

When the advance is executed on a broad front, arrangements must be made to ensure the timely receipt of information by all column commanders.

When the division is close to the enemy, it may be advisable to hold the reconnaissance battalion back and to send forward patrols only.

170. The commander of the divisional reconnaissance battalion executes the reconnaissance mission and sends out the patrols. Should the division commander personally order out patrols, he must advise the reconnaissance battalion commander of these patrols and their missions.

If the divisional reconnaissance battalion commander receives no new

---

*The divisional reconnaissance battalion had a cavalry troop, a bicycle company, an antitank platoon, a heavy machine-gun platoon, and a signal section. Both the cavalry troop and the bicycle company had nine light machine guns each. The heavy machine-gun company had three horse-drawn heavy machine guns. The antitank platoon had three 37mm guns. [*Hartness Report*, p. 29]

orders, or if is he unexpectedly confronted with a change in the situation, he must reorganize and execute the reconnaissance in the manner he believes best conforms to the division commander's intent.

171. Commanders of mounted reconnaissance battalions must maintain firm control of their patrols. The prerequisites for successful patrols include close objectives (10 to 15 kilometers), well defined missions, and rapid and well-planned advances from sector to sector. Contact is best maintained with the enemy through patrols already in contact and the timely deployment of new patrols.

In order to conserve the strength of patrols, it is sometimes best to transport them in trucks with the main body of the battalion prior to their deployment.

172. The assigned strength of patrols is a function of their mission, enemy activity, and the attitude of the civilian population. The number of required reports also is a planning factor. Planners must never forget, however, that it is far more difficult for a larger patrol to operate unobserved by the enemy. A second-in-command always should be designated.

Patrols can be used to provide security for the reconnaissance battalion. They should use available roads as much as possible and advance by bounds from observation point to observation point.

173. Under the cover of the mounted reconnaissance battalion, the individual arms send forward such reconnaissance elements as may be required for the subsequent and timely deployment of those arms. The reconnaissance battalion commander must be advised of all such reconnaissance parties. As the situation dictates, they may be attached temporarily to the reconnaissance battalion.

174. Combat reconnaissance normally is initiated only when units begin to deploy.*

As the distance closes with the enemy, there is a natural tendency to place security requirements above those of reconnaissance. Every commander, therefore, must ensure that reconnaissance is not neglected in favor of security.

175. With the initiation of combat reconnaissance, mounted reconnaissance units to the front should receive one of the following missions: Move clear of the front and reconnoiter the enemy flanks; Continue in zone with the original mission; Occupy key terrain points and be absorbed by the main body; or Withdraw on the main body.

Should the reconnaissance battalion receive no additional orders, it remains to the front, continues with its mission, screens the advancing main body, and withdraws only when forced to by the enemy. Mounted reconnaissance units generally return to their parent units. The divisional recon-

---

*Preliminary deployment, *Entfaltung,* followed by *Entwicklung,* full deployment.

naissance battalions of interior divisions withdraw behind the front after completing their missions.

If a mounted reconnaissance battalion is committed on an open flank it should be echeloned forward whenever possible. This method is equally suitable for reconnaissance support in the flank and rear of the enemy and for the security of friendly flanks.

176. Combat aerial reconnaissance collects information on the deployment of enemy forces; especially his artillery, his bivouac sites, the position and movements of his reserves, his armored vehicles, and any unusual activity behind the enemy front. Combat aerial reconnaissance monitors the course of the battle.

Combat aerial reconnaissance normally is flown below an altitude of 2,000 meters. Low-level reconnaissance is necessary when details must be identified and the advance of friendly or enemy infantry must be monitored. When challenged, friendly units must identify themselves to reconnaissance aircraft by means of signal flares, ground signal panels, hand signals, or similar means.

Combat aerial reconnaissance also produces targeting information required by artillery during the approach march (*Anmarsch*). This information is critical for timely counterbattery planning.

The conduct of combat aerial reconnaissance depends greatly on the overall air situation. Enemy air defenses or fighter aircraft may degrade its effectiveness. Frequently, friendly air defense artillery and fighter aircraft must support combat aerial reconnaissance.

177. Observation from captive balloons supplements combat aerial reconnaissance. Enemy air activity and the range of enemy artillery may restrict the deployment of captive balloons. In calm and clear weather large sectors of the battlefield can be observed from a captive balloon. An excellent picture of conditions can be obtained through the use of enlarged photographs. Captive balloons are an especially effective means of monitoring the enemy front, enemy artillery activity and strength, and friendly forward positions. Their most effective application is observation for friendly artillery.*

178. The senior commander designates the boundaries and often the objectives for the ground reconnaissance by his subordinate units. In the absence of special orders, every unit is responsible for conducting combat reconnaissance within the zone assigned for its advance, its deployment, and its combat action. Units with open flanks also are responsible for conducting their own flank reconnaissance.

When combat reconnaissance elements encounter resistance they can-

---

*Captive balloons often were used for directing the fire of long range, flat trajectory guns. In good weather, an observer could see up to 30 kilometers from a captive balloon. [*Wedemeyer Report*, p. 59]

not break or envelop, they must either be reinforced sufficiently to overcome the resistance, or the main body must assume the reconnaissance function. Combat reconnaissance normally requires concentration of force and unity of effort directed toward a limited objective in the most important zone.

Key information about the enemy sometimes can be collected quickly by small mounted or infantry patrols, which commanders hold in readiness.

If combat reconnaissance is conducted during the night, patrols must be alerted in sufficient time to survey the terrain and to prepare in daylight.

179. Combat reconnaissance takes time. Foresight, therefore, is essential to achieve the advantages of early execution and results. Thorough consideration must be given to the need for time in combat reconnaissance.

180. Combat reconnaissance by the individual arms focuses on their specific requirements. Often it can be executed in conjunction with tactical reconnaissance.

The rapid exploitation of reconnaissance results by all arms is a function of the rapid exchange of information and identification between elements and adjacent units. It also requires the accelerated reporting of critical information to senior commanders, who must ensure its timely evaluation and dissemination.

Combat reconnaissance increases in importance when aerial reconnaissance cannot produce results and when other ground reconnaissance assets are overcommitted.

181. Combat reconnaissance often must reconnoiter the terrain (avenues of approach, areas covered by enemy observation and fire, observation points, and firing positions) and simultaneously serve as close security. If at all possible, other elements should be assigned to the close security mission.

Combat reconnaissance also can be used to identify the friendly front line trace.

182. Observation of the battlefield by commanders at all levels and by specially designated officers is an essential element of combat reconnaissance.

183. The artillery observation battalion* is an especially valuable asset for monitoring the battlefield. Their observers often are in a position to provide the commander with early and important information. During the

---

*A divisional observation battalion included a sound ranging battery, a flash ranging battery, and a survey battery. The flash ranging battery operated from positions where it could observe directly into enemy territory. The sound ranging battery deployed their microphone base behind the line of their own artillery. The techniques of sound and flash ranging were perfected in World War I. They are still in use today, but of course, computerized. In modern parlance, an observation battalion would be called a target acquisition battalion.

course of the battle the flash ranging battery will produce key information.

Intelligence by Special Means

184. The air reporting service monitors enemy air activity and secures key information for the air estimate of the situation. It can produce valuable information about the enemy intent, even prior to the commencement of ground combat.

185. Signals intelligence is collected by monitoring enemy transmissions, both in the air and on the ground. The technical means include listening posts, signal lamp interception stations, and telephone wiretaps. These functions require unified leadership, specially trained operators, and security.

186. On home territory (*Heimat*), important information can be collected by telephone stations oriented in the direction of the enemy. This may help to reduce the work load of other reconnaissance elements.

Prearranged visual and audio signals can be used on home territory for collecting information.

In foreign territory, the monitoring of the public telephone system often can be an effective method of collecting information.

187. The enemy press must be monitored. The senior headquarters will issue special instructions regarding this function.

188. Standard procedures are essential for the interrogation of prisoners and the evaluation of captured documents (orders, maps, pay and notice books, letters, newspapers, photos, films, etc.) Such documents may be found on prisoners; on the wounded; on messenger pigeons and dogs; in villages; in emplacements; or in captured vehicles, aircraft, or balloons. In all situations captured documents must be secured against destruction. Specially trained officers always should interrogate prisoners.

After a short interrogation—which should be limited to the immediate tactical situation—and a cursory review of their papers, prisoners must be transported to the command headquarters by the most direct route.

Quick and skillful interrogation of prisoners is vitally important. They should be questioned about their own unit, adjacent units, higher units, the names of their commanders, their last bivouac position, movements and means of transport, the condition and morale of their units, and any deployments of special weapons. Use of coercion is not permitted by international law. After examination, papers that have no military significance must be returned to prisoners.

The names and unit designations of the enemy dead should be noted and any insignia on their uniforms should be identified.

189. Statements by civilian inhabitants can yield important information. A search of railway stations, mail offices, and similar installations can produce telegrams with military content, keys to codes, call signs, etc. Important information also can be gathered from official correspondence. This category of information turns up often during pursuit operations.

Counterintelligence

190. The enemy will attempt to collect information through methods similar to ours. His efforts can be countered only by the strictest enforcement of security procedures, both at home and in the field. The various broadcasting means for enemy propaganda that might influence troops and the population in enemy territory must be monitored carefully.

The senior headquarters must establish a systematic counterintelligence plan. The secret field police are at the commander's disposal for this purpose. All troops must contribute to operational security, especially in billets or in bivouac. This can be accomplished by observing all suspicious persons, by exercising caution in conversations and telephone communications, and by securing all orders and documents in offices. All suspicious activities must be reported to the secret field police without delay. Any person suspected of conducting espionage activities will be arrested and turned over to the military police.

191. Discretion is essential on the part of both commanders and troops. All signal communications from the headquarters must be tightly supervised.

192. Great care should taken with correspondence, personal memoirs recorded in diaries, and similar records.

Personal correspondence will be censored in certain situations. Letters should not contain any information that might inform the enemy about the situation, the deployment of units, or other such useful information. The regulations governing the field postal service apply to letter traffic.

193. Addresses and unit designations should not be posted on billets. If they are used, they should be removed prior to the unit's departure. Unit designations on motor vehicles and railway cars also can lead to compromise. They should be covered as the situation may require.

Documents that have no further use should be burned. When billets are evacuated, all documents, including the smallest files, should be removed. Such measures require close supervision.

194. Reconnaissance elements, security detachments, and all units in

combat should not carry into the front lines any orders, documents, or regulations that may be of any use to the enemy. In situations where reconnaissance units must carry and maintain written orders, maps, and drawings, these documents will be destroyed when in danger of enemy capture.

IV

SECURITY

195. Security measures are employed to prevent surprise attack and to restrict the enemy's surveillance from the air or ground. Where security measures are employed primarily against enemy surveillance, they also provide screening.

Security is necessary during rest halts, during movement and, to a lesser extent during combat. As the distance to the enemy decreases, security generally is directed against the enemy on the ground. In combat the type and extent of security is determined by the situation. Security measures should at no time impede the execution of a mission.

196. Continuous reconnaissance is the essential element of security.

Paragraph 125 covers the relationship between reconnaissance and security.

197. Security against enemy air activity is executed by air defense units and fighter aircraft; through measures established by higher headquarters for camouflage and the dispersal of units; by using darkness to conceal movements; and through the employment of all air defense measures by all units.

198. Security against the enemy on the ground is generally accomplished by deploying smaller units on a high state of alert to the front of the main body. In certain situations, the main body units themselves will assume a higher state of alert.

The strength, composition, and organization of the security elements depend on the situation, the commander's intent, the total strength, the distance from the enemy, and the nature of the terrain and level of visibility. As far as possible, security forces should maintain unit integrity.

During rest periods, larger units provide their own security whenever local security by outposts or combat outposts is inadequate. During forward movement security is provided by the advance guard; during a withdrawal it is provided by the rear guard. If necessary, flank security is established by flank guards.

Every unit also requires close-in security, which may be organized collectively for multiple units.

199. Security duties increase the demands on units. Therefore, no more force will be committed to this mission than absolutely necessary.

Security During Bivouac

200. Units in bivouac establish outposts or combat outposts, depending on the extent of the threat.

Outposts repel small attacks, secure the main body from disruption, and give bivouacked units time to prepare for combat or movement. They deny enemy surveillance of the main body.

Combat outposts are established when units are in bivouac and a state of partial or full combat alert is anticipated. They secure the immediate avenues of approach for the elements preparing for combat. Otherwise, they function as regular outposts.

Outposts and combat outposts reconnoiter only so far as necessary to provide security for units in bivouac. Wider reconnaissance is the mission of other elements, as ordered by the commander.

201. Because it is impossible to establish procedures for all situations, only general principles are given here. In every situation outposts and combat outposts should be established based on the situation. The more unclear the enemy situation, the greater the requirement for security.

202. Protected sectors make security easier to achieve and make it possible to manage with weaker forces. Wherever possible, trains and service elements will bivouac behind terrain sheltered by natural features.

Unprotected or open flanks must be secured. Based on the situation, the wing may curve rearward, may be echeloned to the rear, or may be secured by specially designated units. Rear area security also may be necessary.

Obstacles and field fortifications reinforce security.

Special attention must be given to defense against armored vehicles.

203. Except in combat, troop movements are confined to roads during daylight, and even more so at night.

It is, therefore, important to occupy and to interdict roads that lead from the direction of the enemy or from open flanks. During day and with good observation, it is normally sufficient to occupy commanding positions with good fields of fire. Such positions that give a similar advantage to the enemy also should be occupied.

Stronger security forces are necessary in terrain where visibility is restricted, during bad weather, and in darkness. Lesser depth in the security echelon and a closer positioning to the main body may be necessary.

204. All security units must establish concealment from enemy air or

ground observation. Favorable rear observation posts may be utilized to observe the forward terrain.

205. Fast and reliable communications are essential between local and adjacent security elements and with units in bivouac positions.

206. Every security element provides its own security through sentries, which vary in number based on the situation.

207. Sentries, outpost sentinels, sentry squads, and patrols of all types do not salute during security duties. They report to their superiors without interrupting their surveillance activities.

208. The relief of security elements must be conducted discreetly. All important information will be passed to the incoming commander, who also must be oriented to the terrain. Security must be maintained during the relief.

209. During an attack, all elements of the security force will be at full alert. They must be prepared to make any necessary sacrifice to fulfill their mission of protecting the bivouacked units.

210. Air defense of bivouacked units is organized as described in Paragraphs 662 and 696. Units on security duty may be integrated into the air defense plan. They are, however, responsible for their own air defense measures, the most important being camouflage.

Outposts

211. The primary criterion for the location of an outpost (*Vorposten*) is the commander's designation of the bivouac area for his units. Other factors include the probable duration of the outpost position and the commander's intent.

The strength and composition of the outpost is determined by the enemy threat; the strength, composition, and type of units requiring security; the terrain; the time of the day; and any special conditions. If other friendly forces are in position between the outpost line and the enemy, the outpost may be correspondingly weaker.

212. The most simple of security measures usually suffice when the enemy is at a great distance (150 to 200 kilometers). This normally includes the direct security of the bivouac area, from which small elements can be deployed as necessary. See Paragraph 677 concerning the security of bivouac areas by outlying pickets.

If this level of security is insufficient, the senior commander or the commanders of the bivouac groups will direct the units nearest the enemy to establish security for the bivouacked main body. A commander must designated for these security elements. In the event of multiple security sectors, a commander will be assigned for each sector. Area or bivouac commanders also are responsible for establishing such security. They direct the action in case of an attack, the state of alert of the main body in bivouac, and the deployment of security elements. Positioning units within the bivouac area can increase overall security.

Cavalry and motorized units establish their own security through long-range reconnaissance and by greater depth of deployment in the bivouac area.

213. An increased level of security can be achieved by establishing an outpost system in the terrain beyond the bivouacked units.

The establishment of such outposts normally does not relieve the bivouacked units from providing local security.

214. Infantry units are the best suited for outpost duties. Other arms can reinforce the infantry as necessary.

Cavalry should be used sparingly and when employed, should be drawn from the mounted elements of the infantry regiments. Bicyclists are effective on outpost duties at night and when roads are good. Artillery is seldom effective on an outpost. If artillery must be used, it should be deployed at night.

A defense by armored vehicles can be reinforced by elements of the divisional antitank battalion.*

Engineers may be committed to establish obstacles and roadblocks.

The establishment of a signal communications net is the general mission of communications units.

215. When units bivouac on the march, the advance guard or rear guard is generally assigned the mission of securing the main body. All or elements of the advance (or rear) guard may be committed to this mission.

The outpost line itself must be established under secure conditions.

If the divisional reconnaissance battalion is available, it may in exceptional situations be assigned to provide security for the outpost line. The outpost line must be informed of any deployment of the divisional reconnaissance battalion. During the night it may be necessary to withdraw the divisional reconnaissance battalion behind the line of forward outposts. Their patrols, however, should maintain contact with the enemy.

216. When the force establishes a bivouac, the overall commander designates the bivouac areas for the units requiring security. If the commander has not delegated such decisions to the commanders of the respective march columns, he designates the units for outpost duty; the outpost sectors; the sector commanders and sector boundaries; the most forward security line;

---

*The divisional antitank battalion had thirty-six 37mm guns. Each infantry regiment also had twelve antitank guns, and the reconnaissance battalion had three, for a divisional total of seventy-five. [*Wedemeyer Report*, p. 36]

the extent and objectives of the outpost reconnaissance; outpost actions during an enemy attack; and communications with adjacent outposts.

The type of defensive—defense or delaying defense—determines whether units of the main body will reinforce the outposts, or if the outpost line will fall back on the main body.

The establishment of a continuous outpost line of linked elements depends on the situation, the width of the units to be secured, and the terrain.

Key roads, railroad lines, and terrain points should lie within the outpost sector. Where gaps occur, the responsibility for their observation must be established clearly.

217. A battalion normally mans an outpost sector, reinforced by other arms as necessary.

The outpost sector commander issues the initial orders for establishing security. These include the occupation of key terrain; the establishment of obstacles on the most important routes and avenues of approach; reconnaissance and terrain information; and the preparation of the defense by the main outpost force.

After conducting a personal reconnaissance, the outpost commander supplements his initial orders by designating the location of the defensive position or the line of resistance. Specific details include actions in case of an enemy attack; instructions concerning contact with other units; field fortifications and signal communications; and air and gas defense measures. The commander also decides whether tents can be pitched and open fires lit, and he designates the uniform of the day. Unless otherwise ordered, field packs are not worn on outpost duty.

The outpost sector commander also determines the location of the reserve, its type of bivouac, its state of alert, its local security measures, and the location of his own command post.

Fast and reliable communications must be established from all elements of the outpost line to the sector commander. His observation post must be connected with the senior commander's. Generally, the divisional trunk line can be used, especially if it has already been established along the route of advance and up to the most forward security elements.

218. Rifle companies deployed in an outpost sector constitute the mainstay of security. In exceptional situations, independent platoons may be deployed in lieu of companies. Rifle companies are reinforced if necessary by infantry heavy weapons, cavalry, or bicyclists. Based on their specific orders, the companies establish themselves in their sectors in position or in a defensive line. Based upon his own orders from the outpost sector commander, a company commander will decide which of his squads will man the positions or the line of resistance, and which can stand down. During daylight and periods of good observation, picket details

(*Feldwachen*) or picket posts (*Feldposten*) generally are sufficient to man the positions or the line of resistance. The company commander will send out patrols to reconnoiter the enemy, to establish security, and to maintain contact with adjacent sectors. Under certain circumstances, he may establish stationary reconnaissance parties (*stehende Spähtrupps*), which occupy appropriate terrain in front of the line of the picket posts. The stationary reconnaissance parties remain in position until relieved.

219. Picket details and picket posts may be pushed forward to advantageous points by the rifle companies. The number, strength, and assignment of heavy weapons is a function of the mission, the location of the most forward security line, the importance of the advanced points, and the proximity of the enemy. In order not to reduce unnecessarily the combat strength of the company, advanced outposts should be deployed sparingly and only where most needed. The company commander, as a rule, specifies the actions of the picket details and picket posts in the case of enemy attack.

220. The strength of picket detail varies from a squad to a platoon.

Picket details provide their own security through picket posts, patrols, and stationary reconnaissance parties.

221. A picket post normally consists of three men, one of whom is designated as the leader. Light machine-gun sections should man important posts. Picket posts normally are not positioned more than 500 meters in front of their supporting unit.

The picket post must have good observation and must be concealed from enemy observation. The occupation of high ground facilitates observation and listening. Day and night operations are different. The posts should be equipped with field glasses and signaling devices.

Two soldiers in a picket post observe simultaneously. They must be compatible with one another.

Picket posts normally dig in. Their orders will specify whether they may sit, lie down, smoke, or remove their field packs.

Picket posts orient in the direction of the enemy. They report any indications of enemy activity as soon as they observe it.

In case of impending threat or attack, the picket posts raise the alarm by firing. They update passing patrols on the situation as they know it.

Picket posts allow known persons to pass in and out. All others must show their credentials or prove their identity. Those who cannot are conducted to higher authority. In the conduct of a roadblock, orders will specify the actions concerning friendly and enemy motor vehicles.

The use of a password enhances security.

All approaching persons halt on the challenge of a picket post. Anyone disregarding the order of a picket post will be fired upon.

During darkness and upon detecting approaching persons, the picket posts will ready their weapons and challenge the approaching party with the words, "Halt! Who is there?" After three challenges without reply the picket posts will open fire.

Enemy defectors or individual enemy officers accompanied by a small escort, and who identify themselves as emissaries or negotiators seeking contact under a flag of truce, will not be treated as enemies. They will be required to lay down their weapons, be blindfolded, and be sent to the next higher commander without being allowed to speak.

In addition to these general instructions, all picket posts receive special orders, which includes information on:

- The enemy and the location
- The position and mission of advanced and adjacent units
- The position of the picket post in relation to the company and the most direct route to it
- The terrain sectors that especially must be observed, including visible road segments, defiles, and bridges that the enemy must use when approaching
- Actions during an enemy attack
- Means of communications with other posts and the transmission of messages
- And other necessary information, including the specific designation of their own picket posts

Whenever possible, the picket post will have a sketch of the terrain to the immediate front, with the local positions marked.

222. Relief within a picket detail is controlled by its commander or by the company commander. The commander responsible for the relief must assure himself that the picket posts know their general instructions, that the relieved post hands over all special instructions to the relieving post, and that these instructions are fully understood.

223. The commanders of all elements of an outpost, down to the picket details, will report as soon as possible to their immediate commanders the specific measures they have initiated for reconnaissance, security, and communications with adjacent elements. Terrain sketches should be included.

224. In order to conserve the strength of the horses, cavalry units should avoid establishing strong outposts. Cavalry units can be used most effectively for relatively light security duties in secure rear areas. This also results in the advantage of a short withdrawal, unless the situation requires that the terrain be held. A withdrawal to secure terrain must be screened by security forces.

At night, cavalry units commit bicycle or attached motorized infantry elements for outpost duty.

The instructions that apply to infantry outposts also apply to cavalry;

but cavalry units generally require more time to deploy in a state of combat readiness. Cavalry outposts can be established with or without horses.

Cavalry units on outpost duty of troop size and larger generally keep their horses. Smaller outpost detachments normally do not have their horses, unless otherwise ordered. If they deploy with horses, a picket detail will consist of a minimum of a squad, and a picket post generally will consist of a half squad. Cavalry picket details and picket posts do not unsaddle. If the terrain is favorable for an enemy surprise attack, the picket posts should remain mounted.

225. If the situation does not require motorized elements to remain in the most forward positions, their mobility makes it feasible for them to bivouac at some distance from the enemy, or to withdraw behind other units for protection.

If separate motorized elements establish outposts, they may include armed motorcyclists, attached motorized infantry, and armored vehicles that can operate behind defiles and obstacles. The vehicles of all bivouacked units must be serviced and ready to move before dark. Their location should facilitate rapid departure. An assembly area (*Bereitstellung*) that is too restricted hinders maneuverability and the rapid deployment of the unit.

Combat Outposts

226. In addition to the special instructions in Paragraph 198, the strength, composition, and organization of combat outposts (*Gefechtsvorposten*) will be determined by the state of alert of the main body, the plan of action against surprise attack, and any other special factors.

Combat outposts must not be established with half measures. Strongly held sectors and effective obstacles and barriers can strengthen a weak combat outpost.

227. Generally, the senior commander determines the mission for combat outposts. He can direct the terrain sector to be occupied by the outpost, its forward line of resistance, connectivity within the outpost, and required actions in case of enemy attack. When attacked, the outpost either defends in place or executes a delaying action, withdrawing in a predetermined direction.

Dependent upon the situation, it may be necessary to establish a position behind the outpost line and to occupy it with units from the main body. This position can be used as a rallying point or assembly area for withdrawing outpost troops.

228. In general, the infantry units closest to the enemy establish the

combat outposts. Outpost troops normally remain attached to their parent units.

Outposts at a considerable distance from the bivouacked main body, and which come from multiple units, may be placed under a single command.

Outposts may be reinforced by supporting artillery or, in special situations, by attached artillery. The reinforcement of outposts by elements of the divisional antitank battalion is also an option.

Combat outpost units establish their own signal communications network.

When contact with the enemy is not imminent, the organization and command of a combat outpost follows the same guidance for outposts.

229. Combat outposts provide close security and maintain contact with the enemy, once it is established. They execute combat reconnaissance in accordance with their orders.

If friendly forces are to the front of the outpost line, their orders must specify whether or not they will be attached to the outpost and the scope of their actions with respect to the outpost.

230. If a combat outpost is established during darkness, it might be advisable to occupy initially the most easily reached points, and then to extend and fully develop the outpost system in daylight.

231. If a break occurs in the battle, the units nearest the enemy will secure their positions by establishing combat outposts. These consist primarily of picket posts, patrols, and stationary reconnaissance parties, which are positioned as close to the enemy as possible or are left in direct contact.

232. Paragraphs 457 and 488 cover special instructions for combat outposts in the defense and during delaying actions.

Security During Movement and on the March

233. Large march columns moving during daylight must maintain a state of alert against enemy reconnaissance and air attack. Whenever possible such columns should be covered by air defense units and fighter aircraft. Primary consideration must be given to protection of the march formation, the start point and release point of the march, water crossings, passages through defiles, and rest areas.

When the road net permits, air defense artillery units should be assigned to routes not used by other units. Air defense batteries often can cover two march routes from one firing position. Motorized air defense batteries and air defense machine-gun companies can be sent ahead to cover points that are vulnerable to low-level air attack. If an air defense unit does not have its own assigned march route, its movement must be coordinated with the common march route. As a rule, air defense units have priority at intersections and defiles.

Air defense units support the patrol and security elements of the command. Air defense batteries provide warning by their fire and by the positions of their air bursts from firing.

234. If the air threat is high but immediate enemy contact is not imminent, air defense units should be dispersed along all available routes. When time is not a critical factor, the march can be extended over a greater period and units can advance as small elements with a specified time interval between each.

235. If the force must accomplish a day's march as a consolidated march unit, the effects of any enemy air attack can be mitigated by extending the length of the column—provided other factors do not prohibit such a dispersion. This deep air defense formation (*Fliegermarschtiefe*) requires every element to double its normal road space. Any reduction in the standard depth of the formation requires specific orders to that effect.

Every unit deploys into the deep air defense formation on order of its commander, reporting the initiation and termination of the maneuver. If the march is being conducted during daylight, horse-drawn trains and horse-drawn rear-service units deploy in a similar manner.

The senior commander orders the assumption or termination of the deep air defense formation. Simultaneously, he determines if the security forces (advance, rear, or flank guards) will maintain, reduce, or eliminate their distances.

The deep air defense formation normally will be initiated at the start of a march. If a column is small, however, it also can be executed during the march. The formation can be abandoned if the tactical situation demands. Halts or rests can be used to facilitate the distribution and separation of units.

236. The wide air defense formation (*Fliegermarschbreite*) is another method of protecting units from air attack during a daylight march.

The execution of the wide air defense formation requires sufficient adjacent routes that run parallel to the main route, or suitable cross-country terrain.

In the wide air defense formation, units deploy on adjacent routes on both sides or to one side of the main march route. Mounted units should be assigned to the longer routes, and motorized elements are assigned to specific routes. The main march route also can be used for motor vehicles, but then other units should march along the alternate routes. If necessary, boundaries are assigned to avoid confusion. The march sequence of units remains the same as if the march was being conducted in a single column. Follow-on units should be notified immediately if congestion occurs.

The march column commander orders the initiation and termination of the wide air defense formation. He also may authorize his subordinate element commanders to exercise their own initiative. If time is critical, every unit commander is authorized to disperse his formation in width.

The execution of a wide air defense formation in great depth is impossible in most situations. Generally, such a maneuver will cause stoppages in the march. Marching in the wide air defense formation slows down the advance, makes it irregular, increases march stress, and complicates command and control. The formation should be used only in exceptional situations, and should be terminated as soon as possible.

237. If a march is executed with the deep air defense formation, the simultaneous execution of a wide air defense formation rarely can be justified. Generally, neither formation is suitable for motorized units.

238. If a combined-arms unit larger than a reinforced regiment marches on a single route and comes under air threat, it can separate into smaller march elements that follow each other at a distance of one to three kilometers. The senior commander controls their forward movement. He can order one or more of the march elements to deploy into the deep air defense formation, provided that the entire column remains within allowable limits. If the total march depth exceeds a day's march, the individual march elements may be permitted to move at different times.

The assumption of the wide air defense formation requires the approval of the senior commander.

239. During darkness cover by air defense units and searchlights is limited to the protection of defiles, bridges, and crossing sites.

The deep and wide air defense formations generally are not used at night.

240. Air defense measures for movements through defiles and across bridges and river crossings must be established before the arrival of the main body.

Defensive techniques against air attack when marching through defiles depend on the type of defile. In short defiles they are similar to those for a march across bridges, ferries, or similar areas.

During air attacks against bridges and crossing sites, the surrounding area is also usually hit. Crossings, therefore, should be executed in small groups if the units are not already deployed into the deep air defense formation. These small groups should be maintained for a certain time after the crossing. Orders must be issued in sufficient time to avoid congestion and stoppages. Ferrying operations are best executed through simultaneous crossings at several points. Troop concentrations close to the banks must be avoided. Air defense units should be positioned on both banks if possible. It also may be necessary to establish a separate communications net for the reconnaissance and security elements. The divisional signal battalion can be brought forward for this purpose.

Crossing operations should be suspended when an air attack against a bridge or a ferrying point is imminent. Crossing operations generally will not be interrupted when only a single aircraft appears.

241. When a single enemy reconnaissance aircraft appears during the daytime, march operations normally continue.

When a formation of enemy aircraft is detected on a low-level approach or is starting a low-level attack, the air guards (*Luftspäher*) will sound the alarm. The air attack signal (five short blasts) will be given on the order of the company commander or any other commander.

On the air attack signal, the infantry will take cover in ditches or depressions alongside the road. Vehicles and cavalry halt in the road and riders dismount and set brakes. Only with sufficient advance warning and in suitable terrain is it possible for them to take cover off the road. Riders and cavalry will not block the center of the road. The cavalry, including its vehicles, continues the march as soon as possible, using available cover. Weapons designated for low-level air defense move into position at once and begin firing. Individual riflemen do not take part in the firing. Gas defense measures also may be necessary.

High-level air attacks against march columns generally occur only when passing through defiles. When an enemy aircraft formation on a high-level approach is detected in such situations, the air guards will give the warning. The air attack signal will be given on the order of the unit commander. Troops react similarly as for a low-level attack. As a rule, only the air defense batteries fire on enemy aircraft.

During the night, enemy aircraft normally attack with the aid of parachute flares. This, of course, provides warning. The air attack signal normally is ordered by the company commander or by other commanders. Foot troops on the march should take cover alongside the road. Other troops cease all movement and take cover. Any movement can betray friendly positions. Only the air defense units execute defensive actions.

Following an air attack, the march is resumed on the order of the unit commander.

When the order to resume the march is given, the commander decides whether the air attack alert status should be maintained.

Units transported by truck operate in accordance with the guidance in Chapter XXII.

242. If a night march extends into a day march, it may be necessary to order a rest period before daylight. At this point, security measures can be initiated against enemy air and ground operations.

243. The divisional reconnaissance battalion has the primary responsibility for securing the infantry division against enemy ground action. The battalion's deployment and operations are described in Paragraph 169. Its execution of reconnaissance is described in Paragraph 170.

The divisional commander may reserve patrols of the divisional reconnaissance battalion for his requirements, but he should not weaken the battalion unnecessarily.

If no reconnaissance element is operating to the front or on an open flank, reconnaissance must be accomplished by other methods.

244. In the terrain between the divisional reconnaissance battalion and the advance guard, the latter must reconnoiter to the front and flanks to screen and secure the advance. Mounted units deployed on the point and those assigned to reconnaissance and security tasks should be drawn from the mounted platoons of the infantry regiments. The commanders of the march columns and the senior commander will make any necessary cross-leveling of the mounted units.

Bicyclists, accompanying machine-gun platoons, antitank weapons, mounted units, artillery, combat engineers, and decontamination units can be deployed in advance to occupy key points along the march route, to keep defiles open, and to emplace or remove obstacles. The exact composition of the advanced force will be determined by the commander of the advance guard, the commander of a march column, or the senior commander, based on the priority of the mission and the units required. The divisional reconnaissance battalion should not be diverted from its primary mission, and therefore will only be used for such missions in exceptional situations.

245. The advance guard must secure the freedom of movement of the main body by overcoming weak enemy resistance. It protects the moving units against surprise attack in the direction of advance. When encountering the enemy it must provide the main body with sufficient time and space to deploy for combat. This should be done without decisively engaging themselves, which would restrict the commander's freedom of decision and action.

In some situations the advance guard must break through unforeseen resistance quickly and firmly hold any key terrain points it has secured.

If a meeting engagement with the enemy is anticipated, the commanders of march columns remain with the advance guard. The position of the division commander is covered in Paragraph 113.

246. The distance between the advance guard and the main body should be sufficiently great so that the main body does not become immediately involved in an advance guard engagement; and not so great that the units of the main body are unable to engage in time. The commander's intent, overall unit strength, and conditions of light and terrain should be considered as well. In general, the distance between the advance guard and the main body should be between two and four kilometers. That distance can be decreased during darkness, in poor weather with low visibility, and with a small advance guard.

247. The strength and composition of the advance guard are deter-

mined by the situation, the commander's intent, the terrain, visibility, and the strength of the main body.

The advance guard should be held to a minimum, with its infantry element between one-third and one-sixth (or less) of the total infantry of the main body. Elements of the divisional antitank battalion, light artillery, and engineers may be attached. The additional attachment of armored vehicles, light artillery columns, ammunition supply columns, or decontamination units might be necessary as well. During the advance, individual heavy artillery batteries (especially flat trajectory), horse-drawn or motorized telephone sections, radio sections, signal-lamp teams of the divisional signal battalion, and elements of the bridge train can be attached if a requirement for them is anticipated. See Paragraph 289 concerning motor vehicles.

As a rule, an advance guard moving at night will consist only of infantry with heavy weapons and engineers. Mounted troops follow about 100 meters behind the advance guard, unless there is some compelling reason to hold them with the main body.* If a night march is extended under the cover of units that have been deployed previously, normally a small infantry force is sufficient for security. Movement in fog is conducted the same as a night movement.

248. The commander of the advance guard organizes his element based on the situation, his mission, the terrain, visibility, and the strength of the forces available to him. It should be divided into a main force (*Haupttrupp*) and a point force (*Vortrupp*), plus any attached faster-moving elements.

The majority of the infantry and the other arms of the advance guard move as the main force. A portion of the infantry and engineers constitute the point force. Horse-drawn sections of the divisional signal battalion also should be included.

The security distance between the main force and the point force is normally about 1,500 to 2,000 meters. A strong point force will normally send a point company about 1,000 to 1,500 meters ahead.

An infantry point, consisting of an officer and one or more squads, precedes the point force by about 500 meters and moves by bounds from one observation point to the next. A mounted point normally consists of a squad. It also is important to assign antitank guns and signal elements (especially signal lamp teams) to the most forward elements.

Smaller elements regulate their march based on the movements of the larger elements.

Paragraph 302 covers communications.

249. Flank security during marches is preformed primarily by patrols. March columns on an open flank assume the security of the flank of the

---

*Each infantry regiment had a mounted platoon of about 48 soldiers.

adjacent column. If patrols are not sufficient, flank guards can be deployed. Such elements are usually designated in the movement orders. In exceptional situations they can be deployed during the march by either the advance guard or the main body. When such requirements occur, infantry sent on a flank guard mission should be alerted and deployed early, because in normal circumstances flank guards travel a longer route.

The threat and the terrain determine the strength and composition of the flank guard. It must be able to reconnoiter continually and rapidly communicate with the main body. On the march, the flank guard operates in a similar manner to the advance guard, but directed to the external flank. It is responsible for its own security, both to its own flank and rear.

The flank guard either accompanies the marching columns, which they protect, or it assumes a position to cover the advance and later rejoins the rear of the column.

If an advance shifts to a flank march (*Flankenmarsch*), the advance guard can be used as a flank guard, and a new advance guard can be constituted from the main body.

Should a strong threat develop against a flank, a force can be deployed against the threat by turning elements from the main body toward the flank. Every such element is responsible for its own security.

250. Reconnaissance and early warning facilitate defense against armored vehicles. Motorized forces are especially capable of early reporting. Warning of the approach of armored vehicles goes first to the unit immediately threatened, or to the commander of the march column by means of signals, messengers, or radio. Such communications must be coordinated in advance.

Antitank guns should be distributed in the march columns, especially those on an open flank. After the flanks are covered, the head and rear of the column also must be covered. Roads leading to open flanks or that come from rear areas can be blocked by engineers or by the units themselves, using mines or other means. Armored vehicles designated for defensive purposes move along the route of march, either in front of or behind the march columns, or on parallel routes.

As soon as an attack by enemy armored vehicles develops, all antitank weapons prepare to engage, the infantry takes cover upon the orders of their commanders, and mounted and motorized troops disperse from the road in small groups. When this is not possible they stop, dismount, block the road in the direction of the enemy using vehicles and other methods, and defend the obstacles. Other personnel remain with the horses and the vehicles.

The order to open the fire normally is given by the subordinate commanders independently.

251. Interference with the march by enemy artillery fire can be coun-

tered by making limited departures from the route of march or by deployment. Air defense batteries should be deployed early to engage enemy artillery aerial observers. If friendly artillery aerial observation is possible, long-range, flat-trajectory batteries should be brought into action quickly.

In terrain that offers poor observation, weak enemy forces usually can be pushed aside quickly by the infantry advance guard partially deploying and committing its heavy weapons. If necessary, the advance guard artillery can be used along the route of march. Armored vehicles can quickly break through this type of resistance.

On open ground or while crossing wide sectors of terrain, the artillery must cover the march. The designated artillery units should be prepared to fire on as short a notice as possible. In some situations, however, it may be necessary to reduce the rate of advance in order to ensure adequate artillery cover to all elements of the column.

The commanders of the march columns draw the overwatch batteries from the artillery of the main body.

During a march along multiple routes, the commander will employ the artillery directly under his command, only if the artillery attached to the march columns has been relieved of the overwatch mission. Heavy, flat-trajectory artillery, however, will not be used for this mission.

All units must ensure that artillery assigned to overwatch (*Überwachung*) missions is also available to engage in battle.

252. The rearguard secures the main body against surprise attack and provides security for rest halts. It cannot rely on support from the main body, and its strength and composition should be planned accordingly. Rearguards are composed of infantry, bicyclists, strong artillery (including long-range, flat-trajectory batteries), antitank weapons, and signal units with radio communications. If necessary, troops to remove wire lines and engineers with materials for barriers and bridge demolitions also will be assigned. In some situations, armored vehicles may be assigned as well. The attachment of chemical and smoke generator units also can be useful. Several rearguards can operate under a single command. A precondition for this is the availability of sufficient communications equipment and other means of contact. The divisional reconnaissance battalion may support the commander of the rearguard, but it will not come under his direct command.

Rearguards withdraw by bounds. March delays of the main body must be anticipated, and influence the distance between it and the rearguard. Mission requirements also must be considered.

During the march, the rearguard is organized for reserve and support, with faster moving units deployed in a similar manner as the advance guard. Their reconnaissance elements maintain contact with the enemy. A strong rearguard may also deploy a rear point company, followed by the infantry rear point, and possibly the mounted rear point.

During a withdrawal it is essential that the main body gain distance quickly. All available routes should be used.

253. Rearguards also can be deployed during an advance, if an attack or disruption from the rear area is expected. Often, small infantry elements, especially if equipped with heavy machine guns and antitank weapons, will be sufficient for this mission. The attachment of artillery might be necessary.

254. During rest halts, security from enemy observation and aerial reconnaissance is best achieved through use of the terrain and the dispersal of units. The senior commander is responsible for establishing air defense measures. Every unit also is responsible for its own security against air attack. When enemy aircraft approach, air guards give the warning. The troops take cover, cease all movement, and conceal themselves from aerial observation. Every element provides its own air guards during rest stops.

If a formation of enemy aircraft is detected approaching at low- or high-level, air guards will give the air attack signal. All troops not performing a specific task take cover as quickly as possible. Air defense weapons commence firing as soon as the attacker is in range. The leader of the halted element cancels the air attack alert condition. If necessary, the leaders of units in a rest halt will issue supplementary orders for air attack signals and air attack alert at the beginning of the rest halt period.

Units provide their own security against enemy ground forces, based on the principles in the section "Security During Bivouac."

Reconnaissance must be maintained during the rest halt.

Security Through Deployment Prior to Combat

255. A marching element that anticipates an early encounter with the enemy increases its readiness for action by deploying into combat formation. This likewise increases the unit's security posture.

An advance guard can be used to secure the deployment of the remaining forces. If the deployment of the main force eliminates the mission of the advance guard, its new missions become consistent with that of the whole force. As a rule, the order for deployment cancels any special unit march dispositions.

256. In addition to the commander's intent, the distance from the enemy, his state of alert, the terrain, and visibility influence the time, the area, and the type of deployment.

Deployment slows the pace of forward movement.

Open terrain, favorable conditions for enemy observation, long-range fire, and strong air threats may necessitate earlier deployment.

Alternatively, the situation may require that the advance continue in its original formation regardless of potential losses. In such cases, areas under enemy observation or fire must be avoided by short detours.

257. An advance in multiple columns can accelerate deployment and give the commander the opportunity of securing early the necessary terrain for the engagement; and in some situations to envelop the enemy flank.

Normally, the force must be assembled for combat. The commander must order this in sufficient time, before the individual subordinate commanders have committed themselves. When necessary for the execution of his intent, the commander also will order an organization in depth.

258. If the commander is unable to assign specific combat missions in his deployment order, he at a minimum designates the direction and objective of the farthest advance. He also establishes combat reconnaissance assignments, unit boundaries, cover to be provided by artillery and other arms during the deployment, and the locations of special units.

A reconnaissance battalion to the front of the division receives orders for its operations as described in Paragraph 175.

259. As a rule, the divisional signal battalion receives orders to establish wire communications to the forward infantry regiments or to the individual march columns. As the deployment continues, communications are maintained and the artillery net is established. The lines should be constructed in such a manner that they can be used for as long a time as possible during the battle. The divisional trunk line (*Stammleitung*) is set up to the rear; forward, it connects to the infantry regiments.* Special observation points for the division commander are connected to the trunk line by branch lines. If divisional traffic overloads the signal battalion and direct wire connection between the division commander and the infantry regiments cannot be established, the regiments will connect themselves to the trunk line at designated points. All available troops of the signal battalion must be employed to establish the communications net for combat. Construction of lateral lines will avoid long lines to the rear when the commander shifts his command post. When the terrain permits, signal lamp communications are valuable as a backup for wire connections.

The timely deployment of signal units is essential for the establishment of the combat communications net.

260. If a deployment is necessary during darkness, security elements must be sent forward as near to the enemy as possible. Units advance by bounds under the cover of the security elements. A deployment during darkness should be executed using existing trails and routes. In some situa-

---

*The divisional trunk line was the main rear-to-front communication of the division. During a march it was laid along the route where the main column and the division commander were moving.

tions, avenues of approach (*Annäherungswege*) should be reconnoitered and marked beforehand. When necessary, the deployment is covered by artillery units, which must be in their firing positions before darkness, or must have made preparations for night supporting fires.

All leaders must remain easy to locate. Communications nets must be reinforced continually.

Screening

261. Screening of assembled forces and unit movements must be provided on all sides against enemy aerial reconnaissance. Screening against enemy ground forces may be necessary to the front as well as to the flanks. Both offensive and defensive methods will be used.

The later the enemy detects a screening effort, the more effectively it accomplishes its mission.

262. Screening from the air is an air forces mission. Screening can be executed for limited periods by strong fighter forces and the bombing of enemy airfields. If the fighter forces are relatively weak, their missions are restricted to countering enemy aerial reconnaissance over the most important friendly positions (Chapter XV). Should air defense units be engaged, enemy attention will almost certainly be drawn to the area being covered.

Screening against enemy air action requires careful camouflage of units, dispersal, and increased use of night movement.

263. Offensive screening is primarily a cavalry mission. Its purpose is to prevent the enemy from reaching the units being screened. Moreover, enemy reconnaissance elements must be attacked and repelled wherever detected.

264. Defensive screening is most effective when the terrain restricts enemy reconnaissance to a few approaches. These can be blocked with defended obstacles. Stronger elements should be assembled to the rear and positioned to counter attempted breakthroughs. Rapid and secure communications must be established between the screen, the front line, and the commander. Reconnaissance elements should be sent far to the front to reconnoiter the enemy.

Cavalry units are well suited for defensive screening missions.

Screening by infantry becomes necessary where the terrain restricts or denies cavalry operations. It may be necessary to reinforce the infantry with other arms for this mission.

The chemical contamination of terrain, in great depth if possible, can strengthen the defensive screen considerably. In the case of a shortage of chemical agents, the contamination of widely dispersed single terrain points can support the screen if those points are selected skillfully.

Dummy emplacements also can be used to reinforce a defensive screen.

265. Enemy signal traffic must be monitored and interdicted by all available means.

266. Signal units contribute to the screening effort primarily through radio communications. They accomplish this by jamming enemy signal traffic, by deceptive traffic, and by maintaining radio silence and the close supervision of their own traffic.

267. Besides its own distinct function, screening directly supports the execution of other missions.

V

MARCHES

268. Unit movements and marches are an important part of warfare. The success of all operations depends greatly upon the secure execution of marches and the fitness of the troops at the end of a march.

269. The march performance of troops will be reduced when they are not regularly trained for marching and accustomed to the exertion. From the beginning of a war, therefore, every opportunity for march training must be exercised. This is especially true for the infantry, for whom even new boots can cause problems.

270. Increases in march performance require careful planning regarding halts and rests; strict march discipline; care of the feet; horseshoeing; and the maintenance of clothing, equipment, saddlery, and harnesses. Medical care and good food for men and horses are the most effective means to maintain and increase march capabilities. Loss rates of men with sore feet and horses with lameness or sore backs are important indicators of the standard of medical and veterinary care provided on the march.

Company and higher commanders must continuously observe foot troops, horses and riders, and drivers and vehicles during the march. They are responsible for assuring the timely march relief for men and horses and the provision of competent care during rest halts and in bivouac areas. Properly timed alternations between trotting, walking, and led distances will minimize the loss of animals from strain.

Chapter XXII also covers marches by motorized units.

271. Vehicle transportation of infantry backpacks and horses' loads provides considerable relief and increases march performance. The corresponding increase in the number of vehicles, however, limits this practice to special situations and smaller units.

On the other hand, unit vehicles, within the limits of their capacity, should be used to transport portions of the equipment of men and horses in need of relief.

Ammunition and emergency rations must be removed from the packs prior to loading them onto the vehicles.

272. Rest days cannot be expected as long as a unit remains under

combat conditions. Every opportunity, therefore, should be taken to relieve men and horses; to inspect and repair vehicles; and to repair weapons, equipment, and clothing.

273. Heat is the greatest enemy of marching troops. It especially affects the infantry, whose numbers can thin out very quickly, and who require well-considered preventive measures.

If possible, marches will be made at night during periods of extreme heat.

If a march must be conducted during the day in the hot season, rest halts should be scheduled during the hottest time of the day.

During periods of extreme heat, the regulation of drinking during the march becomes very important. Drinking can be authorized during short halts or during the march, and must be controlled carefully. Cold coffee or tea can be provided for canteens prior to moving out.

Horses suffer more from a lack of water than from a lack of food. Generally, the adequate watering of a large number of horses can be accomplished only during rest halts.

274. Ears, cheeks, hands, and chins must be protected during cold weather. Infantrymen may sling their rifles from time to time to be able to move their hands. Generally, they march better without their greatcoats, but they should put them on during long halts. Mounted and motorized units will dismount often and will act as guides. Warm meals and drinks should be provided as often as possible.

March speed and performance are greatly reduced in conditions of snow and smooth ice. Troops marching in the front should be relieved on a frequent basis. In deep snow it may be necessary to use vehicles with sled runners or sleighs to break trail for the troops.

Winter equipment requirements for men and horses must be planned well in advance.

275. As far as the situation permits, march routes must be reconnoitered to determine their suitability, construction work, load capacity of bridges, obstacles, heavy snowfall, or other restrictions. Such reconnaissance is especially important for motorized units. Map information about the road network is not always reliable. Photographic reconnaissance from the air can help.

If the possibility exists of damaged routes, engineers with bridging equipment must be sent ahead—or can be attached to the advance guard— to make repairs. Rest halts should be timed to coincide with periods of probable repair work.

276. A night march is more dependent than a day march on reliable maps and on roads in good condition. If reconnaissance is not possible, or should any doubt exist, locally recruited guides familiar with the area should be used—especially when road conditions are bad and in periods of

total darkness. Night marches, especially for motorized units, often require road markings and careful control to maintain the cohesion of the marching elements.

Except in hot weather, a night march is more taxing than a day march.

No lights should be visible if enemy reconnaissance or observation is probable. Otherwise, lanterns at the end of each company facilitate cohesion and connection between march elements. If motor vehicles move without lights, they must reduce their speed.

Total silence is mandatory in the vicinity of the enemy.

To maintain concealment from enemy aerial reconnaissance, assembly for the march and the entrance into bivouac areas should be conducted during darkness. The shorter the night, the less movement time is available, and therefore the shorter the distance covered.

277. Critical situations require higher march performance and even forced marches (*Gewaltmärsche*). The troops should be informed of the reasons for forced marches.

Excessive demands beyond the capabilities of the troops weaken their combat effectiveness and morale.

278. The primary nature of all march orders depends upon the likelihood of early ground contact with the enemy.

If such contact is not anticipated, more extensive provisions can be made for troop comfort. Marching in small units, or in elements composed of a single arm, can reduce both march stress and the risk of air threat.

If enemy contact is possible, however, readiness for action must be the primary focus. This requires the formation of combined arms elements, the selection of a suitable order of march, and the necessary security measures.

279. A march of a combined arms unit along multiple good routes is easier for the troops, accelerates the rate of the march, and increases the combat readiness posture in the direction of the march. On the other hand, the possibility exists that the leaders of individual march columns will engage the enemy in a manner contrary to the intent of the commander, and before he is able to intervene. Such a march along multiple routes makes it more difficult for the commander to deploy his forces to a flank and to concentrate them quickly on one area.

Based on the tactical requirements, the commander can reduce the risk to his freedom of action by deploying the march column in echelon, or by advancing by bounds. To control such a movement, the commander establishes the time and position of the departure of the march columns or the time at which their lead elements must cross a designated phase line.

Changes in the echelonment during the march must be balanced by restraining march columns, or can be adjusted during rest halts.

During an advance by bounds, the march columns should know in advance their required actions—halt or continue the march—upon reaching an intermediate objective. This will avoid unnecessary halts. Rest halts also can be used to synchronize an advance by bounds.

In the absence of specific orders, the march column commanders must inform the senior commander when march objectives are reached.

280. Secure communications must exist between the commander and the march columns, and between the columns themselves. Difficult terrain and periods of poor visibility and darkness require especially careful measures. Communications between the adjacent march columns by radio and signal lamps also require careful planning. During daylight friendly aircraft can provide timely information on the status of the individual march columns and their progress.

281. Boundaries for the march, security, and reconnaissance must be established between adjacent columns.

282. A commander has the best control of his units and the greatest freedom of action during a march in a single column.

The larger the combined arms force on a single route, the greater the requirement for the units to achieve the specified distance.

The greater the column length, the greater the danger from air attack, and the greater the time required for concentration.

283. A night march provides security from ground-based observation and, under favorable conditions, from aerial observation. Night air attacks are difficult for the enemy. Night marches, therefore, are an important method of achieving surprise, and are of particular value when the enemy has air superiority.

If the force moves directly out of a night march into an enemy-held area at dawn, a short rest will help ensure that the troops are committed against the enemy in a fresh and coordinated condition.

284. The decision factors in the formation of a march column include total strength, available bivouac areas, the composition of the force, the order of march, and the tactical situation.

All units must advance in the direction of the march. Detours and cross traffic should be avoided. Units should not be alerted or committed to the march earlier than necessary.

If large bodies of troops must depart from the same position, they should be scheduled to arrive unit by unit, so as to avoid unnecessary waiting, congestion, and exposure to enemy air attack.

Generally, units should be scheduled to join the column based on their bivouac location and their position in the sequence of march. This can be accomplished by moving them into the column from side or intersecting roads. When the bivouac groups are established, commanders will ensure the timely arrival of units and their proper positions in the column.

Trains and rear-area service units must not restrict troop movements.

If the formation of march columns is executed under the cover of out-posts, they must be integrated into the march column in a timely manner.

285. The start-point time is a function of the situation, the length of the march, the weather, and other circumstances. Insufficient rest has a nega-tive effect on the capabilities of the troops.

It may be critically important to complete a night march during dark-ness.

For a day march, it is better for units to leave their bivouac areas in darkness than to arrive in darkness at the new bivouac areas. Mounted and motorized units normally require two hours of preparation time prior to departure. At the completion of the march, they normally stand down later than the infantry. Poorly organized rest halts degrade the recovery of the horses and the maintenance of the motor vehicles. The result is a degrada-tion of operational capability.

286. The order of march determines the position of units in the col-umn. This in turn is based upon their probable deployment in combat. The correct order of march is the first step for success in combat.

287. The order of march of the security elements (advance guard, etc.) usually is determined by their respective commanders. To simplify the orders process, however, the sequence of these elements also can be estab-lished by the commander of the march column.

The order of march of the main body is established by the commander of the march column. He is responsible for the timely entry of the various elements into the main body and for the cohesion of the column during the march. He maintains continuous contact with the advance guard and estab-lishes any necessary flank security. If he leaves the main body, he desig-nates a deputy during his absence. When the march concludes and the col-umn disperses, he reverts to his original status as the commander of his own unit.

288. When an infantry division is advancing along multiple routes, an infantry element normally marches at the head of each main body. The commander of the main body normally positions himself at or near the head of the main body. The column in which the division commander moves usually includes the motorized elements of the division command echelon and the divisional artillery command echelon. These elements are essential for the conduct of battle. The horse-drawn elements of the divisional signal battalion that are not with the advance guard are normally included as well. Horse-drawn light and heavy artillery and engineers not assigned to the advance guard are kept as far forward as the situation requires. This then, determines the positioning of the remainder of the infantry units. The horse-drawn platoon of the medical company follows in the column of the divisional command echelon. Horse-drawn light columns follow their own

units. The horse-drawn elements of the divisional bridge column can follow when they are neither with the advance guard, nor are scheduled to advance later. Antitank guns and air defense machine-gun units are usually distributed within the columns.

Similar organization is required during a divisional advance on a single route.

During a withdrawal, the march order of the main body often will be reversed.

The same principles apply to the main bodies of cavalry columns.

289. Motorized units of the division will be organized into one or more motorized echelons and follow the column of march by bounds—unless they have reconnaissance or security missions or are assigned to the advance guard. When the situation and the road network permit, they can move on special additional routes, together or in elements as a motorized column of march. If contact with the enemy is anticipated, only those motorized units capable of direct combat will be grouped on the special route.

The movement of the motorized echelons and march groups can be altered as necessary by the commanders of the columns on whose route they will be moving. The motorized march columns remain under the direct command of the division commander.

The leader of a motorized echelon or march group has the same tasks during a march as the commander of a main body. Based on the situation, the commander of an entire motorized column has similar tasks as the leaders of the other march columns of the division. See Paragraphs 286–288 for the order of march for the motorized echelons and columns. Chapter XXII covers the procedures for the execution of the march.

Motorized units assigned to the advance guard always must march between the advance guard and the main body. Motor vehicles of the headquarters and other motorized units, such as motorized elements of the artillery, also can be integrated between the advance guard and the main body on an exceptional and temporary basis.

290. The combat trains of infantry battalions, cavalry regiments, and artillery battalions march as an element with their units. Those belonging to command elements and staff are either attached to a unit or are formed independently in the march column. The combat trains of the forward elements of the advance guard march with the advance guard reserve. Detached companies normally keep their combat trains with them. Motorized and mounted reconnaissance units usually have their own combat trains and keep them as close as possible. Should the situation require them to separate from their combat trains for a period, the commander can direct their attachment to another unit.

291. During the advance of an infantry division, the divisional signal

battalion normally establishes a trunk line. (Chapter XVII) Before the start of a march it should be brought as far forward as the situation permits. The leading troops laying the trunk line march with the support element of the advance guard. At key points message centers or telephone stations are established. Their locations must be listed in the march orders.

During a march along multiple routes, the divisional trunk line normally will be installed along the route of the division commander and his staff.

During a retrograde march away from the enemy, trunk lines will be dismantled or destroyed as soon as they are no longer needed.

In addition to the laying of trunk lines, the divisional signal battalion must ensure continuous radio communications to the rear and flanks during both advance and retrograde marches. Communications with advanced elements will be dictated by the situation.

Paragraph 724 covers signal communications during the march of cavalry units.

292. The calculation of the distance of the march and the required time are the essential bases for march orders. The distance to be covered by each unit from the old bivouac site to the new must be considered.

See Annex 2 for march speed and march rate planning factors.*

During cross-county movement, the march rate of large forces with infantry reduces to about 2 to 3 kilometers per hour.

A night march on good roads should achieve the same rate of march as during the day. It decreases rapidly, however, on poor roads and in total darkness.

Bicyclists and motorized units move more slowly at night.

293. Whenever possible, a warning order should be issued for the march. The warning order will state the time and place of the start point, the route of march, and the planned march duration. It also contains instructions for the approach of units to the route of march and their integration into the march column.

294. When corps or army units or larger independent forces follow the march routes of divisions, coordination must be established to avoid friction between the divisional trains and service elements and those following units.

---

*Annex 2 is not reproduced in this translation. The following planning factors were used: foot troops, 5 kilometers per hour; foot troops in small units, 6 kilometers per hour; mounted troops at the trot and walk, 7 kilometers per hour; mounted troops at the trot, 10 kilometers per hour; bicycles, 12 kilometers per hour; motorcycles, 40 kilometers per hour; motor vehicles, 30 kilometers per hour. Large organizations with all their weapons could make 4 kilometers, including time for rest halts. Under forced march conditions, such units could make 5 kilometers per hour. [*Wedemeyer Report*, p. 88]

295. March tables can be established when large combined commands march over a period of several days and in the absence of potential enemy contact. The march table contains information on the routes of march, the daily march objectives, bivouac sites, and staff quarters.

296. As soon as possible after crossing the start point, "route step" should be ordered. Based on the situation, the troops may speak, sing, and smoke.

When units pass superior commanders, they will render the courtesy of "eyes right." Infantry will come to "'shoulder arms" only on order. Further salutes or courtesies will not be rendered.

297. The discarding of clothing and equipment is strictly forbidden. The necessary removal of some clothing items, the opening of tunic collars, and the removal of the helmet should be ordered when appropriate.

298. All units march within the established order of march.

299. Normally, only one side of the road is used. If the march is conducted on both sides, the middle of the road must be kept open for the passage of messengers. Motor vehicles will not pass a column of troops at high speeds.

Units generally march on the right side of the road. During a day march, however, the left side may be used if it is more suitable for the infantry or if it offers concealment against aerial observation. If both sides of the road offer concealment against aerial observation, infantry and cavalry can march on both sides. Motorized or horse-drawn vehicles and bicyclists use the most favorable side.*

On poor roads and during periods of heat, it may be advantageous to march on both sides of the road, leaving the center open.

Dusty summer roads should be avoided.

Units passing other troops should make clearance by moving as far as possible to the side of the road.† The road must be kept clear during rest halts.

300. All units of a march column must maintain established distances and avoid straggling. A uniform rate of march must be maintained in order to avoid tiring halts and stringing out the rearward elements.

301. In order to accommodate the variations in the march depth of individual elements, small buffer intervals should be maintained between march units. Normally these will be ten paces for infantry and fifteen paces for mounted units and staffs.

---

*The infantry normally marched in columns of three men abreast; the cavalry two abreast. [*Wedemeyer Report*, p. 85]

†Road-width-planning factors were 3 meters for horse-drawn vehicles and 2.5 meters for motor vehicles, with 5 meters for passing. [*Wedemeyer Report*, p. 44]

These march intervals cease when a unit assumes the deep air defense formation.

Mounted officers and led horses are considered part of the depth of the march, and not part of the march intervals between units. The march intervals between units compensate for short stoppages, and therefore may be lost temporarily.

Chapter XXII covers the distances between the march units of motorized units.

302. Communications are maintained between the various elements of a march column by horsemen, bicyclists, and motorized troops. For shorter distances, communications are maintained by dismounted connecting elements. In difficult situations, officers will be tasked to maintain contact. At night, in low visibility weather, and in rugged terrain conditions the number of connecting elements should be increased. The commander of the larger unit always is responsible for establishing communications with the smaller unit. When difficulties arise or are anticipated, however, the smaller unit must support the efforts of the larger. Every unit is responsible for ensuring that the succeeding unit follows the correct route. When elements are withdrawn from the column, the commander of the unit following that from which the elements were withdrawn must be informed immediately by the commander who ordered the withdrawal. Connecting elements also should be stationed at key points and road markings and similar indicators should be posted for the benefit of following units, messengers, and stragglers.

Radio and signal lamp elements can be posted between the advance guard and the main body.

303. In addition to a short halt soon after the beginning of the march (for the adjustment of packs and equipment, the readjustment of saddles, and relief of men and animals), each march requires one or more rest halts. The exact number is based on the march length,* the march capability of the troops, the weather, and the type of terrain. A single rest halt is made usually after the greatest part of the distance has been covered. Rest halts generally are made every two hours. During night marches, short rest halts should be made every hour. The time and duration of rest halts should be designated in the march order. Rest halts for feeding and watering horses while unsaddled should not last less than two hours. When marching on multiple routes, the timing, location, and duration of the rest halts can be delegated to each column commander.

---

*An infantry division marching in a single column had a march length of 32 kilometers. In two columns, the main column was 23.5 kilometers long, and the secondary column 8.5 kilometers. In three columns, the main column was 15 kilometers long, and the other two 8.5 kilometers. [*Wedemeyer Report*, p. 37]

Even when speed is required, adequate rest halts must be made on long marches to ensure the troops arrive ready for action. Omitting timely and sufficient rest halts places a heavy responsibility on the commander. The commander may ignore such considerations only when it is absolutely necessary to reach the battlefield or the decisive point with but a fraction of the force.

304. During the day units will be organized into groups and concealed in rest areas close to the route of march. During longer rest halts, units usually are assembled into rest groups. The establishment of such formations maximizes the use of water resources, increases combat readiness, and makes the continuation of the march easier for rearward troops.

Rest halts at night are conducted along the route of march.

Rest areas must be reconnoitered in advance. Factors in the selection of rest areas include: march technique and technical requirements; the air threat; the climate and time of the day; water requirements; shade and protection against wind, rain, snow, and cold; comfort and security of the troops; and the special requirements of the different arms.

305. Troops at rest remain resting when a superior approaches, unless directly spoken to or called.

306. The commander designates the sequence and, if necessary, the distances between units when crossing military bridges. Vehicles whose weight exceeds the load capacity of the bridge must be detached from the column and routed across suitable bridges or crossed by ferry.

307. The bridge commander is responsible for the security of the bridge, for silence and order on the bridge, and for the approach and exit routes. All instructions issued by the bridge commander or by engineer duty officers must be obeyed.

308. Troops and vehicles must not bunch up in the vicinity of the bridge. The approaches and exits should be kept free and the movement across the bridge must flow continuously. Normally, units will be called from assembly areas based on the availability of the bridge.

309. Each unit takes up the necessary march formation at least 100 meters before the bridge and maintains it until the end of the march column is 100 meters past the exit.

310. Infantry crosses in route step. Cavalry dismounts and crosses in pairs, with the men positioned outside of the horses. Cavalry units already across shorten their gait in order to calm the horses still crossing. Horse-drawn units and all single vehicles hold to the middle, drivers remain mounted, service crews position themselves on either side of the horses, and brakes are set. Individual horsemen dismount and lead their horses. The crews of mounted batteries follow their guns, dismounted in pairs.

Motor vehicles move slowly, holding to the middle, with the distances between the vehicles based on the type of vehicle and the bridge capacity.

Units must know well in advance the load capacity of a military bridge. The load capacity also should be marked on route signs approaching the bridge and on a sign at the entrance to the bridge.

311. An order to halt on a military bridge may be given only by the bridge commander or by the bridge duty officer. In an emergency, any engineer officer on duty is authorized to give that order.

During an air attack, the bridge must be cleared quietly and in good order. Commanders of all ranks must prevent bunching-up and increases in the rate of march.

312. Only engineer officers on bridge duty are authorized to cross the bridge in the reverse direction during crossing operations. The bridge duty officer may authorize exceptions.

Military bridges that can be used for simultaneous traffic in both directions must be so marked.

313. Units must prepare in assembly areas prior to conducting ferrying operations. Based on the capacity of the ferrying equipment, units will remain in their tactical groupings whenever possible. Engineer officers will guide the units from their assembly areas, along marked routes, to the crossing points.

Actions during loading, unloading, and ferrying operations must be established in advance. The orders of the ferry crews must be followed.

Swimming the horses accelerates ferrying operations.

VI

ATTACK

314. The attack is executed along its base direction by movement, fire, and shock.

The attack can be launched from a single direction against the enemy front, where the greatest strength usually lies. Normally, however, the attack is directed against the flank or the rear of the enemy. The attack also can be launched from multiple directions. New directions for exploitation develop with the breakthrough of an enemy's front.

315. The frontal attack (*frontaler Angriff*) is the most difficult to execute, but the most frequently used. Even units that are not committed to the frontal attack often must attack frontally because the enemy has a secure flank.

A frontal attack against an enemy of equal strength and in a prepared defense results in long, obstinate fighting for dominance. The frontal attack requires substantial superiority of forces and resources. In general, a frontal attack only leads to decisive results (*entscheidender Erfolg*) if the enemy position is broken through.

316. A flanking attack (*umfassender Angriff*) is more effective than a frontal attack. The simultaneous attack against both enemy flanks requires great superiority. The envelopment of one or both enemy flanks, reaching deep into his rear, can result in the destruction of the enemy.*

A flanking movement is easiest to execute when the forces intended for the envelopment are committed from a distance against the enemy flank or wing. It is more difficult to initiate an envelopment in close proximity to the enemy. The troop movements necessary for such a maneuver are only possible on a battlefield with favorable terrain or at night.

---

*In current U.S. doctrine a very deep envelopment is called a "turning movement." In the late 1930s, the instruction at the *Kriegsakademie* stressed the shallow envelopment almost exclusively, while the U.S. Army Command and General Staff School at Fort Leavenworth stressed the opposite. German tacticians believed that an enemy's reconnaissance assets would make it impossible for a sufficiently large force to move in secret into the defender's rear to affect a deep envelopment. [*Wedemeyer Report*, p. 141]

The envelopment must strike at the main enemy force in a decisive direction. The success of the envelopment depends upon the timing and extent of the enemy's ability to shift his forces in the direction of the threat.

The tendency to extend the wing threatened by envelopment quickly leads to overextension and the dispersal of forces. In an uncertain situation, therefore, it is better to organize the enveloping force in depth.

Any force executing an envelopment also runs the risk of being enveloped itself. The commander must consider this possibility, but he must not hesitate to weaken his own front in order to ensure the superiority of his enveloping flank.

317. An envelopment (*Umfassung*) requires that the enemy's front be fixed.*

The enemy is best fixed frontally when his entire front is attacked. Such an attack, however, requires strong forces, which must be withdrawn from the enveloping wing. The attacker, therefore, often must be satisfied with conducting limited objective or feint attacks. Occasionally a stronger enemy force can be contained in anticipation of a decisive attack.

If the enemy attacks from his front, the friendly front must defend itself or execute a delaying action. In such cases, the follow-through of the envelopment of the enemy will bring success; but the transition from the envelopment into a counterattack will bring even greater success.

318. A flank attack follows from a previous approach direction or from flank marches. It especially is effective when it hits the enemy by surprise and gives him no chance to take countermeasures. It requires superior mobility and the deception of the enemy at other positions.

If the march directions or flank marches make exceptional attacks possible against the enemy rear, great success can be achieved when the enemy is surprised and the friendly forces are sufficiently strong.

319. A penetration attack (*Durchbruchsangriff*) seeks to destroy the continuity of the enemy's front and to envelop the shoulders created at the breakthrough point.

The conditions for success are: surprise; the deployment of the breakthrough force in the area where the prospects for the attacking infantry are favorable deeper into the enemy's zone; and strong forces to exploit the attack after the breakthrough.

The attack must be launched on a broader front than that intended for the breakthrough, in order to fix the enemy on either side of the penetration point. The enemy also must be held in place on the remainder of his front.

---

*Paragraph 317 echoes the elder von Moltke's dictum of Envelop, Encircle, Destroy (*Umfassen, Einschliessen, Vernichten*).

A wider penetration zone will result in a deeper penetration wedge. Reserves must to be positioned to repel enemy counterattacks against the flanks of the penetration.

A successful breakthrough must be exploited before the enemy can initiate countermeasures. The more deeply the attacking force advances, the more effectively it can envelop, thereby frustrating any attempt the enemy might make to close his front by withdrawing to the rear.

Making a change in the front too soon, therefore, must be avoided.

At the operational level, cavalry and motorized units primarily exploit a successful breakthrough. Fighter and bomber aircraft operating against enemy reinforcements support the exploitation.

320. A limited objective attack (*Angriff mit begrenztem Ziel*) is made to achieve only local success. Normally it is conducted where the situation makes such success possible. Such an attack can have a great effect if conducted in an advantageous area. It can be used only to hold or to fix the enemy.

The execution of a limited attack does not differ from the execution of other attacks. The objective can be closer and can be taken with weaker forces, but it also might require the commitment of all forces. The attacker often can organize such attacks with limited depth.

The attack must be well timed. Units should advance beyond their attack objectives only when specifically authorized to do so. Such a decision requires careful consideration.

321. In some situations it is better to allow the enemy to attack first, and then to attack when he has committed his forces. The great difficulty is to grasp the correct timing for shifting to the attack. In such a situation there is a risk that the decision to attack will not be made at the right time or not be made at all.

322. The enemy may accept an attack in order to shift to the attack later himself or to withdraw. These possibilities must be considered when deploying and committing friendly forces.

323. Every attack requires coordinated command. Piecemeal attacks (*Einzelangriffe*) must be avoided at all costs.

The main force and the mass of munitions must be committed at the decisive point (*entscheidende Stelle*). In an envelopment, these forces are deployed on the enveloping wing. Based on the commander's intent, the situation, and the terrain, it is at that point that the effect of all arms will be brought to bear to achieve decisive results. The decisive attack is characterized by narrow sectors; provision for integrated fire of all arms, including that of adjacent sectors; and reinforcing fires by attached infantry heavy weapons and artillery. Fires are increased and armored vehicles are committed during the execution of the attack. The choice of the point for the main effort will be influenced by the artillery, and sometimes by the suitability of terrain for continued armored vehicle operations.

If the decisive point cannot be identified from the start, then the decisive action must be planned in uncertainty and shifted later. If success occurs at a position other than that planned or intended, it must be exploited decisively. Should the point of the main effort shift or be established later in the action, sufficient reserves must be available. The strong and combined effect of all arms must be focused in the new direction.

The shaping of the decisive action must be reflected in the measures taken by all individual commanders. Expediency may require the designation of a point of main effort for individual units.

324. As a rule, every attack passes through a series of crises until it reaches the point of culmination.* It is critical that the command recognizes this point, and possesses the ability to make a decision to immediately exploit the success with all available means, or to prevent failure.

325. If the attack starts to stall under its present organization, then it must be revitalized by altering the organization for combat, by committing fresh forces, or by a reorganization of fires. If this cannot be accomplished, then the attack should be suspended, rather than risk the loss of combat power by continuing.

326. The assigned sector of an infantry unit in the attack must be in proportion to its probable expenditure of combat power. The assigned sector widths depend upon the mission; combat strength, terrain, and fire support of all weapons; and the probable strength of the enemy resistance. The width of a battalion supported on both flanks is usually between 400 and 1,000 meters.

When the terrain is favorable for all arms, 4,000 to 5,000 meters is the usual meeting engagement width for an infantry division of three infantry regiments with sufficient artillery. On occasion, the width of the sector can be increased by grouping forces and by opening gaps. When a unit's sector of responsibility becomes too wide, command and control becomes more difficult, as does support in depth at the decisive point.

The width of an infantry division supported on both flanks and conducting a main frontal attack against prepared defenses should not exceed 3,000 meters. This is especially the case when the division must exploit the attack without reinforcement.

---

*Clausewitz discussed the culminating point of the attack in Book 7, Chapter 5 of *On War*. "Most [attacks] only lead up to the point where their remaining strength is just enough to maintain a defense and wait for peace. Beyond that point the scale turns and the reaction follows with a force that is usually much stronger than that of the original attack. This is what we mean by the culminating point of the attack."

On occasion it may be necessary to refuse combat in one area in order to decrease sector widths and increase the mass of the attacking force.

327. The objective of the attack dictates the direction of attack. It must be designated in the attack order.

The execution and development of the attack by adjacent elements is not restricted by the assignment of sectors of responsibility. These sectors also apply to combat reconnaissance. The calculation of these sectors is a simple method of coordinating the point of the main effort. It is not necessary to fill an entire sector with forces.

The combat operations of adjacent units are coordinated through the assignment of sectors of responsibility. Such sectors, however, do not require units to maintain contact in a rigid and inflexible manner.

Sectors of responsibility establish the necessary boundaries for the other arms, which support the infantry directly, especially the artillery. Such sectors do not restrict the artillery from deploying its observation assets and firing positions in adjacent sectors. This also applies to infantry heavy weapons.

Operational sectors for larger units are assigned based on map inspection; for smaller units, based on direct terrain observation. These sectors must extend far into the enemy's depth, so they can be maintained throughout the course of the attack. Changes can be made as the situation develops. Key points should lie within the individual sectors, unless they are to be attacked by multiple units.

An open flank normally is not bounded. A boundary of separation usually suffices for neighboring but not immediately adjacent units. In some situations, merely the designation of the attack objective will be sufficient.

328. The attack order must clearly designate the intended scheme of maneuver. In the assignment of missions, consideration must be given to the relationship between the necessity for unity of action and the independent action of units. The speed and the force of the attack must not be restricted by orders that are too detailed.

Execution of the Attack and Combined Arms Coordination

329. The objective of combined arms elements in an attack is to support the decisive action of the infantry with sufficient firepower and shock effect against the enemy. This allows the infantry to break through deeply and to break the enemy resistance decisively. The first step in this goal is achieved when the enemy artillery is overrun or forced to withdraw.

All arms committed to an attack must know each other's mutual capabilities and limitations. They must maintain close and continuous communications with each other.

330. The coordination between the attacking infantry and the supporting artillery sets the tone for the course of the attack. Full coordination must exist in time and space throughout the duration of the attack.

The support of the attacking infantry by artillery extends forward from the near limit of the effective range of the guns. At ranges short of this limit, the infantry generally executes the attack with its organic weapons.

331. The senior commander is responsible for the synchronization of artillery fire with the infantry attack. His artillery adviser is the most senior artillery officer present, which in a division is the divisional artillery* commander.

The divisional artillery commander should be positioned as close as possible to the division commander.

If an infantry division has no artillery commander, its senior subordinate artillery commander should establish a command post near that of the divisional command.

The most senior artillery commander of a smaller unit, such as a reinforced infantry regiment, should establish his command post in the best position to support the infantry. Such a command post must provide direct observation of the terrain and secure communications to both the artillery units and to the supported infantry.

Because of the rapidly changing situation of cavalry units, the senior artillery commander usually accompanies the cavalry commander.

The optimal arrangement should be established by mutual agreement. Wherever possible, the commander should defer to the recommendations of the senior artillery officer. If the command posts of the two are separated, communications must be maintained by technical means and the artillery must provide a liaison officer.

332. Coordinated fire control increases the effectiveness of artillery fires and facilitates rapid concentration at decisive points and at decisive moments.

The infantry must have rapid and responsive artillery fire support whenever it conducts an attack against an enemy that is well concealed and is broadly and deeply deployed.

Normally, an infantry regiment will receive direct support from an artillery unit, which may be a battalion or a battery, based on the situation. Artillery may be directly attached if an infantry unit has an independent

---

*The divisional artillery had one light artillery regiment of three battalions of three batteries each with 105mm howitzers; a heavy artillery battalion, with two batteries with 150mm howitzers and one battery with 105mm guns; and an observation battalion (see the footnote on p. 53). All firing batteries had four tubes each. [*Wedemeyer Report*, p. 38] Every infantry regiment also had a cannon company whose guns were not part of the divisional artillery (see the first footnote on p. 95).

mission; when the battlefield is very extended or has poor observation; or when coordinated fire support is impossible for other reasons. The habitual association of fire and maneuver units enhances coordination.

The senior artillery commander directly commands the artillery units assigned for support. He commands the artillery attached to the infantry units through the orders of the overall unit commander, but he must inform the respective infantry commanders of any orders he issues. Artillery units that are attached to the infantry must maintain communications with the senior artillery commander. Commanders can facilitate the rapid execution of other missions by assigning position areas to the artillery.

333. The infantry commander designates to the supporting artillery the nature of the support required. The artillery commander must support the mission. When simultaneous fire missions are received from higher echelons, the artillery commander will determine the firing priorities. In urgent situations, he acts on the basis of his own judgement.

Attached artillery supports the infantry in accordance with the orders of the supported infantry commander. Further subordination to infantry units below the battalion level decreases the responsiveness of the artillery as a whole. Such attachments should be made only in exceptional situations, and must be reported to the senior commander by the commander of the infantry unit.

334. Both the infantry and the artillery are responsible to ensure their coordination by close and continuous communications. The relationship must be maintained, not only between commanders, but also between the forward infantry elements (especially the heavy weapons and their observers) and the artillery observers, who often provide the only means of thorough observation of the terrain of the attack area.

Close positioning of the infantry heavy weapons and the artillery observation posts should be avoided. The senior commander in the area will adjudicate if necessary. Normally, the positions with the greatest field of observation will go to the artillery.

Coordination and the correct choice of objectives are facilitated by rapid and accurate observation and target designation communications between the infantry and the artillery.

335. The establishment of adjacent command posts for both arms facilitates the fastest exchange of information. Artillery battery and battalion commanders often are tied to certain terrain points for the purpose of observation, firing, and fire control. Infantry commanders can sometimes position their own command posts in the vicinity of those of the artillery commanders.

When the command posts of both arms are not in close proximity, they must be connected by communications means or by liaison personnel.

336. An artillery battalion liaison team usually operates where the sup-

port is most required, and where it can best facilitate rapid requests for fire support. Generally it will be attached to the infantry battalion designated to make the main effort. Occasionally, the artillery liaison team will represent the artillery commander at the command post of the infantry regiment. A battery that is operating independently of its battalion may find it necessary to deploy its own liaison element, similar to a battalion's liaison team.

The infantry must support the artillery liaison team. This is accomplished by direct communications between the artillery observation posts, the forward observers, and the most advanced infantry elements.

Communications between the two arms can be augmented through the organic telephone assets of both, by infantry lamp signals, and by low-level aerial reconnaissance.

337. The infantry must know how the artillery is organized; which artillery units support it; the locations of the artillery observation and command posts; what additional artillery observation posts lie within the infantry zones; and the exact terrain sectors the artillery commands with observation and fire. This information is the main basis for the deployment and the fire of infantry heavy weapons.* The infantry likewise must keep the artillery continuously informed of its most forward line and changes in the enemy situation detected by combat reconnaissance.

The artillery must always know the locations of supported infantry command posts and the terrain sectors that the infantry commands with its weapons. It must always know the positions of the most advanced infantry elements and all follow-on infantry plans. The accomplishment of this requires continuous observation of both friendly and enemy lines.

338. The artillery provides its most efficient support against enemy infantry through fire directed by ground observers. Its support is most rapid and responsive if its observation posts and firing positions lie in the immediate rear of the attacking infantry—even during a wide envelopment.

Wherever the artillery cannot deliver observed fires, the attacking infantry must provide its own fire support through its organic weapons. Predicted artillery fire based on the map is not accurate enough to provide direct support to attacking infantry.†

---

*Every infantry company had two heavy machine guns. Every battalion had a heavy weapons company with eight heavy machine guns and six 81mm mortars. Every regiment had an infantry cannon company with six 75mm and two 150mm infantry guns. [*Wedemeyer Report*, p. 35]

†This paragraph seems to reject one of the most significant artillery lessons of World War I. Colonel Georg Bruchmüller and Captain Erich Pulkowski demonstrated convincingly in 1918 that predicted artillery fire based on the map and meteorological corrections was both practical and effective.

339. Whenever possible, enemy artillery is the objective of armored vehicles in coordination with their supporting infantry. As a rule, armored vehicles are committed at the point of the main effort.

An attack by armored vehicles either proceeds in the same direction as the infantry, or comes from a different direction. The terrain is decisive. Too close a contact with the infantry reduces the advantage of the speed of the armored vehicles and may put them at a disadvantage with respect to the enemy's defense. They should be maneuvered in such a way that they either eliminate the enemy weapons that impede the infantry attack—especially enemy artillery—or that they break into the enemy positions simultaneously with the infantry. In the latter situation, the armored vehicles should be attached to the commander of the infantry in whose sector they are attacking.

Occasionally, an armored attack supporting the final phase of an infantry attack can augment the artillery's supporting fires, which become increasing difficult to control in close proximity to the enemy. Direct fire from armored vehicles also can bridge the gap while the artillery displaces forward to extend the depth of its coverage for follow-on operations.

340. The senior commander synchronizes the combat operations of the armored vehicles with the coordination of the other arms. The deployment of the other arms should conform to the operational requirements of the armored vehicles.

Infantry must use the effect produced by the attacking armor to facilitate its own rapid advance. Elements of the infantry heavy weapons should suppress the enemy's anti-armor weapons. If enemy resistance stiffens and threatens to slow the advance by the infantry, that resistance must be broken through as quickly as possible. The commitment of reserve armored vehicles is especially effective for this purpose.

Artillery supports the armored attack. It fires at the enemy antitank weapons; suppresses enemy observation positions or lays smoke screens; neutralizes woods and villages through which an armored attack passes; or isolates those areas to prevent the commitment of enemy reserves. Self-propelled artillery and antitank* guns may accompany the armored attack.

Motorized combat engineers may be attached to armored units. They eliminate obstacles and barriers, reinforce bridges, and facilitate the crossing of ditches and soft ground.

Aircraft provide close air support to armored vehicles by attacking

---

*The Germans had no self-propelled guns in 1933. This turned out to be one of the great weaknesses of the German Army in World War II. As late as 1944, what little self-propelled artillery they had was in the *Panzer* divisions. Most of the artillery in the infantry divisions was still horse-drawn.

enemy defensive weapons, artillery, and reserves. Planes flying deep into enemy territory can maintain communications between the commander and the armored vehicles and can warn of enemy armored attacks.

If weather conditions permit, an armored attack can be supported by a smoke screen.

Liaison is essential between armored vehicles and the arms participating in the attack, especially artillery. It must be maintained by prearranged signals or by other means of communications. All this must be coordinated among the participating commanders prior to the attack.

341. Fighters and fighter-bombers can provide direct support to an attack, or can provide general support by attacking deep targets. These aircraft operate as outlined in Chapter XV.

342. Air defense units provide security for the deployment and the assembly areas of the attacking forces and artillery, and support battlefield aerial reconnaissance units.

Individual air defense batteries should operate sufficiently in advance so they can engage aircraft far in front of the forward line.

The defenses against aerial reconnaissance and air attack in the attack sector must be planned well in advance.

343. Engineers support the attacking infantry by clearing obstacles, eliminating barriers, and by attacking fortified points. They also provide important rear area support by preparing terrain for supply routes.

344. Chemical munitions are effective for attacking enemy artillery and reserves and for reinforcing blocking positions on the flanks. The attacking infantry must know as early as possible when and where chemical agents will be used and their persistence level. This information is vital for the command and control of the advance.

345. If weather and wind conditions permit, smoke can be used to screen friendly units and to blind enemy observation positions and defensive weapons. Smoke is especially valuable for crossing terrain without natural cover. Attacking units must make the best use of smoke's limited duration. The most likely area of a planned smoke screen must be coordinated with the artillery so that it can plan accordingly.

346. As far as the situation permits, the divisional signal battalion establishes and maintains wire communications between the division commander, the artillery commander, and all subordinate commanders. All subordinate commanders must maintain signal communications when advancing and when establishing their command posts.

The point of the main effort determines the operations of all means of signal communications.

The infantry and artillery communications nets are established separately. The artillery net takes precedence.

Signal assets must be held in reserve to ensure continuous communications between committed units, especially between infantry and artillery in an advancing attack.

Cross-communications facilitate coordination between the arms and the rapid exchange of observation results.

347. When direct wire communications to subordinate commanders cannot be maintained during an attack, the divisional signal battalion will advance the trunk line consisting of multiple connections. At the head of the trunk line, an advanced message center must be established to maintain communications with units.

348. The divisional command post must be established early, because its location greatly influences the structure of the entire divisional combat net. The nets of the observation battalion, the air units, and the air defense units augment the divisional net. The divisional signal battalion establishes the connection between these nets and the divisional net.

Assembly Areas for the Attack

349. After deploying, units will assemble for combat whenever reconnaissance determines that the enemy appears to have opted to defend.

350. The assembly order for the attack will specify the infantry assembly areas, security for the assembly areas, the missions of units already engaged, artillery positions, and additional reconnaissance and information requirements. Effort should be made to include as much information as possible in the assembly order for the subsequent execution of the attack. The necessary information includes, the mission for each arm, ammunition resupply, the missions of the light columns, the mission of the wagon elements, and the requirements for medical and veterinary support. Generally, the position of the horse-drawn rations train can be established as well. The inclusion of this information in the assembly order will reduce the size of the attack order.

351. The terrain for an infantry assembly area is favorable when it offers concealment and cover against observation and fire, and it permits the infantry to advance successfully in the most effective direction of attack under cover of the supporting arms. Whenever possible, terrain without natural cover should be avoided when advancing from the assembly area, and should be kept under observation by infantry heavy weapons and artillery. Terrain necessary for observer positions and for the deployment of the infantry must be secured in advance.

As a rule, infantry assembly areas in open terrain should be established at a greater distance from the enemy. Units need not be positioned equally far forward. Those that can be assembled closer to the enemy must facilitate the advance of the more rearward units.

Infantry units in an assembly area in preparation for conducting a wide envelopment must be positioned sufficiently far from the elements making the frontal attack so that inner wings do not converge.

Infantry units perform their combat reconnaissance at the very latest as they are moving into their assembly areas. That reconnaissance will secure the assembly area and the subsequent deployment from those areas.

352. Artillery is deployed so as best to provide cover for the assembly of the infantry.

Prior to the deployment of the artillery, the artillery commander must receive the fire support requirements from the senior commander. These requirements greatly influence the execution of the attack and may require special reconnaissance.

The reconnaissance and selection of observation and firing positions must take into consideration the requirement for coordinated fires on the probable decisive points of the attack. Therefore, the senior commander and the infantry commanders with attached or supporting artillery must inform the artillery of the scheme of maneuver as early as possible.

Wherever possible, artillery must be positioned where it can execute its missions during the attack without additional displacement. Some batteries, especially those assigned counterbattery (*Artilleriebekämpfung*) missions, must occupy advanced firing positions. Terrain, vegetation, site-to-crest masking, and sectors of traverse might impose restrictions on these requirements.

Supporting or attached artillery must remain close to the infantry. This, along with close communications between observation and firing positions, facilitates the speed, reliability, and effectiveness of fire support.

Fire effectiveness must not be decreased when a shift in position cannot be avoided. All displacements should be made by echelon.

Batteries should not be clustered in too tight a grouping.

In divisions strong in artillery, the organization of artillery units into task groupings might be advantageous. Such an organization is especially effective during an attack against a position.

353. Infantry forward of the artillery provides frontal security for the latter. Special flank security may be necessary. The artillery also must provide its own security against surprise. Every artillery unit is responsible for its own local defense, especially against enemy armored attack. Its primary means are close-in security and local observation.

354. When the infantry is in its assembly areas, the artillery makes all necessary preparations to support the infantry attack. It engages high priority targets in adjacent zones, draws out enemy artillery fire, and executes

counterbattery fire against known enemy field artillery and air defense batteries. Artillery aerial observers should be placed under the operational
control of the artillery commander as early as possible, followed by the
observation battalion and a balloon platoon. (Paragraph 358 covers counterbattery fires.) Large troop movements and other high priority targets
should be engaged at long range.

The number of batteries committed to these preparatory missions
should be limited, to avoid giving the enemy early indicators of friendly
intentions and firing positions.

Conduct of the Attack

355. If not already stated in the assembly order, the attack order designates the objectives of the attack; the organization for combat of the
infantry; its sectors and boundaries based on the situation; the task organization, and fire support missions of the artillery; the time of the attack; and
the reserves and their location.

356. The relative strength of the opposing artillery and the ability to
engage it influence the selection of the attack terrain for the infantry and
the time of attack. Some situations may require the more forward positioning of the other arms and combat resources.

Infantry attacking with strong artillery support can cross open terrain
with a high level of confidence. When friendly artillery is relatively weak,
the infantry should work its way forward as far as possible in covered terrain, avoiding observation by enemy artillery and heavy weapons. Darkness
and smoke screens are effective for concealing an advance from ground
observation of the enemy artillery.

357. The infantry attack commences with the advance of light infantry
under the covering fire of artillery and infantry heavy weapons.*

When advancing, the squads deploy at irregular distances and intervals
and with sufficient depth, based on the terrain conditions and enemy reaction. They make maximum use of dead space and cover from enemy fire. In
the face of strong enemy fire, the advance continues by bounds and rushes,
in either large or small groups. During lulls in the fighting, riflemen seek
cover to limit the effect of enemy fire as much as possible. Light machine
guns open fire when in effective range, and riflemen continue advancing

---

*The German infantry attack was built around the light machine gun. A stan-
dard infantry company consisted of three platoons (*Züge*), each platoon consisting
of three squads (*Gruppe*) of twelve men organized around a light machine gun.
[*Hartness Report*, p. 34]

under this covering fire. When closing with the enemy positions, the infantrymen also engage with fire.

Infantry heavy weapons follow in echelon, in coordination with the advance of the light infantry. They must coordinate more closely with the most forward elements as the focal point of the enemy defense becomes clear. At that point in time, it may become necessary to attach elements of the infantry heavy weapons to the most advanced units. In terrain affording poor observation, this may be necessary at the start of the attack. The remaining infantry heavy weapons support the attack from firing positions farther to the rear. They advance by echelons. When engaging with infantry heavy weapons, every effort must be made to concentrate their effect and to augment the artillery fire. It especially is important to employ infantry mortars* against targets that are difficult for the artillery to engage.

The advance against the enemy is executed through the careful synchronization of fire and movement. Exposed advancing units must not lack fire support. While they work forward, adjacent elements suppress the enemy, especially with light machine guns in conjunction with heavy weapons. Up to the point of the decisive thrust, a balance must be maintained between establishing local fire superiority and using that superiority to support rapid advance. Elements unable to advance take cover by digging in. Every opportunity is used to advance. As weak points develop in the enemy line, previously stalled elements must be reinforced and directed against those points.

The independence of action of subordinate commanders and their close coordination will influence decisively the success of the advance.

358. Artillery supports the infantry attack primarily by engaging the enemy artillery and infantry. Both must be engaged throughout the attack, but usually at differing levels of intensity. The engagement of other targets must be limited.

The enemy artillery must be attacked uniformly under the control of an artillery commander. Effective counterbattery fire depends upon reconnaissance and available ammunition. Artillery aerial observers, observation battalions, and captive balloons provide counterbattery target acquisition information through early reconnaissance of the battle area. The counterbattery commander must coordinate with the air defense artillery commander and the air commander to ensure the effective use of the artillery

---

*During World War I the Germans considered mortars as combat engineer weapons. By the late 1930s, each infantry company had three 50mm mortars, with a maximum effective range of 600 meters. The heavy weapons company of each infantry battalion had six 81mm mortars, with a maximum effective range of 1,500 meters. [*Wedemeyer Report*, p. 21]

aerial observers. The suppression of enemy batteries is accomplished through the coordinated surprise fire of multiple batteries firing gas rounds for extended periods.* The suppression of enemy batteries requires high ammunition expenditure and good observation. Larger-caliber guns are the most effective.

The combat effectiveness of friendly infantry is enhanced when friendly artillery engages the enemy's infantry. The effective range of the artillery and that of the heavy machine guns should reach deep into the enemy's sector and on the flanks of the attacking infantry. The fire of the light machine guns and the infantry mortars concentrates primarily on the enemy's frontal elements until immediately before the assault. If the artillery directly supporting the infantry proves insufficient, the artillery commander must augment it with the remaining artillery—preferably by placing it in support of the infantry at the decisive point.†

359. Every attempt must be made to engage the greater part of the enemy's artillery before the start of the infantry attack.

Very often the complete deployment of the enemy's forces and weapons cannot be determined until after the start of the infantry attack. Enemy artillery positions are especially difficult to locate and identify prior to the attack. Consequently, the intensive engagement of this artillery becomes possible only after the various reconnaissance sources have identified it positively.

At the start of the infantry attack, therefore, multiple batteries should whenever possible withhold their fire and lie in wait to engage previously unidentified enemy positions, especially those enemy batteries that had been silent. On the other hand, firing at unconfirmed enemy positions prior to the start of an attack is a waste of ammunition.

360. When there is insufficient strength and observation facilities for the artillery to engage the enemy artillery before the attack, and should engaging the enemy artillery during the attack offer no real advantage, then the mass of the artillery should engage the enemy infantry from the start of the attack.

361. As the picture of the enemy resistance develops, the more important will be the concentration of superior artillery fire against those sectors of the enemy front where there has been limited friendly success. In such situations, the infantry commander should not hesitate to withdraw artillery support from one infantry unit in order to support the attacks of adjacent elements.

---

*In World War I Colonel Georg Bruchmüller established the effectiveness of gas for neutralizing enemy batteries.

†In the original, the term *Schwerpunkt* is used. What was really meant, however, was the decisive point, not the center of gravity as Clausewitz defined the term.

Immediate infantry exploitation of artillery fire effect is decisively important. Should the advance of the infantry require further coordination between the two arms, halts in the advance will become inevitable. The closer the attacking infantry comes to the enemy, the more time will be necessary for the transmission and receipt of fire coordination orders with the artillery.

362. In the course of the attack, the infantry will work its way forward in several places and approach to within break-in distance of the enemy front. When the decision to execute the break-in comes from the leading element, the supporting arms must be notified by light signals or by any available means. As the situation requires, the supporting arms lift their fire from the break-in point and shift it to the direct front of the infantry. Most importantly, they must be prepared to engage immediately those targets emerging for the first time. They continue engaging targets of opportunity until it becomes necessary to lift those fires. As the infantry penetrates deeper into the enemy positions, the suppression of enemy enfilading fire becomes more important. Observers of all supporting arms must follow the leading infantry elements closely.

If prior coordination between the supporting arms and the breakthrough infantry force is not possible, then those arms must employ good observation to determine the intent of the infantry in order to provide the required support. In some situations the supporting arms can give the impetus to the infantry attack by lifting their fire from the most advanced enemy positions.

If the infantry advances on a broad front to within breakthrough distance, and if the breakthrough can be launched uniformly, then the necessary lifting of fires prior to the breakthrough must be synchronized with the infantry. The time and location of the shifting of fires should be coordinated in the attack orders.

363. The size of the breakthrough element determines the scale of the penetration. Any success must be exploited in depth. The infantry, reinforced by reserves, continues the direct attack against enemy strong points and isolated positions. At this point, the attack often evolves into individual engagements. Infantry heavy weapons and other rearward elements protect the flanks and rear of the advance, and should maintain close contact. The commitment of reserves and the steady resupply of ammunition sustain the momentum of the attack. Without such sustainment, the force of the attack will dissipate rapidly within the enemy position. The penetration is enlarged by the rapid and powerful exploitation of initial success.

Immediately after the breakthrough, artillery should start to displace forward in order to remain within range of the advancing infantry. The individual batteries displace either independently or on order. They occupy new firing positions as close as possible to the infantry, establish contact, engage enemy forces that are still holding, repel counterattacks, and support the exploitation with fire.

Antitank weapons follow close behind the penetrating infantry. Air defense elements also should move up rapidly.

364. The rupture of the enemy defense on a wide front is an indicator of approaching victory.

The next task of the attacking infantry is a follow-on advance in the direction of the attack until the enemy artillery is captured. Premature flanking maneuvers should be avoided until the enemy's position is definitely broken through. The units making the penetration must ensure that their flanks are secure. Advancing reserves prevent stalls in the attack, check enemy counterattacks, and sustain the forward momentum. The reserve should be committed to exploit success. Specially designated reserve units also serve as the pivot for rolling up the enemy front. New reserves are formed from remaining units, stragglers, and dispersed elements.

Enemy forces not destroyed in the penetration and the succeeding envelopment must be pursued.

365. If the enemy succeeds reestablishing a defense, or finds cover in his rearward positions, the attack must be resumed. This requires reestablishing coordination in time and space, plus the necessary fire support.

366. When it is not possible to carry the attack through to a decision before the onset of darkness, the attacking units generally will assume a defensive posture during the night. Consideration must be given to the possibility of resuming the attack at another more decisive point the following morning. This may require the shifting of forces during the night. The possibility always exists that the enemy can reestablish his freedom of action during the night and that the attacking forces may face a different situation in the morning. This situation exists especially when an enveloping attack could not be completed during the day. Reconnaissance raids must be conducted to obtain clarifying information. Night attacks can be employed to fix the enemy at the same time.

367. If no fundamental change in the enemy situation is anticipated, the orders for resuming the attack next day must be issued early enough to allow all arms—especially the artillery and the armored vehicles—to make timely preparations. Depending on the situation, senior commanders must be willing to issue orders before they have a complete picture of the day's combat.

The night can be used to advance the infantry closer to the enemy and to establish a favorable departure area (*Ausgangsstellung*) for the resumption of the attack. Night attacks may be necessary to secure key terrain features. Units, including those with exhausted troops, will be relieved only in exceptional situations.

During the night, irregular harassing fire (*Störungsfeuer*) should disrupt traffic within and behind the enemy positions. The advance of reinforcements and ammunition resupply should be interdicted as far as the friendly ammunition situation permits. Aerial bombing attacks should be conducted far into the enemy's rear area.

368. If before dawn the attacking units have secured favorable departure areas for a breakthrough, a coordinated assault can be launched at a fixed hour. The artillery, however, will only be able to support effectively an attack in the morning when the attacking infantry's departure areas and the situation of the enemy are known. The artillery also needs sufficient reference points for unobserved map firing.* Observation in the early morning is often not possible because of visibility conditions. It may be necessary, therefore, to choose a later time for the resumption of the attack.

Fires in lateral areas can deceive the enemy as to the timing of the attack and the intended point of penetration.

369. Although there may be uncertainty whether or not the situation will change fundamentally, all preparations must be made so the attack can continue the next day. The determination of the time of the attack can be withheld.

370. If a fundamental change in the enemy situation is anticipated, the planning of the follow-on attack should be based upon fresh reconnaissance.

371. When the available forces are insufficient to exploit after a successful attack, the terrain already gained must be held. The transition to the defensive, whether temporary or long-term, should be ordered. Emphasis must be placed on the quick reorganization and realignment of the infantry and its heavy weapons, as well as the immediate reorganization of the artillery. The artillery must be prepared to counter enemy infantry attacks as well as to deliver counterfire against the enemy artillery. Friendly infantry units are especially vulnerable in such situations.

Meeting Engagements

372. A meeting engagement (*Begegnungsgefecht*) develops when approaching forces meet while on the march and commit to combat without deliberate preparations.

In a meeting engagement, decisions and actions generally are executed instantaneously and under uncertainty.

---

*The techniques of unobserved map firing by artillery were perfected in World War I. This type of firing is also referred to often as predicted fire. It is most effective when used in conjunction with meteorological corrections.

373. Uncertainty and an obscure situation, which lead to a surprise clash, are the primary causes of meeting engagements.

Even when the approach of an enemy force is known, a meeting engagement can occur when one or both opponents attacks without hesitation or after only a hasty assembly. Commanders execute such a decision to take advantage of a higher state of readiness for action, to seize key terrain, or to achieve other tactical objectives. Such an attack should only be initiated from a posture of relative superiority.

During the course of a battle, individual units also might encounter situations that have characteristics similar to those of a meeting engagement.

374. The meeting engagement will take different forms based on the initial situation. Often, the course of the fighting by the most forward elements determines the course and conduct of the further battle.

During an immediate attack from the march by both opponents, forward and rearward surges can develop in which the skills and independence of action of the subordinate commanders and the combat effectiveness of the units will prove decisive.

The meeting engagement develops differently when both opponents start the battle from deployed positions, when one opponent decides to hold back after the first encounter, or if both try to increase their readiness for action by assembling their forces.

When one of the opponents halts his advance and assumes a defensive posture, the other may be forced to shift to an attack against a fixed position.

375. The side that succeeds in a meeting engagement is the one that anticipates the enemy and restricts his freedom of action. Quick recognition of a favorable situation, quick development of uncertain situations, and immediate decisions are the keys to success.

The surest basis for success lies in earlier readiness for action. This advantage forces the enemy to fight against superiority and facilitates follow-on attacks in the desired direction.

376. The enemy's intent in a meeting engagement will only be clear in exceptional situations. When an important sector of the terrain lies between the opponents, a rapid move of the enemy advance guard should be anticipated. The enemy can be expected to show restraint when he does not have the advantage of readiness for action or the advantage of terrain.

Initial engagements normally bring some clarity to the situation, but such clarity should be waited for only in exceptional situations.

377. When a commander knows of the enemy approach in sufficient time, he will try to dictate the timing and the type of the deployment for the battle, its beginning, and its course.

378. When a commander cannot perceive the situation in sufficient time, it becomes necessary for the individual commanders of the march

columns to make independent decisions. These decisions will be of great significance. The commanders should execute their existing orders so long as the basic planning assumptions do not change. When an adjacent march column becomes engaged, the commander must determine if that action deviates from the mission and the objective of the march and may lead to the loss of greater success.

It is the task of the senior commander to quickly regain control of the situation that his subordinate commanders may have created through their independent action.

379. The mission of the advance guard is to ensure freedom of action for the commander of the march column; to give follow-on forces time to deploy; and to give the bulk of the artillery and the infantry heavy weapons good conditions for observation. These missions can be accomplished offensively or defensively. Decisive action often leads to success. A limited withdrawal may be necessary against a superior enemy and in unsuitable terrain. Such a maneuver can shorten deployment time.

380. The advance guard's preparation for action must be executed rapidly. Early commitment of infantry heavy weapons and the advance guard artillery helps to break the initial resistance, hinders enemy movement, and draws out enemy artillery fire. When armored vehicles are attached to the advance guard, their surprise attack against an unprepared enemy can produce great success.

When an immediate attack by the infantry is required, it is initiated without further preparation. It must move in the decisive direction without delay, under the cover of those heavy weapons that can get into position quickly. If necessary, the infantry will attack after a rapid assembly.

If the advance guard commander decides to defend, the advance guard artillery can assume widely dispersed firing positions to deceive the enemy regarding its strength. This will force the enemy to make detours and exercise caution. The infantry, likewise, will often occupy a broader front than its strength would dictate for a decisive engagement. Early relief of the advance guard by the main body makes such a maneuver feasible.

The advance guard disengages as soon as the forward elements have accomplished their mission.

381. Early advance and deployment of additional artillery will support the buildup of the line of combat. Coordinated employment of the artillery is absolutely necessary. Frequently, however, the commanders of the individual march columns will have to commit their artillery independently. The senior commander should anticipate this situation by distributing the artillery in the march columns and by specifying its attachment. The stronger the artillery he retains under his control and the faster and more secure his communications to the march columns, the earlier he can employ the mass of the artillery in accordance with his intent.

Early deployment of the artillery and its means of observation is the surest way to ensure fire superiority over the enemy. It may be necessary, therefore, to deploy the entire artillery force before the initial engagements have clarified the situation.

Special considerations govern the deployment of artillery in a meeting engagement. The factors to be considered include the situation; previous deployment; the type of initial contact; distribution of artillery within the individual march columns; and the terrain. Every situation is different. Frequently, unified control can be achieved only gradually. Often, the initial order from the senior commander to the commander of the artillery will contain only the general intent and the combat mission of the artillery in broad outline. In the course of the engagement, the senior commander exercises his control over the artillery by assigning missions that develop as the situation clarifies.

382. The commander decides how he will continue the battle, based on the outcome of the initial contact and, if possible, his personal reconnaissance of the terrain.

When he does not believe it necessary to assemble the main force for the attack, and in order to retain the initiative, the commander orders the attack directly from the line of march. He issues attack orders to follow-on units either individually or as a whole.

Unless already specified, the attack order deploys the main body from the line of march; specifies the mission, task organization, objective, and zones or boundaries of the infantry; and specifies the missions of the supporting arms.

For the artillery, the attack order contains the mission, task organization, and the final coordinating details. Artillery not attached to individual infantry units reverts to the operational control of the divisional artillery.

Units deployed from the rear of the formation must clarify the situation to their front through immediate combat reconnaissance. They must secure unprotected flanks against surprise.

In a hasty attack, all commanders are responsible for eliminating confusion and for ensuring coordination between the arms.

383. When the commander's intent and the actions of the enemy make it no longer necessary to continue deploying infantry units directly from the march column into the battle, the commander assembles the uncommitted elements for attack. It is important to anticipate the enemy through rapid action. Units normally should not be withheld pending further clarification of the situation.

If the situation requires the commitment of additional forces before the assembly is completed, it should be done without hesitation.

384. The infantry attack is executed in the same manner, whether or not

it is launched from assembly areas. The attack is conducted as outlined in Paragraphs 355 to 371.

385. The attack should be withheld when the results of the preliminary engagements and the terrain indicate no chance of success, or that the commitment of the main body will not produce results on the same day. The possible commitment of adjacent units also will influence the decision to follow up the covering force engagement by committing the main body.

Attack Against Prepared Defenses

386. The attacker's course of action depends on his intent, the actions of the enemy, the relative strength of the opposing forces, the location and strength of the enemy positions, and the attack terrain.

387. If the enemy position cannot be bypassed or enveloped, then it must be attacked frontally for the purpose of achieving a penetration.

The execution of a frontal attack is determined by the way in which the attacker can bring his forces and means into action in time and space. When these forces and means are insufficient to achieve a breakthrough, the objective of the attack must be limited.

388. The time required to prepare for an attack depends on whether the attacker already holds the terrain in front of the enemy position or must first secure it. A second factor is the amount of time required to assemble the attack forces in their assembly areas.

The more difficult an attack, the more thorough must be the preparations. The defender, however, also can take advantage of the time the attacker takes for preparation.

The amount of force and means necessary for the attack depend on the strength of the enemy defense. An attack made with insufficient force and means can lead to painful reverses.

389. In order to properly deploy the attack force, the commander must know early on the decisive points of the enemy position. This information is necessary for the determination of the point of main effort.

390. Systematic reconnaissance normally provides the final basis for the preparation of the attack and its execution. The reconnaissance combines information both for the approach and the attack. It is especially important to verify the width and depth of any chemically contaminated terrain in front of the enemy position.

A thorough map reconnaissance must be made in advance.

Aerial reconnaissance conducted early may catch the enemy still at work on his positions. Photographic and visual reconnaissance can provide insight into the enemy's defense measures, both his forward positions and in depth. Aerial observers can provide targeting information for long-range guns and adjust their fires. Fighters protect friendly reconnaissance aircraft by attacking enemy aircraft and captive balloons.

Ground combat reconnaissance complements aerial reconnaissance. In difficult situations the combat reconnaissance must be forced through.

Artillery observation assets must be deployed early.

The senior commander is responsible for reconnaissance.

391. When advancing on the enemy position, it is important to recognize where the main battle area commences. The enemy will fight the battle as a delaying action in the area to the front of his positions. Directly in front of the main battle area the attacker can expect to face advanced covering forces and combat outposts.

The attacker should advance quickly and aggressively. Long-range enemy artillery fire must not hold him up. Enemy batteries must be silenced quickly. The advance normally evolves into numerous small attack groups, which will be composed of infantry and artillery as a necessary minimum, as well as armored vehicles if required. They must break through the enemy's forward screen quickly or push the enemy back. The forward enemy covering forces should be bypassed whenever possible, to avoid holding up the advance.

The advance should be made by bounds if the situation in the main battle area is unclear, should the enemy offer stiff resistance, or should the attacker wish to avoid early advance into the effective fire zone of the enemy position. In so doing, however, the freedom of initiative of the units to exploit favorable opportunities must not be restricted.

The goal of the advance is to secure terrain to deploy artillery forward and to observe the main battle area.

392. Encountering an integrated and coherent infantry defense and strong artillery echeloned in depth normally indicates that the enemy's main battle area has been reached. At that point the forward infantry elements should dig in and provide security for the deployment of the artillery observation posts. They must be in a position to repel enemy attacks.

The main body of the infantry and the other uncommitted arms can be held back beyond the effective range of enemy artillery.

393. Follow-on reconnaissance will provide details of the enemy position and for the conduct of the attack. The enemy outposts, therefore, must be pushed back.

Targeting information for the artillery and infantry heavy weapons is obtained through continuous observation of the attack terrain.

Aerial observers, balloons, and observation battalions are committed for target acquisition. They often provide the final information for artillery deployment. These assets, however, should not delay the artillery deployment.

Photographic reconnaissance can establish the probable main battle area. The necessary photos must be distributed to commanders and units.

Opportunities for armored vehicle commitment must be reconnoitered.

Engineers determine the types and the strength of enemy obstacles and barriers.

The signals intercept service (*Lauschdienst*) monitors enemy communications. The security of friendly signal communications against similar enemy action is important.

Artillery fire from varying positions and reconnaissance raids can force the defender to expose his positions and strength. Reconnaissance raids are especially necessary to detect dummy positions and to avoid local enemy strength.

The time allocated for all reconnaissance and information measures should not be limited unreasonably. The proper coordination of all arms can only be achieved through reliable and exact reporting. Later changes are time consuming, complicated, and may result in losses.

394. The commander makes his decisions for the attack based on the reconnaissance and his detailed assessment of the results.

Strong forces must be concentrated against those positions where the full effect of the attack can be brought to bear. Penetration zones should not be so small that the attacking force becomes exposed to the defender's massed fires. Success at one point of the penetration must carry over to others so that the area lying between them can be overcome quickly. Strong points should be bypassed and fixed for later reduction by follow-on elements. High ground from which the defender can coordinate concentrated artillery fire is usually taken faster by advancing on both sides of the position. Points that later will be important for friendly observation and suitable terrain for armored vehicles can have a decisive influence on the choice of the penetration zone. The terrain behind the enemy position also should be taken into consideration.

395. The objective of the attack must be fixed as shallow or deep, depending on the strength of the attacking unit.

If the attack cannot be executed in a single phase, then multiple thrusts with limited objectives should follow in short consecutive sequences as quickly as possible. The rapid and full exploitation of success must not be endangered by this method.

396. When the enemy artillery is ready and in position, friendly artillery should be deployed with great caution. Batteries should be positioned based on their observation requirements and the nature of the terrain.

Artillery ammunition supply and attack preparations require time.

397. The infantry departure areas should be advanced as close to the enemy as possible. They must provide cover for the deployed infantry, and

facilitate observation for infantry heavy weapons and artillery units directly supporting the attack.

Often, the final departure areas must be secured by fighting prior to the infantry attack.

398. The remaining necessary orders will be issued upon the commander's attack decision at the latest. These include orders for the artillery, for the infantry task organization, for the completion of the combat communications net and its connections with the special nets, and for other preparations.

399. On the recommendation of the artillery commander, the senior commander orders the artillery deployment based on its assigned missions. In some situations, some units, especially heavy artillery, will be fragmented and assigned piecemeal. The more difficult the attack, the more important it is to concentrate superior artillery fire rapidly on the decisive points.

When divisions fight as part of a corps and are assigned specific zones of action, the corps commander may opt to specify the task organization for combat of the divisional artilleries and attached artillery units, and to assign these units missions outside their divisional boundaries. Normally, corps artillery units will be limited to heavy batteries for long-range targets.

400. The commander's attack plan serves as the basis for the fire plans of the artillery and the infantry. The commander can task the commander of the artillery to develop a fire plan that is general or specific in form, depending on the difficulty of the attack. When attacking a strong position, artillery fire may regulate of the tempo of the infantry attack and the subsequent securing of objectives.

The fire plans of the artillery and the infantry must be synchronized. All identified targets opposing the attack must be engaged. All targets of opportunity appearing at the beginning or during the course of the attack also must be engaged—especially those in adjacent zones that can affect the advance. The artillery and infantry fire plans also must provide coverage of targets in the depth of the attack zone. All these tasks must be coordinated among subordinate infantry and artillery commanders in their individual zones. They must work together to assist each other, to increase fire effectiveness, and to ensure that targets of opportunity are attacked.

When the fire plans of the artillery and the infantry mortars overlay the same target area, the mortars should be attached to the artillery.

401. Superiority over the enemy artillery must be achieved from the time the infantry crosses the line of departure until they break into the enemy's main battle area. If the enemy has strong artillery that has been well adjusted, such superiority is imperative for the friendly infantry advance. Enemy air defense batteries must be neutralized early as well.

The enemy artillery will attempt to withdraw from the engagement. Sometimes this can be countered by good observation and by active aerial reconnaissance. Otherwise, engagement of the enemy artillery first becomes possible when the infantry attack forces the enemy to reveal his batteries in their final firing positions.

Identified and positively located enemy batteries must be engaged and neutralized prior to the infantry attack. It then becomes possible to suppress these batteries with small units; to place the mass of fire on newly appearing batteries; and to provide effective, sufficient, and immediate support to the infantry. If at the beginning of the infantry attack new and strong enemy artillery units are identified, fire superiority over them must be achieved. Depending on the situation, this may require a corresponding pause in the infantry attack.

The more difficult the counterbattery engagement, the more important becomes the obscuring of enemy artillery observation assets during decisive periods of the attack.

Only rarely will it be possible to begin counterbattery fire with surprise at the beginning of, or just prior to the infantry attack. On the other hand, no other choice may be possible if the infantry attack is not to be postponed and if visibility and observation conditions are unfavorable.

402. The preparations of the attacking infantry in the departure areas depend upon the protection those areas offer against enemy fire, and the time of the start of the infantry attack. If the departure areas are unfavorable and the attack time not yet fixed, they should be occupied late. Covered avenues of approach should be reconnoitered.

403. The success of counterbattery fire, the results of diligent and continuous combat reconnaissance, and the opportunities for preparation in the departure areas form the bases for fixing the time of the infantry attack. That order is issued as late as possible.

404. The infantry advances from its departure areas at the designated time. The execution of the attack and the speed with which it advances depend on the proximity of the departure area to the main enemy position, the nature of the attack terrain, the command which enemy fire has over the terrain, and the strength of enemy positions.

If the departure area is distant and strong enemy artillery fire is anticipated, the initial advance may be made more effectively under cover of darkness. Smoke screens facilitate the crossing of terrain without natural cover. Whenever the infantry is held up by enemy fire, it digs in. Gradually, it works forward at different points, uses the coordinated fires of the infantry heavy weapons and artillery, and digs in again. T he infantry advance can extend over a period of days, if conducted against a strong and well-organized position in difficult terrain. In such situations, the infantry can draw out enemy fire and force him to commit his infantry heavy weapons and artillery at the beginning of the attack, The infantry does this by advancing in a thin line formation organized in depth.

405. Once the superiority of friendly artillery is achieved, the infantry continues to work forward and engages the enemy more closely. When necessary, the most forward elements are reinforced. To achieve maximum effectiveness, infantry heavy weapons should engage the areas artillery cannot reach.

When the enemy defense is weaker, the penetration force can follow immediately behind those elements, working forward to the enemy's main battle position. A staunchly defended position must be prepared for penetration by the combined fires of all arms deployed in depth. The enemy must be worn down and softened up.

The course of the penetration will be shaped by the enemy's strength in his main battle area. Against a weaker defense, it often will be initiated by the individual decisions of the subordinate commanders and will exhibit the characteristics of a penetration in unprepared terrain. When the defense is stiff, it will be necessary to execute a coordinated penetration. The infantry will concentrate its most forward elements during night before the penetration and will attempt to move as close as possible to the enemy, to make full use of supporting fires. Generally, the penetration is a coordinated assault, launched at a designated hour. The exact timing of the attack must be kept secret. The penetration should be planned for the early hours of the day, so as to avoid the attacking infantry being exposed to observed enemy artillery fire in daylight. Following artillery and infantry heavy weapons fire, the infantry pushes directly forward to the attack objective. Engineers may be necessary to eliminate enemy obstacles in a well prepared defense. Elements of the artillery should be held ready, be attached to, and accompany the penetrating infantry. Batteries that see opportunities to advance will move under their own initiative.

406. Following the penetration, the enemy in the zone is suppressed through the coordination of fires and forward maneuver, and the coordination of the effects of the supporting arms (Paragraphs 363 and 364). This suppression is carried out in multiple individual engagements throughout the depth of the position, until the first attack objective is reached, or a complete breakthrough is achieved. Should neither be accomplished, the ground taken must be consolidated for defense and held until the attack can be resumed. New reconnaissance and observation must be initiated immediately.

407. During the course of the attack the enemy may attempt to reestablish his defense in a rearward position, in order to continue the fight from there under more favorable conditions. He likewise might try to withdraw completely. In either situation, he usually will try to disengage from the attacker during the night.

Normally, the leading attack units are the first to detect when the enemy declines to continue the fight in his present position. Close scrutiny must be maintained over all enemy actions.

Likewise, the impulse for pursuit most often comes from the lead units. The intent must be to maintain the closest contact with the enemy by direct pressure in the pursuit. Reconnaissance must be conducted to detect chemically contaminated terrain. If the enemy attempts to delay at a position not far from his rear, the lead units must conduct a reconnaissance to collect information about the new position and its approaches. If the enemy conducts a night withdrawal, stronger units can only follow in daylight. If strong resistance is anticipated—especially by enemy artillery—friendly forces must advance by echelon. They can move forward only when the mass of friendly artillery has advanced to new positions and is ready to fire.

In situations where the enemy withdraws far to his rear, and when pursuit cannot be conducted immediately, the commander specifies the missions of the artillery, controls the follow-up of the infantry, and fixes the positions of the reserve. Often the main body of the infantry will have to wait until daylight to advance beyond the previous front line. Whenever possible, the enemy should be overtaken.

Counterattacks by the withdrawing enemy must be anticipated.

408. An abbreviated attack can be effective when the enemy is shaken by the previous fighting, has not yet prepared his defenses, or if there is an opportunity to surprise him and to exploit friendly superiority. The location and strength of the enemy positions will determine the extent to which the reconnaissance, the required information measures, and the other preparations for attack can be abbreviated. The rapid advance of the artillery and the quick deployment and assembly of the infantry close to the enemy position will facilitate the timely exploitation of the situation. Under favorable conditions, early commitment of armored vehicles will facilitate the attack, and in some cases will guarantee its success. Smoke screens are useful in favorable weather and terrain conditions.

409. Against an enemy fighting a delaying defense, the attacker will reach the objective fastest with a strong attack against a single point. When the attack penetrates fast and deep, the enemy will be forced to evacuate his entire front. If he is able to disengage and withdraw, contact and direct pressure must be maintained through the assignment of deep objectives. The enemy must not be allowed to reform. If he is withdrawing to a rearward position, a new attack should be launched against another point on his front, as the situation permits. The objective is to surprise him and create an opportunity for an early breakthrough. A fresh attack force should be assembled early for this purpose. The mass of the artillery should be kept well advanced, armored vehicles can be deployed, and engineers should be held well forward. Only those absolutely necessary signal elements are brought forward.

VII

PURSUIT

410. Troop exhaustion is never a valid reason for failing to pursue. The commander sometimes must demand efforts that seem impossible. Boldness and daring must guide him equally. Everyone must do his utmost.

411. The preparations for a pursuit must be conducted in a timely manner. The overestimation of an advantageous situation can lead to a serious setback. Forces launched into a pursuit too early can endanger success.

412. The victor pursues on a broad front, always intending to outflank the enemy, to overtake him, to take positions in his rear, or to cut him off from his rearward communications.

Obstacles placed in the enemy rear can assist the pursuing units.

413. When aerial reconnaissance, reports from adjacent units, advancing friendly forces, or the slackening in enemy action indicate that the enemy cannot hold his position, the senior commander must inject his subordinate commanders with the will of victory (*Siegeswillen*). He orders all available forces to move in the direction of decisive pursuit, and as soon as possible he advances reformed or newly formed pursuit forces. Rapid and highly mobile weapons should advance with the lead units. Lucrative missions will emerge for cavalry and stronger motorized forces. Motorized engineers, antitank weapons, and air defense elements should accompany them. When the pursuit cannot be executed by outdistancing the enemy, or if the distance is too great, the pursuing units must be pushed through the penetration breech. At such points a coordinated chain of command must be established.

414. Fighter aircraft and bombers will operate against the retreating enemy main body, even at the expense of other targets. The action of the air units accelerates the disintegration of the enemy and creates disruption in his rear area, along his routes, and at his railheads.

Reconnaissance aircraft monitor enemy withdrawal routes and watch for advancing reinforcements.

415. From the very moment the enemy begins to retreat, the subordinate commanders who are closest to the enemy initiate the pursuit, immediately and without waiting for orders. They must act boldly and independ-

ently. All weaknesses of the withdrawing enemy must be exploited. Coordination with adjacent units is essential.

The reporting of objectives overtaken must not be forgotten during rapid pursuit.

416. Ammunition supply for all arms is a prerequisite for the intensive execution of pursuing fires.

417. Artillery is especially effective in pursuit operations because of its long-range fire and its mobility. Wherever possible, it maintains the maximum rate of fire.

Some artillery elements will remain in position as long as the withdrawing enemy can be engaged with planned and observed fires. Long-range targets in particular should be engaged, but the advance of the pursuing infantry must not be restricted. Long-range, flat-trajectory batteries* lay their heaviest interdiction fires on the enemy's withdrawal routes and railheads.

Strong artillery elements advance together with the pursuing infantry, prevent the enemy from consolidating positions, engage counterattacks, and gradually assume the fire missions of the rearward elements.

418. The infantry assures the complete defeat of the enemy through fire and intensive pursuit. When necessary, it engages the enemy with hand grenades and bayonets.† Infantry heavy weapons must not hesitate to assume positions close behind or among the forward elements. Strong enemy resistance should be bypassed and left for elimination by follow-on forces, which advance where the pursuit is most successful. A shift in the front too early should be avoided.

419. Chemically contaminated terrain should be bypassed and marked to warn follow-on forces. Motorized units can push through such areas. In areas that can be decontaminated easily (roads, uncovered terrain), passage should be forced as soon as possible.

420. Engineers not ordered to overtake and block enemy withdrawal routes will repair roads and routes in the rear of the pursuing units.

421. Signal communications units maintain contact between the senior commander and the pursuing units. Often, communications will be maintained through radio.

The divisional signal battalion pushes the trunk line forward in the main direction of the pursuit, closely behind the leading infantry. If the

---

*Devastatingly effective in World War I, most long-range, flat-trajectory guns were 150mm and larger. In 1933 and 1934, Germans still had no artillery pieces larger than 105mm, in compliance with the Versailles Treaty. The German Army reintroduced the 150mm heavy gun in 1938.

†In the infantry companies a rifleman carried 100 rounds of ammunition and one hand grenade. [*Wedemeyer Report*, p. 19]

enemy resumes combat, an advanced message center should be installed on the trunk line for communications to the flanks and to the rear.

Signal intercept units must make every effort to intercept enemy messages and communications.

422. All commanders accompany or closely follow the pursuing units.

423. Enemy covering positions and rearguards should not divert the pursuing forces from the decisive axis and should not tie down stronger forces. Every effort must be made to close with the enemy main force. The reserve should be pushed forward. When necessary, new attack elements are formed from the reserve, which can push the pursuit forward with renewed energy.

If the enemy makes a stand on terrain from which he cannot be dislodged immediately, the attack must be recoordinated and supported with strong artillery fire.

424. Organization of the units' ammunition supplies, combat trains, and rations will be made while advancing and must not restrict the rapid advance of the pursuit. The commander must relieve the pursuing units of supply and evacuation concerns.

425. During a night pursuit, the infantry pushes frontally along the roads, while the artillery extends its interdiction fire to maximum range. Individual batteries attempt to follow and to occupy firing positions based on map reconnaissance. In doing so, they extend the depth of interdiction fires. As the situation permits, they also can provide close support to the infantry.

In order to prevent pursuing units from being hit by their own artillery fire, the advanced elements must send reports to the rear on the objectives they have taken.

Night aerial attack can supplement artillery fire on the enemy's rearward terrain.

Units designated for an encirclement mission should advance during the night if possible.

426. The pursuit can only be halted by the order of the senior commander.

The pursuit cannot be halted in only a single sector.

VIII

THE DEFENSIVE*

427. The defensive (*Abwehr*) is based primarily on firepower. The defender, therefore, must try to produce the maximum fire effect. Accomplishing this requires a detailed knowledge of the battle area, which in turn facilitates the use of the terrain by means of field fortifications. Such positions provide better cover and make possible superiority of fire against the moving attackers.

428. Since the defensive does not have the advantage of the initiative, it requires the earliest possible contact with the enemy using all means of reconnaissance to determine the direction of his advance and the composition and strength of his forces. It is important to establish security as early as possible in all directions from which immediate attack is possible. During the organization of the defensive the defender mush be prepared to counter a surprise attack. Units must be deployed in this manner from the beginning.

429. The defensive terrain itself dictates the position of the forward elements. Good observation for the artillery and the infantry heavy weapons is usually the most important consideration for effective fires. Terrain that provides concealment for the infantry from enemy observation may be an overriding requirement. Cover against armored vehicle attack may require the use of natural barriers, such as rivers, swamps, and steep slopes.

Terrain that is strong to the front is useless if the flanks are vulnerable. Sometimes open terrain with good observation that can be covered by fire during the day will produce the best possible defense of a flank. Chemical contamination of selected areas can reinforce the overall defensive.

---

*During World War I on the Western Front, the German Army perfected most of the tactical techniques we now associate with modern defensive combat. Using combinations of defense in depth, flexible defense, and reverse-slope defense, master tacticians like General Fritz von Lossburg brought the French and British Armies to a standstill up until the start of 1918, when the Germans themselves shifted to the offensive.

120   *Truppenführung, Part I: 1933*

The defender will seldom find terrain that is equally suitable in all areas, especially not in a large sector.

A planned resumption of the offense also will influence the selection of the terrain.

When the situation permits, the terrain should be reconnoitered from the enemy's point of view.

430. When the natural strength of the ground is used skillfully and the positions are well camouflaged, the natural terrain picture can be preserved. This in turn will hinder the enemy's reconnaissance efforts. In certain situations, less favorable terrain can be more advantageous than stronger terrain from which the enemy can easily determine the organization and intent of the defender.

Terrain must be reinforced where it is not naturally strong. Initially this can be achieved with obstacles and barriers. When sufficient time and forces are available, even unfavorable terrain can be made exceptionally strong by using natural features.

431. Every effort should be made to surprise the enemy. Deception measures should mask the true nature of field fortifications, manning and strength of units, the type of defensive, and its tenacity.

432. Unless the plan calls for surprising the enemy by opening fire at close range, effective fires should be delivered at maximum ranges—as long as the ammunition situation permits. An advancing enemy should encounter increasingly stronger defensive fires.

The commander is responsible for fire planning. An established communications net is essential for effective fire control.

433. As a rule, firepower will be committed first in repelling an attack. Based on the situation, it also may be committed during the enemy approach, as soon as information about the deployment of his forces and his main attack points become clear. This in turn dictates the focal points of the defensive and provides the basis for the deployment of friendly forces.

Strong reserves are necessary to secure open flanks, but the firepower of a defensive front must not be weakened by the retention of strong reserves.

434. If contact has not been made with the enemy, the commander generally is free to select the defensive terrain and the deployment of his units. The timely delay of the enemy approach will result in additional freedom of action.

If the direction of the enemy approach remains uncertain, friendly forces should be deployed in a defensive assembly position. The intended defensive posture must be assumed as rapidly as possible.

435. If the defensive is assumed immediately before or after the initial contact, the selection of the terrain can no longer be based on time-consuming reconnaissance. In unfavorable terrain it might become necessary to

withdraw to more favorable terrain. If it is necessary to assume the defensive immediately, more favorable terrain may be seized from the enemy through a hasty attack.

The assumption of the defensive is most quickly executed from the march in multiple columns or by a direct deployment from the march.

436. When in the course of an attack it becomes necessary to transition to the defensive, it must be established immediately. The most pressing requirement is for flexibility in the forward line, while the forces are organized in depth. Based on the situation, the line may be required to advance or withdraw in various places in order to secure the best defensive position.

The transition to a delaying defense will be executed from the defense.

437. The operations order must state clearly the intended type of defensive: i.e., defense (*Verteidigung*) or delaying defense (*hinhaltender Widerstand*).*

Defense

438. The terrain on which a unit defends itself is its position (*Stellung*).

The most important part of every position is the main battle area (*Hauptkampffeld*). It must be held to the end.

Advanced positions and the covering forces deploy to the front of the main battle area. Their operations are covered in Paragraphs 456 and 457.

439. A position can only achieve its purpose when it forces the enemy to attack, or it prevents him from attacking. The establishment of the position must be based on the forces available.

A flank position should force the enemy to attack in a direction different from his intent. Such an attack is forced on the enemy when he cannot avoid the flank position and he cannot attack its flank.

440. The optimal situation for the defender is when the enemy is forced into a frontal attack. In order to counter an envelopment of the position, the defender must be able to bend back or echelon the threatened wing.† Local attacks must to used to prevent the enemy from flanking the position.

441. If the defender advances against the enemy in front of his own defensive position, it must be done in such a manner as not to weaken the security of the position. The attacker also should not divide his forces in the process.

---

*The two different forms of the defensive recognized by the Germans, defense and delaying defense, are roughly analogous to the two forms of the defense currently recognized by the U.S. Army, area defense and mobile defense, respectively.

†In older military literature this technique is called "refusing the flank."

442. The main battle area must be organized in depth. Its purpose is to divide the enemy fires; to concentrate friendly fires from the rear; to facilitate local withdrawals in the face of superior enemy fire; and to facilitate the continuation of the defense—even when the attacker has penetrated the main battle area. Organization in depth requires that the mass of the infantry heavy weapons and as many light weapons as possible must be able to fire to the front of the main battle area.

Authorization for a local withdrawal in the face of superior fire can be delegated to battalion commanders by the next-higher commander, and to subordinate commanders by the battalion commander. Such a withdrawal should not endanger the cohesion of the defense and should not make it possible for the enemy to establish himself in the main battle area.

443. The width and depth of the defense are closely related.

Flat, easily observed terrain permits greater width than hilly and broken terrain. Strong natural barriers can make it possible to manage with only security elements. Spent and exhausted units require narrower sectors. Darkness and poor visibility weather require stronger manning of the front line. Greater width can be achieved by deploying forces in groups. Ordinarily, a defense of long duration requires a continuous line of occupation.

Exact standards cannot be established for sector width. As a general rule, however, in favorable terrain it can be about twice as wide for defense as for attack.

444. Depending on the time, the work forces, and the means available, the position will be either a hasty or a prepared one.

A well-constructed main battle area normally consists of a chain of mutually supporting positions with obstacles, trenches, and individual firing positions. The positions should be distributed irregularly and in depth, and are established in the sequence of their importance. Strong points for combinations of weapons should be laid out in the most important positions. The plan of defense should be difficult to identify from the ground or from the air. Adjacent positions must be able to provide mutual support; but too great an emphasis on flanking support must not detract from the frontal defense. Adequate frontal defenses are especially important during periods of darkness or poor visibility weather.

The interlocking of all defensive positions must be established gradually.

The defensive position layout is completed with the establishment of obstacles, dummy positions, surveyed terrain points to the front, the removal of identifying features, camouflage, observation posts, and communications trenches.

445. The commander designates the general position of the main battle area on the map, and from the map he indicates the general trace of the

main line of resistance (*Hauptkampflinie*). This line forms the base of the continuity of the defense.

The subordinate commanders establish the main line of resistance on the ground. The decisions regarding the details of the defense, the exact location of the line, and its manning, can only be made on the ground.

The main battle area should be situated sufficiently far in front of the observation posts of the artillery and the infantry heavy weapons. The observation posts should be located so that enemy observation and fire has minimal effect. The enemy should be deceived for as long as possible as to the exact location of the main line of resistance. The terrain, therefore, must be analyzed from the standpoint of enemy observation and the defensive positions adapted accordingly. In hilly terrain, the main line of resistance can be positioned on the reverse slope if the danger exists that it will be detected early on the forward slope; and if a forward slope position appears unlikely to be held effectively against long-term enemy fire.

446. The defense of the main battle area must be conducted in such a manner by all arms that the enemy attack culminates in front of the main line of resistance. All arms must accurately monitor the enemy's situation.

447. During the fighting to the front of the main battle area, the artillery and infantry heavy weapons observation posts must provide distant observation into the enemy's depth.

In some situations, limited observation must be accepted to the front of the main battle position. If the leading edge of the defenses (*Verteidigungsanlagen*) lies on the reverse slope, artillery and infantry heavy weapons should position advanced observers on the forward slope and under the security of an outpost. High ground should be used where possible for rear and flank observation.

Paragraph 334 covers the siting of artillery and infantry heavy weapons observation posts. Auxiliary observation posts must be established in advance.

448. The position is divided into sectors for the purposes of reconnaissance and security. Sector boundaries should be drawn in such a way that they do not split defense installations. Special measures may be necessary to secure sector boundaries, especially at night or during bad weather. In such situations security elements should be specially designated for this additional mission.

449. Reserves assigned to deployed infantry sectors have the following missions: reinforcement of the forward elements; counterattack against any enemy elements that gain a foothold; and local relief.

The commitment of the commander's reserve depends on the situation. The most dangerous contingencies must be anticipated.

450. In the course of a prolonged defense, it will be necessary to relieve units. Reliefs normally are conducted during darkness. Each relief

should be conducted under secure conditions, and the time of the hand-over must be stated clearly in the operations order. The simultaneous relief of infantry and artillery units will seriously disrupt operations.

During a relief, unit familiarity with the terrain, the enemy, and the situation will be degraded for a short period.

451. Rearward positions should be designated and laid out. Normally, a withdrawal to such positions is made only in extreme situations. Rearward positions should be far enough back to force the enemy to displace his artillery. The establishment of these positions depends upon the situation and the time and forces available.

The withdrawal to a rearward position should be ordered when the forward position can only be held with unacceptable losses, and the situation permits such a move.

Conduct of the Defense

452. The same principles apply in a hasty defense as in a deliberate defense.

The defender's course of action is determined by his intent, his forces and means available, the natural and reinforced strength of the position, and the time available for preparation.

453. Arrangements for the defense must ensure the coordination of all arms, and must consider the limitations on the various arms imposed by the terrain. The close coordination and full commitment of all arms in time and space may require command-directed details that normally would be left to the discretion of the subordinate commanders.

454. The defender must derive the enemy's attack plan as early as possible. He monitors the reconnaissance and intelligence-gathering systems of the attacker, he monitors the enemy radio nets, and he tries to determine the strength and deployment of the approaching forces. Areas behind the enemy's front, traffic, airfields, and advanced landing fields also must be kept under observation.

Key factors for the defense can be derived from reconnoitering the terrain on which the attacker may concentrate or deploy. Artillery firing positions, observation posts, armored vehicle avenues of approach, and favorable attack terrain are especially important.

Fighter aircraft, air defense artillery, radio silence, and other assets can be used to screen friendly preparations.

Unity of command is essential for all reconnaissance, screening, and intelligence evaluation efforts.

455. Forces operating forward of the position execute a delaying action. Normally they operate under the direct orders of the area command-

er. Increased speed and mobility are their primary advantages. They should be strong in artillery and infantry heavy weapons. Coordination with adjacent units must be established through higher echelons. Obstacles and natural barriers facilitate the execution of delaying actions to the front of the position. Artillery within the position must be able to engage the approaching enemy. The area commander controls the withdrawal of the screening forces into the defensive position and their combat missions within the sector.

456. Advanced positions (*vorgeschobene Stellungen*) prevent the attacker from early occupation of commanding ground forward of the outposts.* The use of advanced artillery observation positions makes it possible to deceive the enemy as to the location of main positions and to force him to deploy his artillery too early. Generally, advanced positions should be selected far enough forward that they can be supported by elements of the artillery in the main battle area.

The area commander orders if and where advanced positions are established and under whom they operate. When they are subordinated to a sector commander within whose boundaries they lie, that commander can assign the units, the strength, and the missions of the advanced positions.

Advanced positions should be sufficiently equipped with heavy machine guns, antitank weapons, and light artillery batteries. The advanced positions should not be exposed to defeat in detail. They must be withdrawn in adequate time. Their return to the main battle area must be covered. Their withdrawal should not restrict the operation of the combat outposts, if at all possible.

457. Combat outposts provide the units in the main battle area with the time to prepare for action, to reinforce observation in the direction of the attack, and to deceive the enemy as to the location of the main positions. They must have specific orders regarding the extent to which they participate in the engagements of the advanced positions, and how long to continue in that action. The strength of the outpost line, its distance from the main battle area, and its specific missions are based on the overall mission and the terrain. It should not be located beyond the effective range of the light artillery in the main battle area.

The combat outpost line can be weak as long as advanced positions are forward of it and in terrain easily observed in daylight. Normally, the infantry units in the main battle area establish the outposts.

The commander establishes the approximate strength of the combat outpost, their most forward line of resistance, and period during which they

---

*Advanced positions essentially were a second outpost line in front of the main outpost line. [*Hartness Report*, p. 37]

must be held. On a wide front, the different sectors of the outpost line can have different missions. Coordination must be established with the combat outposts of adjacent sectors.

Combat outposts should be withdrawn in a such way that they do not restrict fires from the main battle area and are not exposed to those fires. Prearranged signals facilitate coordination between the combat outposts and the main battle area.

Small, deliberate, limited objective attacks launched under the cover of the combat outposts can disrupt the enemy's attack preparations and produce important information.

458. Planned and coordinated fires from all arms are the key to the defense of the main battle area. Such fires are laid out in a fire plan as described in Paragraph 400.

The senior commander and the sector commanders are responsible for the planning and coordination of the required fire support. That support includes long-range fires; their synchronization; coordination between the artillery and infantry; fire concentrations; and the rapid massing of fires on threatened positions.

The entire terrain to the front of the main battle area, to include long ranges, must be covered by fire without gaps. The individual arms must augment each other based on their capabilities and the nature of the terrain.

Fire should be concentrated increasingly on the enemy as he closes on the main battle area.

The coordinated fires of all arms must be brought to bear against the enemy in the case of a local penetration of the main battle area.

459. The artillery engages the approaching enemy from advanced positions, and if necessary, from positions to the front of the main battle area. Interdiction and harassing fires are executed with the aid of observers, pushed well forward and using radio communications. Artillery aerial observers and elements of the observation battalion are committed for this mission. Under certain conditions existing telephone lines or prearranged light signals can be used. The situation may required limiting the number of batteries committed to such missions in order to deceive the enemy as to the overall friendly strength.

The artillery must be organized in depth as the defense of the main battle area is established. Both this organization and coordination with the infantry must be established early. Every effort must be made to assure that the majority of batteries—even those without advanced and main observation positions—can fire on the attacker and can engage successfully any enemy elements that penetrate the main battle position. If there is a chance that the enemy has determined their positions, it may be necessary for batteries to shift firing positions during the night preceding an expected attack.

Artillery must be used with great mobility to achieve its full effect. Its

versatile employment requires careful preparations of observation positions, firing positions, firing data, position changes, camouflage movements, and the approaches to and exits from positions.

460. The guns of the divisional artillery must be able to lay concentrated fires, both deep and close, in front of the main battle area. The artillery
commander controls the firing for as long as possible. The task organization of the artillery and the assignment of fire missions must be based upon
this principle.

Having assigned his corps artillery assets to the divisions, the corps
commander can issue instructions for the task organization of the artillery
(attached and assigned) within the divisions, and can assign combat missions outside the divisions' immediate sectors. In general, the corps commander retains only heavy batteries under his control for commitment
against deep targets.

The division commander determines the artillery task organization, the
infantry units with which the artillery units will work, the units to be directly supported by artillery, and those that will have artillery attached. In order
to retain the ability to influence the battle decisively, the division commander must hold a proportionately strong artillery element under the
immediate control of the divisional artillery commander.

Artillery units that directly support infantry units in the defense of the
main battle area must establish communications with the infantry commanders. The commanders of both units maintain the communications.
Other aspects of the coordination between artillery and infantry are covered
in Paragraph 329.

461. When the situation and the ammunition supply permit, the
artillery will fire at maximum range.

In order to make the enemy approach more difficult, friendly artillery
fires on the enemy artillery when it occupies positions; its observation
points; and its communications and supply. It engages enemy field and air
defense batteries as described in Paragraph 358. The enemy's artillery fire
must be drawn out early so his batteries can be located and engaged. When
this is not possible, the enemy batteries should be engaged gradually, as
they are located. If the enemy is superior in artillery, early engagement
should be avoided in order to achieve surprise.

Enemy infantry moving into assembly areas, command posts, and communications and supply points are engaged with interdiction and surprise
fires, in conjunction with the infantry heavy weapons. Assembly areas also
should be taken under fire.

The mass of the artillery should be employed against the enemy
infantry as it occupies its assembly areas for the attack. The engagement of
enemy infantry heavy weapons is especially important. Attention should be
given to the avenues of approach and assembly areas of armored vehicles.

Only the most necessary artillery units continue counterbattery firing. At decisive moments the enemy observation posts should be blinded by smoke or neutralized by observed fires.

462. The infantry opens its fire as soon and as strongly as possible. Its fires are based on the fire plans of its heavy and light weapons. When friendly forces are weak in artillery, the approaching enemy should be engaged at long range with heavy machine guns and mortars. For this mission, a portion of the infantry heavy weapons are located forward in the main battle area, or even in front of it. As the enemy approaches, those units positioned deeper in the defense also engage. The heavy weapons of the reserve units are committed when necessary. The heavy machine guns should be deployed in concealed positions, and must have alternate, covered positions from which they can deliver flanking fires. Infantry light weapons engage in the firefight progressively as the attacker closes.

If enemy fire creates gaps in the infantry fire defense, the local commander must restore the situation immediately.

Reconnaissance must determine the options for the commitment of the support and reserve units. Those units dig in and prepare their own local defense. Under strong enemy fire, they may be permitted to relocate to areas that are not as vulnerable.

463. Should a portion of the main battle area be penetrated and taken by the enemy, all efforts should first be made to eliminate them with fires. Friendly infantry elements and supporting weapons in the immediate area of the penetration attempt to eject the enemy through hasty counterattacks before he can establish himself. These elements can be supported effectively by artillery fire laid in the rear of the enemy. These elements, however, should not be dependent upon artillery support.

Should these measures fail, or should the enemy make a major penetration, the senior commander decides whether a deliberate counterattack will be made to restore the position or whether the main battle area is to be reestablished farther to the rear. Whenever possible, the counterattack is launched against an enemy flank. The counterattack requires thorough preparation, especially when launched by strong forces. A single commander must control the assembly areas, timing, objectives, boundaries, artillery support, and the commitment of armored vehicles and air units. Too much haste leads to failure.

Reserves intended for the counterattack must be so assembled, or during the course of the attack so shifted, that they are readily available.

464. At all times all arms must be prepared to repel a surprise attack by night, during periods of low visibility weather, and in terrain with poor observation.

Normally, defensive fires are laid immediately in front of the main battle area. These fires must be planned and are executed upon order or special signal. Such fires are limited in time and space. The light artillery and infantry heavy weapons place their fires on areas that infantry light weapons cannot reach. The execution of defensive fires, the weapons engaged, the duration, the ammunition allotment, and the commitment of reinforcing batteries must be well planned. The specific authorization to initiate defensive fires must be established clearly. A battery should be tasked to deliver defensive fires only on an area that it can cover effectively.*

The enemy avenue of approach must be identified early. Increased reconnaissance, listening posts, and terrain illumination facilitate this task. Enemy elements that penetrate the main battle area are thrown back by hasty counterattack (*Gegenstoss*),† if necessary with bayonets.

Every soldier must know his immediate actions during a surprise attack.

465. The secure transmission of orders and information requires a close-knit communications net, organized in depth. Such a net must be established to the greatest extent possible. Lateral communications are important. If possible, radio silence is maintained until the start of the battle.

In addition to maintaining radio communications with the sector commanders immediately under the division commander, the divisional signal battalion has the primary mission of establishing communications between the artillery commander and his units, and facilitating coordination with artillery aviation, the observation battalion, and the balloon units. As time permits, special nets can be established gradually for infantry, artillery, balloon, air defense, and air forces units.

The mass of the signal assets is employed in the main battle area. Outposts and advanced positions must be connected. Radio is especially effective in this situation, but alternate means must be established. Signal communications from the main battle area to the rear must be maintained and improved. The wire net is laid by heavy field cable, based on the time and the forces available.

Signal monitoring is important. Friendly message traffic must be restricted and screened.

The commander controls the assignment of and changes in light signals.

466. Engineers are employed forward of the main battle area to estab-

---

*In defensive barrage fire, a light howitzer battery could cover about 150 meters, a light battalion 500 meters. [*Wedemeyer Report*, p. 111]

†The distinction between an immediate or hasty counterattack (*Gegenstoss*), and a planned or deliberate counterattack (*Gegenangriff*) grew out of the German experience while on the defensive on the Western Front between 1915 and 1917.

lish obstacles and barriers. Within the main battle area they establish obstacles, communications, and camouflage. Engineers may be attached to infantry units assigned difficult missions. In general, the commander places the engineers in reserve at the beginning of the defense, in order to commit them where their technical capabilities become most necessary.*

467. Tanks are committed offensively. They are a decisive reserve in the hands of the commander, and are especially effective for deliberate counterattack (*Gegenangriff*) or for the engagement of enemy tanks.

Ordinarily, the tank assembly area is far to the rear, out of effective enemy artillery range. Direct observation of the battlefield is desirable. The various options for their commitment must be reconnoitered.

In general, tanks are committed on order of the senior commander, who controls the time and objective of the attack and the coordination of the other arms.

468. Smoke can be used to conceal the shifting of reserves and the repositioning of artillery. Such movements can only be concealed against aerial observation if they start from one naturally covered position (woods, village, etc.) and lead to another, and the gaps are sufficiently obscured by smoke.

Likewise, batteries that must fire during active aerial reconnaissance can be camouflaged if smoke screens are placed not only over the batteries, but also over areas where batteries are not firing.

Gas and chemical weapons are covered in Chapter XVIII.

469. Air forces support the defense. Fighter units disrupt enemy aerial reconnaissance. When sufficient strength is available, friendly air units can be used to attack approaching enemy ground forces. As a priority, bombers attack enemy airfields and railheads.

The primary missions of attack and bomber aircraft are executed during the period immediately preceding the attack on the main battle area. Simultaneously if possible, strong fighter elements are committed to suppress enemy aircraft. Sectors not under attack must be stripped of aircraft to support this mission. At the same time, enemy assembly areas, reserves, firing batteries, and observation balloons should be attacked.

470. During the enemy approach, friendly air defense artillery must counter enemy aerial reconnaissance. To accomplish this mission, air defense batteries are pushed well forward, in front of the main battle area, if necessary.

With the beginning of the enemy artillery deployment, air defense artillery will be used to protect friendly artillery and ammunition dumps.

---

*The divisional engineer battalion had one motorized and two nonmotorized companies, a bridge train, and a signal platoon. [*Wedemeyer Report*, p. 39]

The protection of the reserves and the artillery is important immediately before and during the attack. Friendly air defense assets should be concentrated in the area of the enemy's main effort, if known. In areas where attack in depth is imminent, individual air defense batteries or air defense machine-gun companies are pushed well forward.

471. If the defense is to be reestablished in a rearward position, the breaking of contact, the withdrawal, and the resumption of the defense must be well planned. The maintenance of cohesion of the withdrawing units is especially important.

The commander must make his decisions and the preparations must be executed in such a way that the enemy cannot derive his intent. All measures must be executed in a deliberate manner. The withdrawal must be secured and executed in conjunction with adjacent sectors. If low visibility weather, smoke, or favorable terrain cannot be exploited, then the withdrawal should be executed at night.

For as long as possible, the enemy must be deceived into believing that the original defensive position remains fully manned. The maintenance of fire of all arms from their original positions will contribute to this deception. A following enemy must be delayed to the maximum extent possible. This is best facilitated by friendly artillery firing from their new positions. Should the new defensive position lie far to the rear, the artillery will have to use intermediate firing positions. Chemical contamination of areas in and behind the former positions is an effective delaying measure.

472. If the enemy attack breaks down, the defender should shift to the offensive if adequate forces are available. When attacking out of a defensive position, friendly forces must assume that the enemy is organized in depth and has artillery superiority. Should it prove impossible to suppress the enemy artillery or to break through the enemy positions, the attack will lead to a protracted frontal struggle with indecisive results. An envelopment offers the best chance of success. In some situations, the organization of an entirely new operation may be required.

473. If the defender intends to shift to a delaying defense he must reckon with a fully deployed enemy. Therefore, the first rearward line of resistance must be set well to the rear.

474. Should the battle end indecisively, or should a lull settle over the general operations, a situation can result in which the opponents stand opposite each other in small unit combat and the conditions approach those of positional warfare. In this situation the decision must be made to hold the former position, or to establish a new position farther to the rear. In the latter case, the old position can be used as an advanced position or as the outpost line of the new main line of resistance. If the main battle area is held, it is further strengthened and weak areas are either reinforced or abandoned. Outposts are pushed forward as far as possible.

The combat units, the reserves, and the support units should be reorganized in order to conserve the force. Obstacles are reinforced and dugouts for men and ammunition are constructed. Chemical defense measures are increased. Positions farther to the rear can contribute to the strength of the defense.

In addition to these measures, provisions for the care of the troops are made in and behind the position. Such provisions include water and care for the wounded and the sick.

Delaying Defense

475. Delaying defense may be forced by enemy superiority or it may be executed deliberately. In the latter situation it fulfills its mission only if superior enemy forces follow. It often can be employed advantageously as a preliminary to a battle, or as a supplement to a battle.

476. A delaying defense is executed from a line of resistance (*Widerstandslinie*) and, based on the situation, continued from other rearward lines of resistance. The action may offer strong resistance or may be conducted without close contact.

The defensive at the line of resistance must force the enemy to deploy early in force, thereby expending time and resources.

The defensive between the lines of resistance must delay the enemy and buy time for the preparation of the next line of resistance.

477. A line of resistance is favorably located if observation and fires are effective far into the approach terrain; if it lies along a strong position; or if it is fronted by defiles from which the enemy must deploy. Should the line of resistance lie in a wooded area, the observation and fire effect conditions are equally unfavorable for defender and attacker. On the other hand, the defender can better exploit the terrain for resistance, while the attacker is limited in movement and cannot fully exploit his superiority.

Covering terrain within and behind the line of resistance facilitates the breaking of contact and the withdrawal.

Obstacles of all kinds can strengthen the defensive from the line of resistance and between the lines of resistance. Field fortifications are an exception. Dummy positions can be valuable.

478. The commander designates the general location of the line of resistance.

The distance between the lines of resistance is a function of the terrain, observation, the intent, and the actions of the enemy. In terrain with favorable observation, the distance must be so great that enemy artillery is forced to displace forward. In wooded areas that distance may be short.

479. Ordinarily the line of resistance marks the position of the obser-

vation posts of the artillery and infantry heavy weapons. These weapons are located close behind the line of resistance.

When the terrain to the front of the line of resistance is open, the task of the units in the line normally is limited to the security of the observation posts and firing positions. Should the line of resistance lie behind stream lines or defiles, this advantage should be exploited by stronger forces and a defense of greater duration. As a rule, stronger forces are required in terrain with poor observation. In wooded areas, the infantry normally bears the brunt of defense.

480. The duration and strength of the defense at each line of resistance and in the intermediate terrain varies according to the situation. The commander exerts his influence through the organization and distribution of his forces and the allocation of ammunition.

481. The defense at a line of resistance must be organized to facilitate a well-regulated withdrawal to the next line of resistance and the resumption of the defensive. In general, open terrain that affords the enemy good observation should be evacuated early.

482. Based on the situation, the commander establishes the time of withdrawal to the next line of resistance. In terrain over which observation is difficult and on wide fronts, he can delegate the decision as to the time of withdrawal to the subordinate commanders; or he can designate a general line, which when crossed by the enemy in strength, triggers the withdrawal.

483. A unit fighting a delaying defense should have forces already in position in the rearward line before starting the withdrawal from one line of resistance to another.

If the withdrawing units cannot be supported from the second line, they generally should break contact early, retire while not under pressure, and select the next line of resistance well to the rear. Limited forces should be committed to facilitate the break-off of the forces in contact and to prevent the enemy from following immediately.

484. The longer the delaying defense is continued, the more necessary it is for rearward units to receive the withdrawing forces. Those rearward units should come from the forward command. The width of sectors depends upon the number of troops required in the rearward position.

There is no general rule for the width of a front. As a guide, the sectors for a delaying defense in favorable terrain can be about double the width of those in the defense.*

485. The terrain for a delaying defense must be divided into sectors.

---

*Wedemeyer reported divisional widths of 10 to 12 kilometers in the defense, and 15 to 18 kilometers in a delaying defense. [*Wedemeyer Report*, p. 37]

Boundaries are established for the lines of resistance, intermediate positions, reconnaissance, security, defense, and withdrawal.

Ordinarily combined arms units are committed in a sector. These units are assigned missions that they must coordinate with adjacent sectors. The strength and composition of the units are determined by the mission, the width of the sector, and the terrain.

The forces within each sector form resistance groups (*Widerstandsgruppen*). They support each other with flanking fires (*flankierendes Feuer*). In darkness, low visibility weather, and in terrain with poor observation, these groups must maintain close contact. By retaining some artillery under his immediate control, the commander retains the flexibility of supporting the individual units and of relieving them of the responsibility for deep interdiction and harassing fires.

Conduct of the Delaying Defense

486. Reconnaissance, intelligence, and screening are covered in Paragraph 454.

487. The movements of the enemy should be harassed and delayed far to the front of the line of resistance whenever the distance to the enemy, the terrain, and friendly strength and mobility permit.

488. Outposts with infantry heavy weapons and individual artillery pieces in front of the line of resistance can restrict the enemy approach. In covered terrain, light machine guns and riflemen can delay the enemy's approach and deceive him as to the type of the defense and the location of the line of resistance.

Gradually, all elements forward of the line of resistance withdraw to it. They reinforce the line or are deployed the next line to support the later withdrawal.

489. The defense from the line of resistance starts with timely artillery harassing fire against the enemy approach, supported by the forward elements. Artillery forward observers and aerial observers engage as well. The commander may delegate to the artillery commander the execution and control of the interdiction and harassing missions.

Gradually, the friendly artillery engages the enemy to the front as he prepares to attack. From the first, the preponderance of the artillery fire must be directed against the enemy infantry. The synchronization between artillery and infantry heavy weapons and the distribution of missions must be controlled by established orders or through coordination.

If the ammunition situation and other circumstances permit, every attempt must be made to deceive the enemy through aggressive artillery fire from widely dispersed positions.

490. Using its heavy weapons, the infantry primarily executes the defense from the line of resistance. In general, they fire from covered positions. In open positions, they should be advanced only so far as to permit their ready withdrawal. Light machine guns and riflemen are deployed if there is favorable cover in or in front of the line of resistance.

491. The breaking of contact is most easily accomplished if the line of resistance can be held until dark without becoming decisively engaged. In this case the retiring units usually withdraw en masse to the next line, while under the cover of the rearward elements.

Should the situation require that the line of resistance be held until dark, and close combat results, units must shift to the defense. The determination of the defensive position requires careful consideration.

492. If a line of resistance is evacuated during the day, the infantry heavy weapons and the artillery must deploy in depth. Communications between those units and the most advanced infantry units must be maintained.

If the enemy is to be held up by an intermediate position (between the lines of resistance), the units assigned to cover the withdrawal from the forward line of resistance execute this mission. In a deep intermediate position, it may be necessary to support the units therein, and to cover their withdrawal before they reach the next line of resistance. Such action may require leapfrogging the units in the intermediate position.

493. The unified command and control of all units is facilitated by early reconnaissance and determination and of the next line of resistance.

In certain situations it may be necessary to designate a line to which a withdrawal can be made in one day.

494. The duration of the defensive at a line of resistance depends essentially upon whether or not the enemy recognizes the delaying defense. If the enemy prepares to make a penetration, it is essential to withdraw from the threatened area in adequate time.

By no means does the withdrawal from one area along an extended line of resistance require a general withdrawal, or even the withdrawal of adjacent sectors. Any such withdrawals are based entirely upon the situation. Sectors of the front that hold their original positions can deliver effective flanking fire against a hastily advancing enemy. The effects of such flanking fire can be multiplied by advancing elements of the friendly front. The units remaining in position are responsible for adequate security of their own flanks.

495. The orders for the occupation of the next line of resistance must be issued as early as possible. All units must reconnoiter that line, and preparations must be made for its occupation.

496. As the withdrawing units approach the new line of resistance, some of the artillery and infantry heavy weapons must be in position there

already. Rifle companies are employed to the full effectiveness of their defensive capabilities as security elements in the line of resistance.

497. The command and control of all units demands reliable communications between commanders at all levels.

The senior commander and the sector commanders should be connected by wire. The sector commanders also should be connected laterally. The artillery commander must have immediate and direct communications to the firing units under his control.

Frequently, communications to individual areas must be limited to radio. In such situations, motor vehicles, horses, and prearranged signals must augment radio.

To the extent that the communications net permits, commanders should be as far forward as necessary to maintain proper command and control of their units, and communications with adjacent units. Commanders often must exert personal influence to meet these requirements.

The senior commander issues the orders for the removal or the breaking-down of the fixed communications systems. All commanders are responsible for the timely removal or the destruction of all communications equipment from the line of resistance.

498. Engineers should be committed early to construct major obstacles to the front of the line of resistance and in areas between the lines.

499. Antitank units should be deployed along avenues of approach and in open terrain to prevent enemy armored vehicle penetration.

500. Air defense units restrict enemy aerial reconnaissance. In rear areas they defend against enemy air attacks.

In exceptional situations, air defense units can perform deception missions.

501. In certain situations, armored vehicles can support the withdrawal of units by making short advances. During a delaying defense, however, armored vehicles are seldom available.

502. Smoke can provide ground cover on open terrain, but its use might favor the enemy.

Terrain contamination with chemical agents can restrict the enemy's follow-up.

IX

Disengagement and Withdrawal

Breaking Contact

503. An engagement can be broken off after its purpose has been achieved; when the circumstances require the use of units at another position where their redeployment seems more advantageous; when continuing the engagement may not lead to success; or when defeat can be avoided only by breaking contact.

The breaking of contact can be deliberate or forced, and executed on the decision of either the immediate commander or the next higher commander. Subordinate units should be informed of the reasons for a deliberate break in contact.

504. The situation, the intent, the actions of the enemy, the condition of friendly forces, and the terrain are the determining factors for the timing and the execution of the break-off.

505. Almost always, units that break contact require a rearward position for their reception—especially during heavy fighting.

The focus of the enemy's main effort is often the point that must be held for the longest time. A prepared rearward position is essential for units with this holding mission.

506. The more a break-off can be screened and concealed, the easier it is to execute. It becomes more complicated with close contact with the enemy and severe fighting.

507. A break in contact is easier after a successful action.

508. If an action must be broken off short of a decision and in daylight, heavy casualties often will result. In most situations the withdrawal should not be started before dusk. This may require units to hold a tenuous position until then. If this is not possible, a delaying defense must be conducted until nightfall and the start of the actual break-off. In some situations, smoke can provide the same concealment as darkness.

509. Breaking contact after losing freedom of action is very difficult. It is important for all commanders to encourage their units in such a situation

and to maintain discipline by personal example, coolness, and quiet and dependable orders.

If the senior commander still has reserves available, it is normally better to group them with the artillery still capable of displacement to the rear. These units should be moved into a new defensive line farther to the rear, instead of risking them in a hopeless fight.

Fighter and bomber aircraft, armored vehicles, and smoke generator units can assist a withdrawal.

510. Breaking contact can become necessary in any kind of engagement.

In the attack, the transition to the defense is the first stage of breaking contact—unless the enemy has been defeated or the friendly attack has culminated.

Contact can be broken during the pursuit by simply halting.

Paragraphs 471 and 479 cover breaking contact in order to establish a rearward defense, and for executing a delaying defense.

Paragraph 513 covers breaking contact with an undefeated enemy.

Withdrawal

511. The decision to withdraw may be made only when all options for a successful decision have been exhausted, and the continuation of the engagement would lead to defeat or to losses disproportionate to the mission.

Only extreme necessity, therefore, can justify a withdrawal from a battle. All too often a battle is lost because a commander believes it to be lost. Local failures or defeats in themselves do not necessarily justify a decision to withdraw. Commanders must persevere in uncertain situations. No subordinate commander is authorized to initiate a withdrawal contrary to his orders because of an untenable situation reported in another position. Even when the situation is bad, the commander must wait for superior orders.

The intention to withdraw must to be reported immediately to the next higher commander.

512. During the withdrawal it is essential to gain distance from the enemy. No unit should reengage without a compelling reason, because it will make disengagement from the enemy more difficult. Units that have disengaged from the enemy must maintain accelerated march rates. Multiple march columns facilitate the withdrawal. March discipline must be maintained at a high level, especially in the trains and rear service echelons.

513. Disengagement from a battle and the coordinated execution of a

withdrawal requires thorough preparation, farsighted orders, and purposeful command.

514. The commander designates the unit to form the covering force and where it will operate.

If at all possible, the covering force should consist of artillery and machine guns, protected by sufficient mobile forces. This will permit the infantry to withdraw without halting.

Positions established by the rear guard should cover the withdrawal route and force the leading enemy units into time-consuming deployments. In some situations, a covering position astride the flank of the line of withdrawal can be very effective.

There always is a danger of an encircling enemy pursuit overtaking the withdrawal. Countering such a threat requires rapid mobile forces, preferably equipped with antitank weapons.

When the intent is to defend from a new position, that position should be selected as far to the rear as possible. It should be far enough to the rear so as to force the enemy to reorganize his attack completely. The commander designates by map reference the position, the deployment of forces, and their sectors. He orders the immediate reconnaissance of the position and the routes to it. All arms send out reconnaissance elements. The deployment of the observation battalion in the new position must be timely.

515. Baggage and service trains are set in movement to the new position, under escort if necessary, to establish the support echelon.

Medical elements should be retained forward to provide care for the wounded during the withdrawal.

516. Combat units that are not needed should displace without delay. Assigned boundaries facilitate movement during the withdrawal. Individual units may be assigned to specific routes.

The position of the new airfield must be established early.

517. Traffic must be regulated. Officers with the necessary troops and equipment must be assigned to regulate traffic in towns and at defiles and bridges. These personnel should be provided with identifying insignia.

518. Radio traffic must be limited and strict communications discipline maintained in order to restrict the effectiveness the enemy's intercept capabilities. Under such conditions, signal lamps will be an important communications means.

Communications circuits no longer needed should be dismantled. If there is insufficient time to salvage them, the lines necessary for the initiation and execution of the withdrawal are destroyed after their purpose has been served.

Signal units should be sent back early to establish the communications network in the new position.

519. Obstacles are valuable for facilitating a withdrawal, especially in the face of an enemy pursuit. Friendly units must know the locations and the types of obstacles. Withdrawing units must not be jeopardized by chemical contamination of the terrain.

Engineers should be sent back early to repair roads, build or repair bridges, establish obstacles, and destroy bridges not used by friendly units.

520. A strong air defense system must be established early to secure threatened points, especially river crossings and defiles.

521. The supply of ammunition, fuel, and rations must be secured. Ammunition and ration dumps should be established along the line of withdrawal.

522. The senior commander designates the sequence and the timing of the disengagement, the security forces to be employed, and their strength and missions.

523. Using all routes perpendicular to the front, the infantry withdraws on a broad front while maintaining the combat formation held prior to the withdrawal.

Elements of the artillery maintain their fires for as long as possible, both as a deceptive measure and to cover the withdrawal of the infantry. Those remaining elements maintain their positions as long as possible, even sacrificing guns if necessary. The main body of the heavy artillery should be withdrawn first, the light artillery last. Elements of the artillery should be sent back to the new position or to a covering position.

The overall commander and the artillery commander should move back quickly to the new position, once they have assured themselves their orders for the withdrawal are being executed and their presence forward is no longer required. Otherwise, they should send their deputies back to the new position. There, they complete the reconnaissance and issue further orders. The subordinate commanders stay with their units to maintain cohesion and order.

524. The rearguard covers the withdrawal of the main body and deceives the enemy that the position is still manned in force. These elements are formed from the units in closest contact with the enemy, either as complete tactical units or elements from several. They must be fully supplied with ammunition. It often is not possible to designate a single commander on wide fronts. Orders must be issued establishing the time to break contact, and the required reaction if the enemy attacks early. These units can either follow immediately behind the main body, or remain in contact with the enemy until he begins his advance.

The sooner the enemy follow-up is anticipated, the stronger the rearguard must be in artillery and infantry heavy weapons. They make maximum use of the original positions. Combat engineers are deployed to establish obstacles. Smoke and chemical agents facilitate the mission of the rear covering forces.

It is an advantage if the existing communications net can be left for the rearguard. In such a situation it may not be possible to destroy the net, and part of it may fall into enemy hands. All efforts, therefore, should be made to simulate normal communications traffic in the original position.

The rearguard normally will be supported by and received into the covering positions.

525. The covering positions are abandoned after the rearguard's mission is accomplished and the main body has gained sufficient distance.

526. With increasing distance from the enemy, the withdrawing units will be able to form their march columns under the security of the rearguard. Rearguard missions, strength, composition, and organization are covered in Paragraph 252. Where the situation permits, the rearguard will be formed from fresh units. The units used for manning the covering positions also may be used to form rearguards. Conducting a delaying defense, they gain time for the main body. A thorough blocking of the enemy's avenues of approach is essential. If the enemy advances strongly, the withdrawal must transition to the defensive, even at the risk of severe losses. Limited objective attacks must be made when there is no other way to guarantee the necessary time and distance for the main body.

If bicyclists and mounted and motorized units cannot operate against the enemy's flanks and rear, they must hold tenaciously against the enemy to the last. Their mobility and speed permit them to withdraw rapidly and to close up with the remainder of the force.

Fighter and bomber aircraft can be used effectively to slow down the enemy pursuit. As far as the protection of the main body permits, air defense units can be deployed for deceptive measures and to restrict enemy aerial reconnaissance.

527. The rearguard falls back in bounds (Paragraph 252). Their halts should take full advantage of the cover and concealment afforded by the terrain.

528. Adequate and secure communications must exist between the rearguard and the senior commander, or the commanders of the individual march columns. These commanders maintain contact with the commander of the rearguard and designate the timing for the rearguard to follow.

529. When enemy action no longer requires the rearguards to withdraw in deployed formations, they form march columns. The withdrawal then becomes a retirement march to the rear.

530. In the course of the march to the rear, constant effort must be made to increase the distance from the enemy, thereby gaining more freedom of action for the commander. This requires an increased march rate,

night marches, or early starts, as well as increased security against encirclement by enemy forces.

Railroads will be used only if adequate preparations have been made. Enemy use of railroads should be restricted by destruction of the lines and air attack against the unloading points.

X

DELAYING ACTION

531. The objective of a delaying action (*hinhaltendes Gefecht*) can be achieved by defense, by limited objective attack, by feints, and by avoidance of combat. The determining factors are the intent, the situation, the strength and the actions of the enemy, and the terrain. The enemy can either be awaited or sought out. Opportunities to inflict damage upon the enemy are created or exploited. The objective is to conserve friendly forces and to inflict high losses on the enemy.

The longer the duration of a delaying action, the greater the area necessary for its execution.

532. Delaying defense is the primary means of executing a delaying action.*

533. Defense is only a temporary measure.

534. Based on the situation, limited objective attacks will be executed against the wing, the flank, or the rear of the enemy, or against a weak point in his front.

In order to exploit favorable situations quickly, subordinate commanders must have freedom to exercise their initiative.

535. Feints can be employed defensively or offensively. They lack staying power, however, and will be effective only when the enemy, based on the situation and the terrain, is anticipating severe fighting and his reconnaissance has been restricted.

Deception of the enemy must be achieved primarily through artillery fire and infantry heavy weapons. Dummy positions can support a feint.

536. Variations in action, mobility, speed, surprise, concealment, and deceptive measures increase the effectiveness of delaying actions, give

---

*The Germans took great pain in their doctrine to distinguish *hinhaltendes Gefecht* (delaying action) and *hinhaltender Widerstand* (delaying defense). Curiously enough, this distinction does not come out at all in Wedemeyer's report. Surely he would have come away from the course at the *Kriegsakademie* understanding this important facet of German doctrine. Perhaps he thought the distinction too subtle to try to explain to an American audience.

friendly forces temporary freedom of action, and delay the enemy for longer periods.

In open terrain with good observation, however, it is difficult to deceive the enemy for any length of time regarding friendly intent. This is especially true when he has superiority of aerial reconnaissance.

537. The great widths necessary for executing delaying actions often require the concentration of forces and ammunition at the decisive point. The remainder of the front operates with limited forces, which often must execute difficult missions.

538. All subordinate commanders must know the purpose of the delaying action, how it will be executed, and the missions of adjacent units. This is essential for coordinated action among subordinate commanders, who often are required to make rapid decisions based on their own initiative.

XI

COMBAT UNDER SPECIAL CONDITIONS*

Darkness and Fog

539. Actions that continue until darkness or sudden clashes at night normally result in a standing fire fight or the suspension of combat activity. A night engagement, therefore, should be executed only after thorough planning and the timely deployment of forces.

540. Darkness makes troop leadership more difficult. The direct influence of commanders is minimized. The determination of routes, reconnaissance, security, movement, contact and especially the engagement itself, all become far more complicated. Friction and the influence of chance are greater than during the day. The complexities are greater for the attacker. High troop morale is essential for successful night combat.

541. A decisive commander will not hesitate to attack at night to complete or exploit a success, to gain key terrain for subsequent operations, or to fix the enemy. The estimate of the enemy's combat power is an important factor in the decision to attack at night.

In exceptional situations, a night attack against a stronger enemy can result in success that could not be achieved during the day.

Commanders also should consider the use of night feint attacks.

542. Generally, the scope of a night attack must be restricted and its objective limited. This, however, does not apply to the pursuit of a decisively defeated enemy.

543. Prerequisites for successful night operations include simplicity in planning, careful preparation, surprise, and the use of the simplest formations. These prerequisites also apply to small-scale operations, like scouting and minor raids.

---

*Despite the space the manual devotes to this chapter, Wedemeyer reported in 1938; "River defense, mountain fighting, defense of defiles were not stressed in the instruction. . . . The instructor merely emphasized that the tactical doctrine we had learned continually applied, and that only the technical handling of the situation differed from the other types of operations." [*Wedemeyer Report*, p. 114]

Night attacks are executed primarily by units in the front line and in close contact with the enemy. The initiative often will originate with those forward units, and the actions are best left in the hands of the forward commanders.

If new units execute a night attack, they should be briefed thoroughly concerning the terrain, the direction, and the objective. Reconnaissance is indispensable. Orders for a night attack must be issued to units as early as possible.

544. The designation of the exact time of the attack should be withheld for as long as possible.

An attack launched in the first hours of darkness will allow the enemy little rest, will deny him time to establish himself in position, and will prevent his evacuation before daylight. An attack during the final hours of night masks friendly intent for a longer period, and facilitates the immediate follow-through of a daylight attack.

545. If forces committed to a night attack are required to conduct an approach march, it must be short and must be executed under the security of units already in contact. The route of approach and the assembly areas must be established in advance. Compass directions and guides are essential. Concealment from enemy observation is essential for an approach march during twilight.

The approach march by small units is best conducted in march column. Multiple attack units require sufficiently large intervals and even separate missions to avoid interference and mixing.

Short halts during an approach march will help maintain unit integrity.

546. If the attack is not launched from an assembly area, units should deploy as late as possible. A relatively tight skirmish line is the preferred formation for the final advance. Reserve and support forces follow as closely as possible in narrow, deep echelon. Horses and vehicles are left in the rear. Flank security is essential.

Infantry heavy weapons accompany the forward line, establish flank security, and then follow with the reserves and support forces. If they support the attack from rear positions, measures must be established to ensure their fire does not interfere with the infantry advance.

The situation may require individual artillery pieces to accompany the forward elements.

547. Light and noise discipline during movement are essential until contact is made with the enemy.

Identification procedures are essential for friendly forces.

In general, it is better to leave rifles unloaded. This is especially true for rearward units. Bayonets should be fixed.

548. When the attack is launched without artillery preparation, the attacker seeks to gain success by surprise. He throws himself at the enemy

with shouts and cold steel. Infantry heavy weapons and artillery remain ready to seal off the attack area by fire, or when there are multiple attack elements, to cover the terrain between them. The target areas should be registered in. In addition to these missions, the artillery engages identified enemy artillery and infantry mortars.

When the attack is launched with artillery preparation, it should be limited to short* and heavy fire strike (*Feuerüberfall*), followed by a scheduled and coordinated fire advance. The attack is conducted in the same manner as if there had been no preparation.

In all cases the firing data must be computed during daylight.

Upon contact with the enemy, the situation may require the illumination of the battle area with flares. Any such action should be planned in advance.

549. Actions following the attack must be specified in advance in the orders.

550. Darkness gives the defender the advantage of better knowledge of the terrain.

Delaying actions at night normally are executed by weaker forces, which fight and withdraw along roads and trails.

The defender who anticipates a night attack reinforces his front and shifts his positions when he believes that the enemy has identified them. In stronger combat outposts, the defender secures against a surprise attack by conducting aggressive reconnaissance and by irregular illumination of the forward terrain. Defensive fires must be on call and tightly controlled, in order to limit ammunition expenditure.

551. Heavy fog can influence combat operations in the same manner as darkness, and therefore the same principles generally apply.

Battlefield illumination is impossible in fog, and visibility is generally more restricted. On the other hand, commanders must operate under the assumption that the fog can lift at any time. Any decision based on the use of fog requires rapid execution and must take into consideration the possibility of sudden lifting.

The sudden appearance of fog or low-visibility weather can facilitate a surprise advance.

Combat in Built-up Areas

552. Operations can be affected severely by combat in and around towns, villages, cities and other built-up areas.

---

*10 to 30 minutes. [*Wedemeyer Report*, p. 117]

The importance of built-up areas during an engagement depends on their position relative to the terrain, their type of construction, and their size. A concentration of groups of buildings, such as extended industrial and mining areas, have the same significance as built-up areas. Large cities themselves can become battlegrounds.

553. Built-up areas offer concealment from ground observation and restrict aerial reconnaissance. When solidly constructed, they provide limited protection against small arms fire, light mortars, medium-caliber artillery, small aerial bombs, and armored vehicles. On the other hand, they draw enemy fire and air attack, they increase the fire hazard, and they prolong the persistence of chemical agents.

In favorable terrain, built-up areas form natural strong points and can become the focal point of an engagement; but they also can become a greater disadvantage than an advantage to the forces using them. Built-up areas lying within the enemy's zone of fire should be traversed only in dispersed formations. Small, easily observed built-up areas should only be used only by smaller forces. They should not be used for the position of the reserves.

Built-up areas that do not lie in the forward zone should be secured against artillery fire and chemical agents.

554. Combat in built-up areas wears forces down very quickly, often without having a decisive effect on the action. Such combat is fought at close range and its outcome often hinges on the independent actions of subordinate commanders.

555. During an attack, the main force usually bypasses built-up areas. Any enemy within such areas should be suppressed by fire or chemical agents, or blinded by smoke. The built-up area can be taken later from the flanks or rear by follow-on forces.

556. A frontal attack against a built-up area becomes more difficult the wider and the deeper it is, and the longer the time the enemy has to fortify it. Careful reconnaissance, including aerial photographs, is essential. If reconnaissance indicates that the built-up area is defended tenaciously and in depth, a detailed plan of attack will be necessary. Intensive preparation fire is essential. In order to eliminate flanking fire, the salients around the built-up area must be taken first. The attack then advances to the edge of the built-up area under the cover of artillery fire, infantry heavy weapons, and mortars. As the infantry approaches, the artillery fire lifts. When infantry heavy weapons are insufficient, individual artillery pieces or firing platoons are attached to the infantry. They follow as closely as possible. Their value increases as the normal artillery fire can no longer support directly the infantry at fixed distances.

As the artillery fire lifts, the infantry rushes the built-up area with bayonets and grenades. The leading elements push as deeply as they can without being diverted by skirmishing. If possible, they push to the far side of the built-up area. As necessary, they advance along streets and through yards and courts.

An attack normally will advance only by phases against a determined enemy defending in depth. Initially the attack may have to advance by bounds. Heavily defended houses and farmsteads should be softened up by artillery and mortars before the infantry assault. Combat engineers with demolition charges and flamethrowers can provide valuable support. The attacking forces should not bunch up, and reserves should be held ready to counter any setbacks.

Upon securing the built-up area, it should be cleared of the enemy and organized for defense. Special measures must be taken to neutralize booby traps. Follow-on forces accomplish these tasks.

557. Built-up areas often will be integrated into a defense, especially when they offer protection against armor attack.

The forward edge of the main battle area should not lie along the edge of a built-up area. It will run either in front of, or through the built-up area. Defensive power is increased by field fortifications. Houses, courts, and hedges that form salients can be used for flanking fire along obstacles and along the edge of the built-up area, and for sweeping the streets with fire. Large built-up areas must be organized for the defense in their entire depth. Individual farmsteads and buildings are used as strong points. If the enemy penetrates the built-up area, each sector and group of buildings must be defended. The reserves are committed to repel any enemy force that breaks in.

Forces inside the built-up area deliver flanking fire to prevent the enemy from bypassing and outflanking it. Forces outside the built-up area counter any enemy attempts to go around.

Units in built-up areas that have been surrounded and cannot break out, can nonetheless inflict serious damage on the enemy by tenaciously defending their position.

558. During a delaying defense, built-up areas can be used advantageously to screen the type and strength of the defensive from the enemy.

Combat in Woods

559. Wooded areas facilitate the approach of units to the battlefield. This is especially true for weaker forces. Normally, stronger forces can be supported more effectively in open terrain through their organic assets.

Combat within and for wooded areas can influence significantly the course of an engagement.

560. Woods provide concealment from ground observation and from

aerial observation, depending on the season and the density and type of trees. The foliage can restrict observed fires, provide some protection against armored attack, facilitate the positioning of obstacles and barriers, and reduce the effectiveness of fires.

In large wooded areas, the maintenance of effective communications is difficult, especially with adjacent units. Roads and paths can facilitate the determination of direction, but their use in heavy fire areas often results in severe losses. Except on well established roads, direction in the woods can only be maintained with a compass.

Commanders can easily lose control of their units. In the forward lines commanders only control their immediate proximity. Limited observation and the pressure and increased tension of close combat lead to confusion for both friendly and enemy forces.

Combat in woods is especially strenuous. The subsequent reorganization of the force is difficult and requires time. Units that have been engaged in heavy combat in large forests often require extended recovery periods.

The larger and denser the wooded area, the greater the restrictions on movement and combat action.

Smaller wooded areas are especially good targets for artillery fire, are favorable for the employment of gas, and are easily observed from the air or ground. They should be avoided if possible.

561. Infantry close combat normally decides the action in wooded areas. Light machine guns, rifles, hand grenades, and bayonets are the primary weapons. Heavy machine guns are especially effective in providing fire at close ranges. In many situations heavy machine guns and the light and medium mortars must fill the role of artillery.

Combat engineers establish obstacles and barriers or open routes through enemy obstacles for infantry and horse-drawn elements.

Flamethrowers are very effective in the attack. Their effect lasts for a considerable time and is very destructive.

As a rule, massed artillery can be committed only outside of the wooded area, and generally can only engage the enemy rear areas or cleared areas within the woods. Firing positions for howitzer or gun batteries are the easiest to site. Individual guns or firing platoons generally should be attached to the forward infantry units.

Telephone lines of any distance must be laid along roads and trails. Ordinarily, messenger dogs and radio provide quicker communications.

562. The attacker will attempt to secure small wooded areas by envelopment. Artillery suppresses enemy flanking fire or it lays smoke in the wooded area. Smaller wooded areas can be gassed or contaminated, precluding their use by friendly forces.

563. The attack against a wooded area is directed initially against any salients, which are engaged first with artillery and mortars. These weapons

must maintain direct fire support for as long as possible, facilitating the infantry approach to the edge of the woods.

In shallow woods, the attack pushes through directly to the far edge.

Immediately after entering deep woods, units are assembled and reorganized if necessary. The type of woods determines the nature of the reorganization. In thin woods with little undergrowth, the attack often can be continued with the formation used for entry. Support forces and reserves, however, must move close behind and the flanks must be secured. In large thick woods with considerable undergrowth, reconnaissance units should be deployed on a broad front. The main body should be deployed in depth and on narrow fronts.

Columns, rather than skirmish lines, are generally the best formations for advancing through woods. All commanders must exert maximum efforts to prevent their units from assembling on or near roads and trails, where the strongest enemy resistance will be encountered. During the advance the enemy should be attacked away from the roads and trails. Movement by bounds may be necessary to prevent friendly troops firing on each other as a result of uneven advances. Reserves are held sufficiently far back so they do not become prematurely engaged in the forward fight. They should be committed to reinforce success.

Units should be reorganized prior to emerging from wooded areas. Artillery and infantry heavy weapon support must be laid on. Observation posts should be advanced to the forward edge of the woods.

Vehicles can only advance along roads and trails in thick woods. Their movement must be carefully controlled. They should not be allowed to bunch up or to block the routes. In woods of lesser depth, the vehicles can be held outside the wooded area until friendly forces have reached the far side.

564. In general, defensive positions should not be established at the edge of a wooded area. They should be established either well in front of or deep in the woods. If positioned deep, the combat outposts should be advanced to the edge of the woods. Individual rifleman or light machine guns can fire effectively from positions in the trees.

In woods, the necessary fields of fire must be prepared and contact must be established between the units of the main battle position.

Some situations may require the establishment of strong points at road intersections within the woods.

Machine guns and mortars provide effective flanking fire, especially over open spaces.

All kinds of obstacles can be used to restrict the enemy's advance and deployment, to channel his movement, and to bring him under flanking fire.

Direct artillery support is difficult in wooded areas. In general, the principles in Paragraphs 460 and 461 apply to combat in woods.

Routes forward and to the rear of all positions should be reconnoitered and made known to all concerned.

If the possibility exists for the enemy to attack on either side of a wooded area, the defending forces must be able to engage him with flanking fire from the woods. Elements should be positioned outside the woods to repel his advance.

565. Wooded areas can be used for a delaying defense as effectively as for a defense. Woods can be used to deceive the enemy as to the size and intent of the friendly force. The unit executing the delaying defense can permit a closer approach by the enemy, can withdraw more easily, and can regroup and resume the defense at shorter distances than is possible in open terrain. On the other hand, the broader the front of the delaying forces, the more difficult it is to command.

566. Combat in wooded areas requires independent action by all subordinate commanders and individual soldiers. Personal courage in hand-to-hand fighting is more important than superior numbers. In woods it is often hand-to-hand combat that proves decisive. Bayonets must be fixed when sudden close contact with the enemy is imminent. As the enemy is engaged, he is overwhelmed with fire or aggressively attacked with bayonets and grenades.

Crossing and Defending Rivers and Other Bodies of Water

567. Rivers that cross the direction of approach are an obstacle to the attack and an advantage to the defense. They facilitate screening against enemy ground reconnaissance.

The strength of a river sector increases with the width, depth, and speed of the river. Its natural strength also is based on its course, the condition of the banks and adjacent terrain, existing fords,* islands and tributaries, the type of riverbed, and the season and weather (frost, ice, rain, drought, storm, etc.).

Water courses of little consequence themselves may become significant obstacles as the result of swampy banks, high water, or artificial dams.

Water barriers, especially when they have muddy bottoms and steep banks, are the most effective tank obstacles.

568. In the situation of a destroyed bridge or a forced river crossing,

---

*Planning depths for fording operations were 1 meter for infantry; 1.3 meters for cavalry; 0.6 meter for artillery and infantry heavy weapons; and 0.9 meter for armored vehicles. [*Wedemeyer Report*, p. 44]

routes must be reconnoitered and engineers and ferrying and bridging equipment must be assembled at the necessary sites in a timely manner. In larger commands, the senior engineer officer will be in charge of all preparations. The senior engineer on the staff essentially becomes the engineer staff officer for the river crossing. He must be briefed as early as possible on the situation and the commander's intent.

569. The rapid securing of the far bank is the primary objective of a river crossing.

Existing bridges must be taken quickly. When necessary, engineers are positioned well forward to repair damaged bridges. Precautions must be taken against delayed action demolition charges.

Bridges constructed of prefabricated or field expedient material can supplement or substitute for fixed bridges. The greater the number of bridges, the more rapid the crossing. As a rule, bridges that are to be used by heavy loads and supply columns must connect between hard surface roads.

The construction of bridges using field expedient material often requires considerable time and manpower. Troops must be specially trained for this task.

Hastily constructed bridges have limited carrying capacity.

The construction of bridges in daylight is preferable but requires strong air defense cover. In the absence of such cover, ferrying operations only should be conducted in daylight. Ferrying operations require considerably more time and manpower than bridge construction.

Annex 3 lists the carrying capacities of bridge and ferrying equipment.*

570. Security against air threats must be established early, both by the crossing units themselves and by supporting air defense units. Fighter aircraft can be committed to this mission.

571. Smoke can be used to conceal bridge construction and large ferrying operations from ground observation, but not from aerial observation. During initial ferrying operations smoke can restrict the effectiveness of enemy fire. If enemy ground observation is to be effectively blinded for sufficient time and in an area of sufficient width and depth, the employment of smoke requires favorable wind and weather conditions, an abundant supply of chemicals, and sufficient chemical units.

Short duration smoke screens over a small area can effectively deceive the enemy.

---

*Annex 3 is not reproduced in this translation. It listed two basic types of pontoon bridge: 100 meters in length with a 4-ton capacity; and 80 meters in length with a 7-ton capacity. Both bridges had a 2.8-meter-wide roadway, and both took two to four hours to emplace.

When smoke is employed, the routes leading to the bridge and ferry locations must be marked effectively.

572. Obstacles in the river, individual guns, and machine guns are used to protect against self-propelled mines and fires floating toward the bridges.

573. If the enemy is still approaching the river, friendly forces should advance as quickly as possible on a broad front, cross the river, occupy the far bank, and in all situations facilitate future crossings by securing both sides of the river.

574. If the enemy is already at the river, the key conditions for a successful crossing are the maintenance of secrecy and the screening of the crossing preparations in order to deceive the enemy as to the intended crossing site. Crossing feints will contribute to any deception effort.

575. If a surprise attack is feasible, the preparations should be shortened. Strong elements must be put across immediately. A surprise attack in daylight is only possible in fog or over a narrow river. As a rule, an attack over a wide river should be made just before daylight.

If the enemy appears to be executing only a delaying action at the river, the guidance in Paragraph 409 applies.

576. An attack against a defended river line is executed on the same principles as an attack on a position. Ordinarily the enemy's main battle position begins at the river's edge. Often weak enemy forces will be on the friendly side of the river, deployed to delay the advance.

577. As a rule, multiple groups launch the attack. The objective is to use favorable terrain; to execute the initial crossing on a broad front using light equipment; and to deceive the enemy as to the decisive action and to force him to disperse his forces. The strength and composition of the attack groups are determined in accordance with their specific missions and the general plan of attack.

The intervals between the adjacent groups should be synchronized, so success by one group can be exploited by another.

578. The selection of a crossing site depends upon the situation, the terrain on both sides, the current, and the river conditions.

579. Favorable conditions for an attack include a good, hard-surfaced road net; routes of advance concealed from aerial and ground observation; good assembly areas; dominant terrain along the near bank; bends in the river that envelop enemy banks; clear observation over the river; open crossing areas; and favorable terrain for follow-on attack beyond the river.

Technically, the execution of a crossing is easier at narrow widths, with steady currents, with easily accessible banks that have easy and firm slopes, and when auxiliary material is available.

580. Ordinarily, ground reconnaissance can be conducted up to and across the river only after the enemy forces on the near bank have been

driven back across. Possession of the near bank is normally necessary in order to reconnoiter and determine the details of the crossing. In order to acquire additional information on the far bank and beyond, a wide flanking ground reconnaissance may be necessary.

581. Aerial photography will most rapidly identify the initial indicators of favorable crossing sites. Aerial photographs supplement maps and provide additional information on the conditions of the river.

The commander initiates the ground reconnaissance, or assigns zones of reconnaissance responsibility to the subordinate commanders.

The commander of each attack group can assign individual missions to the officers of the separate arms, or he can direct them to accompany the reconnaissance parties.

Based on the assigned mission, reconnaissance parties are provided with light crossing equipment, measuring instruments, means for route marking, and maps.

Signal officers reconnoiter the crossing area to determine the placement of permanent lines on the near side of the river and the sites for pushing the field lines across.

The commander evaluates all results.

582. If the attack requires assembly in great depth, weak forces should advance to the river to screen friendly forces and to restrict enemy reconnaissance.

In uncertain situations, the assembling of units and equipment in depth will provide the flexibility to shift the area of decisive action. Marked routes and closely regulated traffic facilitate the subsequent advance to the river under conditions of poor visibility.

583. Based upon the engineer commander's recommendations, sufficient engineer personnel and materials are attached to the attacking forces to support their crossing on a broad front. Secrecy in the assembly of engineer equipment and auxiliary materials requires careful preparation. In normal situations it can only be done at night.

Strong engineer elements must be committed from the start. Engineer and equipment reserves must be assembled sufficiently far from the river. They serve to reinforce the crossing at the decisive point or at the area where the crossing is most feasible. Engineer reserves replace losses and construct bridges.

When their attachment to the attacking units is no longer necessary, they revert to the engineer commander.

584. The divisional signal battalion connects the engineers' command posts to the division main trunk line and to the command posts of the attacking units. The engineers establish the communications necessary for their technical operations.

585. In exceptional situations and if time is available, the attacking

units may be echeloned for the initial crossing. Reinforced or increased fires should not be allowed to alert the enemy to the start of the attack.

Any islands in the river should be secured first.

586. Execution of the attack begins when the light equipment of the crossing units has been brought forward to the final covered positions on the near side of the river. The first wave crosses on a broad front and establishes a bridgehead. Follow-on waves cross based on the situation. Areas where enemy fire is suppressed should be exploited. The massing of units at the river should be avoided. The success of the initial crossing depends primarily on the initiative and capability of the subordinate commanders. Rearward forces and equipment advance to where the crossing is most successful. Movements to the flank on the riverbank should be avoided. Footbridges can be used over narrow streams that are not too rapid. Infantry heavy weapons, artillery, signal equipment, ammunition, and in certain situations armored vehicles follow on ferries. Horses swim across if possible. Vehicles essential for the construction of ferries must be assembled at key points. After the ferries have started operating, the simpler means of crossing often can be suspended.

The senior commander initiates the preparations for subsequent bridge construction, and all bridges are constructed in accordance with this order.

587. Automatic antiaircraft guns and antiaircraft machine guns must advance early to the far bank to provide cover for ferrying, bridge construction, and bridge traffic. All efforts must be made to position air defense elements on the far bank before bridge construction starts. The mass of the air defense weapons should remain on the near bank until most of the combat units have reached the far side. Air defense units must cover key bridges used for supply and special traffic until the crossing is completed.

588. Artillery remaining on the near side of the river must provide flank protection for the infantry elements already across. The initial attack objective, therefore, must be observable from the initial artillery observation posts. Artillery observers equipped with communications equipment should accompany the lead infantry elements.

Elements already across in sufficient strength and with adequate artillery support should push straight ahead. The bridgehead should be expanded as far as possible so the enemy cannot employ ground observation for fire against the bridge area.

The bridgehead must be reinforced immediately. Lateral communications between bridgeheads must be established without delay.

589. Initially, communications between forces on both banks will be exclusively by radio. As soon as possible, the divisional signal battalion establishes the trunk line over or through the river to the far side. The attack groups connect to the line when it is pushed across.

590. The artillery should push individual batteries across the river to

protect the forces advancing into and holding the bridgehead. Later, the artillery commander must advance the mass of his artillery across the river, retaining some elements on the near bank. The first batteries across should be attached to the infantry. All measures, including ammunition supply, must be taken to repel counterattacks and to prevent the defeat of the units already across. Reliable communications are vital.

The commander crosses to the far bank when communications have been established.

591. If a surprise crossing fails at individual areas, a renewed attempt in those areas should be delayed until fire effect or success at other areas can assure success.

592. The commander orders the initiation of bridge construction as soon as the situation permits. As a rule, the construction is conducted in darkness. The main body of the engineers and the bridging construction material normally are assigned to the engineer commander. Ferrying operations continue as long as they do not delay bridge construction.

A bridge under enemy fire can be withdrawn and later installed at the same location or at another place. The course of action depends on the volume of fire, the situation, and the available time. The removal of bridges and the subsequent detouring of traffic cost time. Auxiliary bridge locations must be reconnoitered and prepared as far as available personnel and material permit.

Air attack can force a temporary suspension of ferrying and bridge crossing.

593. The defensive value of a river line depends on the situation, its natural strength, and the defending force. The advantage of its frontal strength is offset by the disadvantages of the river becoming an obstacle when the defender wants to restrict the enemy's ability to shift his forces, or when the defender wants to exploit the defeat of an attacking force with a counterattack. Moreover, the river as a strong frontal obstacle loses value if the enemy is not forced to attack the river line. In such a situation the best course of action is to place the mass of the force in assembly areas initially.

594. Elements that are forced to withdraw from the far bank should use crossing sites to the flank and outside the zone of the enemy's effective fires. As an alternative, they can use established crossings in their respective zones. As far as possible, field expedient material should be used for this purpose. Units on the near side cover the withdrawal. Patrols and reconnaissance groups remain on the far side to determine the assembly areas and crossing sites that will be used by the enemy. If necessary, these units recross by swimming.

595. By effectively using the river as an obstacle, units executing a delaying action not only force the enemy into time-consuming attack

preparations, but they can repel weaker crossing attempts. Special attention should be paid to probable crossing points, roads leading to the river, likely bridge positions, and salients in the river line.

Breaking off the action and withdrawing are more easily accomplished from behind a river line.

596. In the defense, the forward defensive line of the main battle position often will lie along the near riverbank. The defending forces must be able to command the river from the main battle position. It should be covered with overlapping fields of fire concentrated on the probable crossing sites. If the enemy bank dominates open terrain in the friendly main battle area, and especially in salients created by the river's course, those areas should be weakly held in daytime and covered by fire from rearward positions.

Illumination of the river is essential. Outpost boats should be used on very wide rivers.

The wider the sector covered by the artillery, the greater must be their fire maneuverability, so when necessary they can concentrate their fire on initially unknown enemy crossing sites. Where frontal fire is difficult, small artillery detachments can be pushed forward to execute flanking fire along the river.

Engineers emplace obstacles at probable enemy approach routes, assembly areas, and crossing points. Mines placed in the water in probable crossing areas are effective in delaying the enemy. Floating mines, fireboats, and similar devices should be held in readiness.

The primary mission of the air defense units is the prevention of enemy aerial reconnaissance. The air defense units are deployed in favorable crossing areas and far enough forward that enemy aerial reconnaissance can be countered effectively everywhere. Preparations must be made for their rapid displacement to threatened areas.

The signal net must provide rapid communications from the forward lines to the commander, and the quick transmission of his orders to the artillery and the reserves.

If the river constitutes only a weak obstacle, the situation and the terrain may dictate a rapid and deliberate counterattack by strong forces held in reserve against the enemy's anticipated crossing site. In such situations, the enemy's artillery and infantry heavy weapons generally will be in their original positions on the far side of the river.

597. Should the river line be used as the base for attacking and defeating the enemy as he is astride the river, the friendly attack must be launched at the correct time, in the correct area, and in the decisive direction. In such a situation the friendly defense of the river should only be strong enough to force the enemy to execute prepared fires for his crossing and to distinguish

between his decisive and his feint crossings. Simultaneously, the friendly defense gains time for the execution of the counterattack. The mass of the units remain in readiness to the rear. They advance to attack as soon as the main enemy crossing point is identified. The attack, including the direction of advance, requires thorough preparations. Artillery must be able to concentrate its fire in this direction. The enemy must be hit with strong forces before he can establish himself in a bridgehead. Artillery observation on the far side must be blinded or eliminated. The commitment of armored vehicles against those enemy forces already across, and combat aviation against enemy forces in the process of crossing can produce significant effects. The highest state of combat readiness and rapid communications are the prerequisites for the effective commitment of units.

598. During a withdrawal or a retreat under enemy pressure, the leading march columns should be directed to those available bridges that are out of enemy artillery range. If bridges do not exist or if there are not enough of them, the preparation and construction of adequate crossing facilities must be initiated. When sufficient time is available, field expedient material should be used. All available air defense units provide cover from both banks for the construction of bridges, ferries, and the withdrawal across the river. Motorized columns and essential vehicles cross first. Elements of the artillery and some of the long-range, flat-trajectory guns should be deployed early on the far side of the river. Detailed instructions concerning the march sequence (especially for motorized elements), route marking for night marches, and the maintenance of strict traffic control facilitate the withdrawal across the river.

Those elements still in contact with the enemy must delay him so he cannot bring effective fire on the mass of friendly units as they cross the river. These elements will be brought across to the near side on a broad front on prepositioned ferries and boats constructed as much as possible from field expedient materials. The units on the near side cover their crossing.

Bridges constructed from prefabricated material should be removed as soon as they are no longer needed. Fixed bridges and those made of field expedient materials, as well as organic ferrying and bridging equipment that cannot be saved, should be destroyed to prevent their use by the enemy.

Combat in Mountains

599. The basics of combat and command of the combined arms in mountains correspond to those employed in lowlands. The peculiarities of

mountainous terrain, including limited routes and differing weather conditions, present many challenges to the employment of those principles. The differences depend on the type of the mountains.

600. Those differences increase in higher mountains. In general, only specially trained mountain troops have the necessary mobility, combat skills, and supply capabilities to operate in higher altitudes.

In mountains of medium height, the operating differences decrease. In small or low-level mountains the differences become unimportant. In mountains of medium size and height that are heavily snow- or glacier-covered and with extended bare, high, or rocky areas, the difficulties that must be overcome are nearly as great as for high mountains. Extended foliage often requires the same combat techniques as in forests, especially on mountains that are not rugged. Except for weather conditions, wide, cultivated, and gently sloping areas on medium altitude mountains present no problems that are significantly different from those encountered in lowlands. In normal conditions, even in winter, all types of units can be committed in medium altitude mountains, provided they have suitable clothing and equipment and sufficient time for preparation.

601. Differences in operating altitudes require careful calculations of time and space (see Annex 2).* These differences, combined with the fewer roads, slow down all troop movements as well as communications and supply operations. The differences can restrict the operations of the various arms and increase the level of strain on the troops.

Movement and deployment are restricted. The courses of the valleys and the locations of passes often will force the directions of movements. This can have a decisive effect on operations. The size of operating forces also will be limited. The quick deployment and commitment of reserves will be restricted. Adjacent units frequently will not be able to support each other directly. Conversely, combat in mountains can produce situations in which the attacker needs fewer forces than the defender. Small units will have many opportunities for independent, rapid, and bold action. There will be numerous opportunities to deceive the enemy.

The commander will be restricted in the choice of his command post. All commanders must remain well forward.

Firing in terrain of varying elevations is difficult and requires special procedures. Dead space can be used for concealed approaches, assembly areas, and for surprise attacks. Conversely, high ground provides observa-

---

*Annex 2 is not reproduced in this translation. It noted that march time calculations in mountainous terrain were highly dependent on road conditions and weather. In general, foot units and larger combined arms units required the addition of 60 minutes to normal march time increments for every 200 to 300 meters of climb, and every 400 to 500 meters of descent.

tion at greater distances and simplifies fire control. Heights also facilitate the command of terrain at great distances with relatively weak forces.

The weather in higher areas often changes quickly and sharply. Rapidly developing fog and low cloud cover restrict observation, direction finding, and leadership. These same conditions favor surprise attacks. Special preparations must be made for deep snow and protection against the cold.

The lack of towns and settlements and of water must be considered. Planning for water supply is vitally important were local supplies are not available. Winter and difficult terrain normally require special arrangements.

Terrain reconnaissance is indispensable, especially before combat operations. Such reconnaissance, however, should not result in the loss of valuable time. Reconnaissance by commanders is more difficult in mountains. Thus, every method of reconnaissance must be used.

Local inhabitants can provide valuable information about weather patterns and can serve as guides. Weather station reports must be obtained early.

602. The command's influence on movement and combat is restricted by a many factors. In general, it is not possible to control a battle on a wide front. Independent engagements will be the norm. On the other hand, the positioning of friendly forces on a wide front is the only way to force the dispersal of the enemy, and thereby achieve local superiority at key points. The commander, then, must decide upon his course of action early, and his planning must result in local superiority at the key points through the skilful deployment of his forces. An envelopment or a turning movement should be considered in the initial planning stages. These forms of maneuver are especially effective if the enemy withdrawal will be limited to certain routes. Subordinate commanders must be able to execute their tasks independently. Their missions, therefore, must not be too limited and they should have adequate forces and supplies.

Larger reserves should be formed only when they can be committed quickly. All commanders must pay constant attention to flank and rear security.

603. In mountains where the conditions are difficult, the following principles apply to the various arms operating in support of the infantry.

Reconnaissance must be conducted well in advance. Fire missions must be assigned early.

Changes are time-consuming once weapons have been deployed and are in position. All firing positions should be able to provide the infantry support from their initial positions up to the penetration of the enemy line.

As far as possible tactical units should be deployed as units; but quite often individual rifle platoons and individual guns must be committed separately.

The mass of the infantry heavy weapons is normally deployed well forward. Lack of space will not normally allow their deployment in depth.

The frequent opportunities for overhead and flanking fire must be exploited. Weapons that are unsuitable for overhead fire in level terrain often can deliver effective overhead fire in mountains. An effective technique is to fire over the heads of troops attacking uphill, until they break into the enemy positions.

Direct fire weapons normally should avoid the highest points as firing positions. Concealed firing positions on a slope serve the same purpose. They conserve time and forces and restrict enemy observation.

In areas where dead space cannot be eliminated by flanking fire, individual riflemen and light machine guns should be sent far enough forward to cover those areas.

Supply complications make ammunition economy necessary in all situations.

604. In mountains, and especially in bad weather, the infantry is the most reliable arm and the best force for reconnaissance and observation. Infantry patrols can do excellent work when operating sufficiently far forward and when equipped with adequate communications equipment.

Riflemen, and especially sharpshooters, play a decisive role. They can most easily overcome difficult terrain. In high or inaccessible places the self-reliant infantryman depends on himself alone.

In rough and difficult terrain light machine guns can assume missions that would be assigned to heavy machine guns in lowlands.

In addition to their most important role of supporting the infantry, heavy machine guns firing from well-concealed positions can interdict roads in valleys, crossings, and mountain trails. In such positions they are relatively secure against enemy action. Their employment from covered firing positions can be exploited by observation posts on high ground to the rear.

Mortars are best for covering dead space. They also can substitute for artillery.

605. Artillery generally is limited to roads and passable trails. Mountain artillery can move with the infantry through more difficult terrain. Therefore, individual guns and platoons attached to the infantry should be drawn from mountain artillery units.

High-angle fire is least restricted in mountainous terrain. Flat-trajectory fire for the most part can only be used at long ranges. Mountain artillery and high-angle-firing artillery, therefore, often must assume positions well forward of the flat trajectory artillery. Heavy flat-trajectory guns positioned far forward can be very effective in special situations.

Larger artillery units generally must be positioned in valleys or in clearings, because on high ground artillery normally can only be deployed as individual guns or in platoons.

In order to secure effective observation, the observation points should be carefully reconnoitered and assigned. Forward observers should be used extensively. Sound and flash ranging will be restricted greatly. Aerial observation and adjustment will be difficult. In this situation, ground observers become very important and must be deployed early.

Gas and smoke can produce good effects in valleys and ravines.

606. Engineers emplace or remove obstacles, repair or build roads, and construct bridges. They use organic equipment and field expedient materials. They must be committed sufficiently early.

607. Radio provides the fastest and most reliable means of communication in difficult mountain conditions. Visual signal communications can produce excellent results, but they are sensitive to visibility conditions. Visual communications sometimes require time-consuming reconnaissance. Wire circuit connections require much time and equipment.

Messenger dogs can be used in nearly all conditions. Messenger pigeons can be used only in limited situations because of the hazards from birds of prey.

608. Combat aviation will be restricted by the lack of good advance landing fields and even of air bases; by the necessity to fly at high altitudes to clear mountain crests; and by the weather conditions. Terrain features often will restrict low-level attacks against troops in valleys and passes. On the other hand, combat aviation may be very successful in such situations.

609. The commitment of air defense units often will be restricted by the lack of good roads, insufficient bridge capacity, and limited observation in the area to be covered. In open terrain, therefore, air defense machine guns should be deployed as soon as possible. Antiaircraft artillery should be deployed in terrain vulnerable to high-level attack. Points that must be covered include entries and exits from the mountains, intersections in key valleys, and passes.

610. Opportunities will be limited to commit cavalry, bicycle units, and motorcycle units. These units will be important during pursuit operations.

611. Armored vehicles can operate in wide valleys and on plateaus.

Antitank defense also is easier in these areas.

612. Tactical aerial reconnaissance is an important supplement to ground reconnaissance against an enemy that is moving slowly and is confined to a limited number of good roads.

The use of suitable high ground for observation will facilitate the combat reconnaissance of the various arms.

Ski patrols should be used in snowy areas.

613. The following points should be considered in organizing the march:

The troops must not be exhausted when they reach the enemy.

In areas with considerable differences in elevation, the distances between elements are prescribed best in units of time rather than in units of distance. Greater distances than normal may be required.

In general, advance and rear guards must be stronger and their security distances from the main body will be greater.

Since it is not possible for the various arms to displace forward from the rear, the march columns must be organized on the basis of probable commitment of the arms in time. Engineers should be well forward. When contact with the enemy is established, the mass of the artillery units should be able to occupy their firing positions from their locations in the column.

The dispersal of friendly march units along all usable routes will restrict and fragment enemy air activity, increase the possibility of breaking through the enemy resistance, and make better use of available quartering areas.

Flank guards on the high ground on either side should secure a march through a valley. The lead time they will require is a function of the terrain and the situation. In some situations, fresh forces should relieve the flank guards at valley crossings. If necessary, the main body will halt. If parallel roads are not available, flank security will be limited to the occupation of dominant ground astride the march routes. Units with flank guard missions normally reestablish contact with the main body only after a considerable loss of time.

The main body frequently must advance by bounds, even at the expense of time.

Rests halts depend upon the mission, the length and difficulty of the march, and the condition of the troops. On long marches, frequent short rests halts should be made, in addition to the standard long rest halts.

614. When the enemy is restricted primarily to roads, friendly security during rest halts should focus directly on those routes. The occupation of high ground should be avoided if it gives the enemy observation over friendly forces. The situation dictates the extent to which terrain must be secured, other than that in immediate proximity to the roads. A continuous line of security is seldom feasible.

615. Superior leadership always plays a dominant role in mountains.

Quite often the attacker needs only local superiority in numbers and firepower. Apparently strong hill positions, rocky positions, and single plateaus can be defeated by envelopments or flanking movements or by penetrations on a narrow front. Normally, the effect of such attacks is faster and more decisive in mountains than in lowlands.

The defender, therefore, must secure weak positions with forces that can counterattack immediately in planned and reconnoitered directions. Such attacks will be successful if they are well timed and hit an enemy who is exhausted after a climb. A counterattack from above on favorable terrain and at the right moment also gives the defender physical and moral superiority.

616. Meeting engagements generally are limited to the most leading elements, which must strike rapidly.

In uncertain situations and in difficult terrain, units should advance on a broad front and by bounds.

In difficult and broken terrain assembly areas for the attack should be closer to the enemy in order to reduce the effects of a long and tiring approach. Dead space must be exploited fully. During longer descents or ascents it is important to suppress the enemy fire until friendly forces engage.

The reinforced battalion is usually the largest element that can operate as an attack unit in difficult mountain areas. Decisive action often will be achieved by smaller units. Everything depends on resolute exploitation of these successes.

The width of the valleys; their passability; the terrain of the adjacent hills; cover and concealment; the weather; and the strength, composition, and equipment of the committed units all determine whether the attack will be made along valleys or on the hills. When making enemy contact, larger forces normally attack simultaneously along the valley and the immediately adjacent high ground. This especially is the case when the valley can be commanded by fire from the heights. The adjacent high ground will increase in importance as the pace of battle slows.

The objectives of the attack should be terrain features such as passes or hills that dominate the exits from the valleys or the mountains.

In a turning movement, an envelopment, or a penetration, the attacker should be less interested in rolling up the enemy front than in cutting off his line of retreat. As a rule, that line must follow fixed routes.

617. The more that terrain protects the retreating enemy from the pursuing forces and fire, the more the pursuit should be directed against the enemy's avenues of retreat.

When an encircling pursuit is greatly restricted in winter and at high altitudes, it may become necessary to limit the pursuit to the roads the enemy is using. Even in such situations, the encircling pursuit can be conducted by ski troops.

618. The conduct of a defense in the mountains generally requires stronger forces than in lowlands.

The defense of the main battle position is executed by groups. The most important positions should be laid out for all-round defense. Careful reconnaissance must precede the determination of the main line of resistance and the establishment of contact areas between adjacent groups. If the terrain permits little depth to the main battle position, individual machine-gun positions and combat groups should be deployed well forward. These elements also cover dead space with fire. If an advance is not possible during the day, infantry mortars and mountain and high-angle artillery must cover the dead space. The assignment of sectors should be done in such a way that flanking fire or fire from the rear will cover any gaps between sectors. If necessary, special units are assigned the mission of covering the gaps.

The more complicated the defense of the main battle position, the more important it is to stop the enemy early by using forward forces and outposts in combination with gas, barriers, and obstacles. Carefully managed observation assets must constantly watch and report on the approach of the enemy.

Forces for a counterattack against any penetration of the main battle position must be kept well forward.

619. Delaying action will be facilitated by observation points on high ground that have deep fields of view; by terrain that restricts the enemy to few routes of advance; by streams; and by opportunities for obstacles and barriers. Often, the resistance only needs to concentrate against the roads and valleys, with the intervening ground being kept under observation. Units not required in the main resistance are deployed in the next line of resistance or in the intermediate ground.

The unified command and control of forces withdrawing along different routes requires reliable communications. In the absence of such communications, the use of specifically assigned missions is the only way to achieve centralized control. In exceptional situations, the withdrawal of separated units can be regulated by a timetable.

620. Withdrawal in mountains is especially complicated if contact cannot be broken early enough. All side roads, even those that seem unpassable, must be secured to prevent their use by the enemy in an encircling pursuit, and to keep them open for use in the withdrawal, if necessary.

A withdrawal initiated in a timely manner can make good use of the terrain. Skillfully commanded small units can effectively deceive and delay a following enemy by striking him in the front and flanks.

Combat at and Around Defiles

621. Defiles restrict room for maneuver and combat. They facilitate the emplacement of obstacles and barriers.

Defiles favor enemy aerial reconnaissance and air attack. Defiles also multiply the effects of gas and smoke.

Defiles increase in importance with their depth and in relation to the difficulty of the surrounding terrain (mountains, lakes, swamps). Roads through dense forests that have few routes, bridges, and dams all can have the same effect as defiles.

Generally, defiles favor the defender and restrict the attacker, who can operate superior forces only incrementally and then not completely against the defender.

622. When advancing against a defile not yet occupied by the enemy, the advantage is with the force that arrives first. Gaining control of a defile before the enemy can greatly influence the outcome of an action. Units do not have complete freedom of action until they pass the defile.

623. When the enemy holds the exit to a defile, it is better to conduct an envelopment or a turning movement.

In the situation of a meeting engagement in a defile, the attacker will achieve success more quickly through an envelopment.

If it becomes necessary to fight to secure the exit from a defile, the time, direction, and extent of the attack should be screened until the last moment. In mountains the deployment of forces requires considerable time. Quite often it will not be possible to displace the decisively important forces.

624. When an attacker operates against multiple defiles simultaneously, he can commit stronger forces against the enemy. He also can use the advance in one defile to facilitate the movement of forces in adjacent defiles.

During an advance from multiple defiles in the face of strong resistance, all the exits should be secured before proceeding in order to avoid piecemeal defeat of the separate columns.

625. If the enemy reaches a defile first, all opportunities must be exploited to attack him as he emerges.

626. During a pursuit the objective should be to advance quickly to the far side of a defile, using all adjacent routes for an encircling movement to block the exits. In some situations it may be possible only to commit attack aviation and long-range artillery. These forces should be used to create delays.

627. The defense of a defile can be mounted from the front, from within, or from behind the defile.

If the defile must be held open for follow-on forces, the defense is conducted in front of the defile. If friendly strength permits, the main line of resistance should be far enough advanced so that the exits of the defile are protected against enemy artillery fire. If necessary, the terrain required for the main battle area must be taken by attack. The defile itself must be secured.

The defense of a defile requires that the adjacent terrain, to the greatest extent possible, precludes an envelopment or a turning movement by the attacker. In mountains, the heights on either side of a valley should be integrated into the defensive position, especially if a defense of long duration is anticipated.

The main battle area behind the defile must force the enemy to make his exit at the point of the most concentrated fire. If the enemy attack is repelled, and if the situation permits a shift to the offense, every effort must be made to penetrate the defile either before the enemy, or at least simultaneously.

628. A delaying action makes best use of a defile:

In short defiles, behind the defile;

In long defiles, within the defile.

629. During a withdrawal through a defile, the entrance must be secured against the pursuing enemy. Movement must be tightly regulated and controlled. Countermovement must be prevented. If necessary, cover will be established behind the defile. The emplacement of obstacles and defensive measures against envelopment during the passage of the defile is important.

Frontier Guard

630. Frontier guard secures the borders against enemy ground forces. Normally it is conducted with minimal forces. The frontier guard force can compensate for its numerical inferiority by superior knowledge of the local area; by exploiting the resources of the area; through familiarity with the mission; by selecting and reinforcing favorable terrain; by emplacing barriers, obstacles, dummy positions, and demolition charges; by rapid and secure shifting of forces; by adequate and secure communications—especially by making full use of the existing telephone system; and by making wide use of deception measures.

631. The general local tasks of frontier defense are:

Screening the border.

Obtaining a reliable picture of the enemy in the border area.

The defense of border crossings.

632. The mission and terrain requirements will determine the allocation of frontier guard units to a border area and their assignment to frontier guard sectors and subsectors. The great width of frontier guard sectors usually requires that the forces be concentrated where attacks by the enemy are most probable.

633. The immediate security of the border is established through reconnaissance patrols and stationary reconnaissance parties.

The main forces of the frontier guard are located at a frontier guard position. Depending on the distance of these forces from the border and upon the terrain, advanced frontier guard positions may be established to support the forward security elements and to provide security for the main force. Outposts should be established in front of the main frontier guard position.

The senior commander determines the general location of the frontier guard position. If his forces are weak, he will shorten the front sectors and exploit the terrain to support his intent. Frontier guard positions, therefore, usually will not conform closely to the line of the border. Positions also should be far enough back from the border to be out of artillery range. Frontier guard sector commanders are responsible for the detailed locations of the frontier guard positions, for their preparation and construction, and for establishing the advanced frontier guard positions. The senior commander is responsible for communications between adjacent sectors.

Reserves should be established in such a way that the proper occupation of the position is not jeopardized, either locally or overall.

Reserves of larger frontier guard forces should be held at a state of readiness in positions from which they can be shifted rapidly over long distances. This movement can be accomplished by trains held on standby, trucks or other vehicles, or bicycles.

Reserves of smaller frontier guard forces can be positioned in key rear areas as security against surprise attacks.

Frontier guard missions of longer duration require regular relief of the units and occasional shifts in positions.

634. Surveillance and blocking of the border prevents the crossing of unauthorized traffic. In the forward defense area it secures the border against scorched-earth tactics and looting; facilitates the evacuation of the area; screens military activities; and prevents ground reconnaissance and intelligence collection required for an enemy attack. As the situation requires, the sector commander also is responsible for blocking roads and railroads and for cutting telephone and telegraph lines.

Customs, postal, police, and forestry officials; territorial defense units; and other civilian agencies are required to cooperate in the execution of frontier security tasks. These include defense against enemy intelligence activity; security of overhead or underground telephone lines, radio facilities, and carrier pigeons; control and masking of friendly signal traffic; and security of installations and key public works against sabotage or other enemy agent activity.

635. Reconnaissance by the frontier guard includes carefully planned

and continuous observation of the area on the far side of the border. Observation towers can be erected for this purpose.

If the frontier guard is authorized to cross the border, it should collect information on the enemy by sending out reconnaissance patrols and surprise raids. Guides familiar with the area should be used. In general, the size of the frontier force does not permit large-scale offensive operations.

Any method of collecting information should be used. Once established, contact with the enemy must be maintained.

636. Any weak enemy force crossing the border should be pushed back immediately.

Defense against a strong enemy force begins at the border.

In the case of a delaying action, the frontier guard position (Paragraph 633) becomes the initial main line of resistance. Should the intent be to give up this line, the withdrawal to the next line will be made, either under pressure or not under pressure, as the situation dictates. Every effort must be made to provide flank security for the lines of resistance.

637. In case of a breakthrough, or should the frontier guard falls back before superior forces, adjacent frontier guard sections that are not under attack or that are advantageously engaged must provide support. If the situation to their front permits, they attack the advancing enemy by fire, feint attacks, operations against his rear communications, and by night raids into his flanks. Similarly, the operations of strong reserves against the enemy's flank, as a blocking measure or for attacks with limited objectives, can be more successful than committing them on the withdrawing front.

If the frontier defense is broken in any area, the units should be reassembled and committed at another location.

638. The operational area of the frontier guard should be established well in advance. The terrain to the rear of the frontier guard position must be reconnoitered and prepared for potential combat operations.

639. Frontier guard commanders normally operate independently when their units are deployed in groups on broad fronts and at great depths. Such commanders must be selected carefully and briefed thoroughly on the situation and their mission. The rapid transmission of orders and intelligence is essential and command posts must be selected accordingly. Commanders must remain mobile and be able to move quickly from area to area.

640. Frontier guard units can expect only limited resupply of ammunition, weapons, and equipment. All commanders and soldiers are responsible for tightly managing the available assets.

641. The frontier guard must maintain contact with aerial reconnaissance and ground patrols in the border area.

Partisan Warfare

642. Partisan warfare (*kleiner Krieg*) is a method of supporting the main force through small secondary attacks that complicate the situation for the enemy. In general, partisan warfare is only effective when used in conjunction with other operations. A hostile and belligerent population can make partisan warfare impossible. Wherever the opportunity for partisan warfare exists, its use depends on whether the forces and means employed will produce a worthwhile effect.

643. Partisan warfare is conducted against the enemy's front, his flanks, and especially his rear.

644. The principal missions of partisan warfare are to disrupt, damage, and deceive the enemy; to divert enemy forces; to restrict his reconnaissance activities and his transmission of orders and intelligence; and to disrupt his rear area operations—especially his logistics.

645. Small raiding parties are most effective for mission execution. Their strength, equipment, and mobility are based on the intent and the mission. The ability of the leader and the experience and reliability of the force are more important than superior numbers, which actually may work against mobility and surprise.

Tight security and need-to-know access are requirements for mission success.

646. Offensive actions by raiding parties should be executed as surprise attacks. Deception and cunning should be applied to the maximum extent. Encirclement of the enemy is the preferred form of maneuver.

Terrain should be selected that restricts enemy observation and mobility, but that facilitates friendly surprise attacks and rapid withdrawal.

Careful preparation and reconnaissance, good maps, and guides who are familiar with the area facilitate mission execution. A rallying point must be designated in advance. After the execution of the mission, all troops assemble there immediately.

Night operations are the preferred option. All movement should be made by night if possible. During the day the force must remain under cover and away from towns and roads.

Raiding parties operating in the enemy rear area require especially bold leaders and soldiers. They must be supplied and equipped for extended operations.

If multiple raiding parties operate simultaneously, their operations must be coordinated in time and space. Elements must operate in their assigned areas.

Changing operating methods, deception, and the spreading of false information all facilitate surprise. The enemy must be kept off balance by a continual threat and by the neutralization of his countermeasures. In all situations movements must be kept secret from enemy forces and the enemy population.

647. Roadblocks and obstacles are most effective against enemy traffic on routes that must be used and where detours are not available.

The destruction of bridges and other such installations in the enemy rear will complicate his logistics operations.

The senior commander normally establishes the type and scale of destruction. The smaller the raiding party, the more it must concentrate its efforts and limit its destruction to the most important installations. Mission commanders must know the purpose and the technical functions of the objectives to be destroyed.

648. The senior commander must be kept informed of the progress of operations so he can influence the actions of the raiding parties and provide them with orders. Reliable communications, therefore, are essential.

649. Area defense against partisan warfare is the mission of all units. In the rear of the operational area, specially designated forces may be required. Such units should be kept on alert and located at key positions. Their rapid commitment must be well planned. Armored vehicles and armored trains often can be used for such moves. The necessity for the immediate transmission of information from the raiding parties may require the establishment of special communications networks.

If enemy raiding parties are operating in the friendly rear area, they should be surrounded and destroyed. Detailed mopping-up in the rear area may be necessary, but stronger forces usually are required for this.

XII

QUARTERING

650. Units assigned to rest periods will be provided with one or a combination of all three categories of quarters: town quarters (*Ortsunterkunft*) in buildings in towns or cities; bivouac in the open; or town bivouac (*Ortsbiwak*) partly in the open and partly in towns.

651. Town quarters provide shelter against the weather and cold, and afford the opportunity to care for men and horses and to repair weapons, equipment, and clothing. Even a small and sparse billet gives the troops more protection than a bivouac in the open. Any sort of shelter is preferable for the horses.

652. Town bivouac protects those troops quartered in towns, provides greater overall comfort than a bivouac in the open, and has a higher posture of combat readiness.

Those units not quartered in the town bivouac nearby.

For those elements under shelter, the procedures for town quarters apply. For those not in quarters, bivouac procedures apply.

653. All units will bivouac if the use of town quarters or town bivouac is precluded by the proximity of the enemy, the mass of units, a lack of building space, or other tactical considerations that restrict units to a certain area. The threats of air attack, long-range fires, gas, or other security requirements also may be reasons to avoid towns and cities.

654. Units in bivouac must be organized and prepared for movement or action on short notice.

The bivouac is not fixed in a specific location. It must be readily reachable and be positioned based on the tactical situation. It must be out of range of enemy ground reconnaissance and be secure against aerial reconnaissance and attack, long-range fires, and chemical attack.

655. Organizing bivouacs by units or march elements facilitates the selection of sites and increases readiness for movement and action, especially in larger commands.

The organization of the bivouac will generally be based on the tactical situation. The front will face in the direction of the enemy; but considerations for concealment and subsequent movement may dictate variations.

The key factors in determining the groupings for a bivouac include, the terrain, accessible and adequate water and wood, and the special requirements of the different arms. Good entrance and exit routes are especially important for motorized units. If necessary, such routes must be constructed, but concealed from enemy aerial observation.

656. The bivouac area should be dry, be on firm ground, and if possible should provide good shelter against the wind and weather. Light woods normally meet these requirements. Meadows are generally unsuitable, even if they look completely dry. Lakes, swamps, and ponds should be avoided because of fog and other related health hazards.

During cold weather troops must have the means to keep warm. Techniques include digging in the tents, warming with hot stones, using double shelter halves filled with straw and leaves, fires, and similar measures. Protection from the wind can be secured in and behind woods, behind steep slopes, and in defiles.

657. If ground contact with the enemy is unlikely, the first priority should be comfortable quartering for the troops. The factors that determine the extent of the quartering area include: the number and size of the towns in the area; their location in relation to the route of march; the depth of the marching units; the distance covered and the next planned march; and the time set for the resumption of march. Generally, it is easiest and most comfortable for the troops when the assigned quartering area equals the march depth.

The distribution of units in towns will be determined by the existing troop distribution or the distribution intended for subsequent marches. The towns along the route of march should be occupied to their capacity. When various arms are quartered together, all available rooms and stables must be used fully.

If there is a shortage of town areas, bivouacs must be established along the route of march.

The baggage trains can be sent forward to join their units.

658. If ground contact with the enemy is imminent, tactical requirements take priority. The bivouac area generally will be smaller. Strong infantry units will be assigned bivouac areas to the front, on unprotected flanks, and in some situations in the rear. They will be supported by antitank elements. Units that cannot defend themselves against a surprise attack should be bivouacked with the infantry and in a secured area.

In towns it often is necessary to ensure an increased level of readiness for individual elements or for the entire bivouac. This can be accomplished by using close billets and by requiring specific pieces of equipment to be maintained at the ready. Every close billet must have a light and a guard. If necessary, and as far as the required traffic flow permits, the exits of a town will be blocked and the billeting area will be readied for defense.

In bivouac it may be necessary to establish defensive measures against long-range fires and air attack. Such measures may include camouflaged trenches.

Trains should be bivouacked at the greatest possible distance from the enemy—when possible behind stream lines.

The advance of the baggage train depends on the situation and the intent of the senior commander.

659. If units are close to the main enemy force, troops should bivouac based on the tactical situation.

Engaged units will rest in place during pauses in the battle.

660. Cavalry and motorized units have special quartering requirements. See Paragraphs 212, 224, and 225.

661. When selecting headquarters for senior and subordinate commanders, the emphasis must be on the frictionless transmission of messages and orders in the shortest time. Both signal communications requirements and the condition of the roads should be considered.

The responsibilities of senior and subordinate headquarters down to the regimental level require that their bivouac sites should be placed in towns or houses whenever possible.

662. Air defense units recommend the level of air defense cover provided for bivouac sites. During an extended bivouac, air defense cover normally is limited to densely occupied areas or to supply distribution points.

Air defense weapons will be deployed independently by air defense units, or on order of the bivouac commanders. The senior commander is responsible for establishing coordination between the air defense units and the organic air defense weapons of the other units. Air Defense personnel assigned to other units will distribute themselves among the observation and warning elements of the air defense units, or may be positioned independently. There should be no restrictions on opening fire on enemy aircraft.

The air defense effort is augmented by passive measures when in bivouac. These include: avoiding small and narrow villages and small but conspicuous woods, using ground cover or suitable underground quarters for the bivouac, keeping the bivouac away from conspicuous landmarks, and the establishment of dummy positions. Vehicles must be camouflaged and hidden and parked irregularly. In towns it is necessary to determine the location of cellars and other possible areas that might afford cover during air attacks. Town bivouacs must be blacked out at night.

663. All communications assets in the bivouac area should be used to conserve the resources of the signal units. If this is not possible and if the bivouac area is sufficiently far from the enemy, wire communications can be established by tapping into the divisional trunk line. If the enemy is

close, it will be necessary to connect the bivouac groups to the commander with a special wire circuit.

664. The bivouac area should be identified and announced early, if possible in the order for the march or during the march. When the bivouac area is identified late, units will rest along the route of march and eat while the bivouac area is reconnoitered and prepared. Unnecessary halts and route reversals should be avoided.

665. As far as the situation permits, bivouac areas should be prepared in advance.

666. If possible, billeting in towns will be coordinated with the civil authorities and the quartering parties will notify the units of the arrangements. Precautions should be established against enemy intelligence activities. Quartering dockets will facilitate orderly billeting and should always be used if time is available. Even if the distribution of the units is established during the march, quartering parties will ensure a quicker transition from the march to quarters.

The civil authorities and the local population must be questioned about disease or epidemics. Houses and stables with contagious diseases must be marked and will not be used. The horses of the different arms can be mixed in order to maximize the use of the stables.

667. When there is insufficient time for a full reconnaissance and questioning of local officials, a hasty quartering method is to assign sectors of the towns to units, and streets and houses to their subordinate elements. Staffs should be billeted together. When possible, officers should be sent forward to take over the areas of assignment. Preferably, the senior officer will be from the staff of the town or area commander. Officers from the units and the individual staffs will be attached to him.

668. The various sectors of the town quarters must have easily identifiable boundaries. In the assignment of those sectors, consideration must be given to their defense and the suitable quartering of the troops.

669. Everyone in the town quarters must know the location of his immediate superior. Every leader must know the location of his immediate subordinate.

670. The bivouac commander, accompanied by officers of the various units, should precede the march to reconnoiter and establish the sectors.

Every arriving unit establishes its bivouac immediately. Any later displacement of units means less rest for the troops, and should be done only for the most compelling reasons.

671. Billeting groups often are assigned multiple and various types of quartering areas. Such groups are formed if the quartering and the transmission of orders during rest halts are accelerated. As a rule, the billeting groups correspond to the existing or planned march or combat groups. The

© 2007 Lauren Staanitti Photo
Item1 0735955 R 0001 F 0407

quartering of a billeting group is left to the group commander. He reports his dispositions and instructions to the higher commander.

672. Unless otherwise specified by the senior commander, the senior officer within each town quarters also is the town commander. Regimental commanders and higher are authorized to delegate this duty to another officer, including staff officers.

If not already accomplished, the town commander assigns the area to be occupied by each unit. He is responsible for external security measures, the readiness of the command, and interior organization. He especially is responsible for determining the size and missions of the security and the interior guards. He complements the instructions issued by the various units regarding readiness and alerts, and he issues instructions for control of the traffic, the civil population, and for operational security. He also controls the street patrols, the confiscation of weapons, the security of supplies, and fire fighting. He issues instructions regarding wells and water supplies and the sources to be used by the various units. He issues instructions concerning medical and veterinary service provisions for sick and wounded personnel and animals and, when necessary, chemical decontamination measures. He ensures that units arriving later are properly quartered.

When a portion of the force must remain in bivouac and the remainder is in town quarters, the town commander issues the necessary orders for the use of the town's facilities by the troops in bivouac. The water supply must be controlled so that the town will not be endangered by fire. All units are responsible for complying with the orders of the town commander.

673. The unprepared occupation of larger towns and villages with many units—including towns taken in combat—requires that the town commander immediately receives strong, and if possible, fresh troops to establish the necessary security and guard details. The initial measures include an adequate guard and the deployment of numerous patrols to search houses, to detect demolition charges, to confiscate weapons, and to locate and guard abandoned enemy equipment.

674. In the absence of other orders, the bivouac commander is the senior officer present. He determines the external security measures against enemy air and ground threats, as well as the construction of necessary obstacles and barriers. He designates the areas to be occupied by the various units and controls the use of resources, including wells and springs. He especially is responsible for the immediate and equitable distribution of all available material (straw, wood, etc.) so that the troops can take shelter quickly and make best use of the rest period. Based on the situation, he authorizes or prohibits fires.

675. In every town or bivouac, the town or bivouac commander designates an officer of the day. In the larger towns this officer may be a staff

officer. He is responsible to the commander for the execution of all external security measures and for the interior guards.

The officer of the day is the senior officer of the guard detail. He is responsible for their postings, instructions, and inspection. The guards and outposts are under his command at all times. In bivouac, an officer of the guard handles the interior guard.

Inspecting officers are used as required.

676. The town or bivouac commander designates the medical and the veterinary officers for town or bivouac duty. They advise the commander on all medical and veterinary matters and must be available at all times.

Every element (infantry or artillery battalion, cavalry regiment, etc.) designates a duty officer and every smaller seperate unit designates a duty NCO. As soon as their units reach the quartering area, those representatives report to the town or bivouac officer of the day to receive appropriate orders. Within their jurisdictions, they are responsible for quiet and order and for the execution of all orders issued by the town or bivouac commander and their respective unit commanders.

When a single unit occupies a town or a bivouac position, the guard and bivouac duties are combined.

677. In many situations, direct security requires exterior guards positioned beyond the perimeter of the town or the bivouac area. They ensure security in accordance with the principles outlined in Paragraph 212. Their mission, strength, and composition depend on whether or not other security forces have been posted farther out. If necessary, they assume responsibility for air attack warning (Paragraph 662). When required, they control the outgoing traffic and prevent the entry of civilians into the bivouac areas. Communications with adjacent positions must be maintained.

678. Interior guards are posted in every rest area. They also can be tasked to provide warning against air and ground threats.

In town quarters, every unit is required to provide troops for interior guard duty. Policing considerations, close quartering, a large number of positions to be secured, and an uncertain attitude on the part of the local population may require large and numerous posts.

In bivouac every unit posts its interior guard based on its own requirements and orders. The strength of the interior guard depends on the number of posts, which should be kept to a minimum.

The interior guard is conducted in the same manner as in garrison, but in bivouac the guards and posts do not salute.

In small units and in a bivouac, exterior guards can assume the duties of the interior guard. Their execution of the exterior guard function remains the same.

679. Each guard detachment must have an attached bugler.

680. The quarters of the town commander, the officer of the day, and

the command post must be clearly marked and recognizable by day and night. The routes to those positions must be marked. Guards and posts must know those locations so messengers can be directed quickly.

The command post of the town commander should have posted a sketch showing the communications net and a list of the staffs and units that are billeted in the town. The sketch should also show where the connections to the various staffs and units are established.

The positions of special installations, such as fuel points, hospitals, and air raid shelters, should be indicated by signs and markers indicating the routes to them.

The quarters of troop units are identified in the normal manner, through the use of flags.

681. The bivouac commander establishes his own position in a location easily identifiable to all guards.

682. Staff offices must be marked and clearly identifiable by day and night. When officers and noncommissioned officers are temporarily at a headquarters to receive orders, their horses or other means of transport should be maintained close by.

683. When the presence of staffs or units in a certain area must be kept secret, it may be necessary to limit or completely restrict the normal methods of identification.

684. When the attitude of the local population is uncertain, it may be necessary to initiate special security measures. These may include threats of punishment, the seizure of hostages, and the requirement that all houses remain unlocked and accessible.

The inconsiderate treatment of a passive population is wrong. In all situations, restraint and reserve toward the population is the best policy.

Counterintelligence measures are covered in Paragraphs 190 and 193.

685. In town quarters, horse-drawn vehicles that cannot be held near the animals should be placed on the side away from the enemy, and in such a way that the animals can quickly be brought up, harnessed, and driven away. Motor vehicles require good roads in and out, an accessible supply of water, and good parking ground. Gasoline tank trucks must be positioned at least 50 meters away from buildings because of fire hazards. Smoking in their vicinity is forbidden.

During the night, vehicles parked along streets should be marked by lanterns.

686. Necessary medical and veterinary measures must be carried out in town quarters. Drinking water sources must be marked. Water from doubtful sources must be tested and boiled when necessary. It might be necessary to construct latrines in town quarters.

In bivouac, garbage and refuse from butchering must be buried deeply enough to prevent it from being dug up by animals. Latrines also must be dug deeply for similar reasons.

Increased sanitary and medical measures are necessary in warm weather.

687. For long stays in one quarter, medical and veterinary measures must be enhanced. The special establishment can be extended and made similar to those in permanent garrison. Arrangements for the comfort and convenience of the troops are essential.

688. Order, cleanliness, and discipline must be maintained in the quartering area.

In town quarters, troops extend the same military courtesies as in garrison. It might be necessary to close stores early, to forbid the sale or use of alcohol, and to require troops to retire earlier.

Stringent measures must be taken against the misuse of weapons; wanton damage to or destruction of supplies and stores and property belonging to enemy personnel; and other unauthorized actions by individuals.

689. Alert assembly positions must be designated for the individual units in a town quarters. These should be selected in a way that units can assemble quickly and can reach their positions without mutual interference. Traffic to these points must not be blocked. The alert positions for horse-drawn and motorized units can be at the vehicle locations.

In bivouac, the alert assembly position of an individual unit generally is its bivouac area.

690. The alert will be signaled by the bugle call "Alarm." The order to do so is given by the senior officer or the town or bivouac commander. When danger threatens, every guard recognizing the threat must relay the alarm. Every officer and platoon commander is authorized on his own initiative to sound the alarm.

691. Silent alarms should be developed and practiced so that every unit, town quarters, and bivouac can be brought quickly to a state of alert and be rapidly assembled without unnecessary noise and bugle calls.

692. Upon the alert signal, troops assemble fully equipped at their alert assembly positions, or man their previously designated points. All vehicles must be prepared to march. When only a single unit is concerned, the unit commander issues the detailed orders for actions when the alarm is sounded. Otherwise the town or bivouac commander issues such orders.

Mounted and motorized units, trains, and vehicles require special procedures, especially during night alerts.

When mounted units are billeted in a town, the decision must be made either to evacuate after delaying action, or to defend the town with all available forces.

Each alerted unit must maintain silence and discipline.

The town or bivouac commander establishes the conduct of the exterior guard. The unit commander establishes that of the interior guard.

693. The time required for the execution of an alert will be shortened by a higher state of readiness. This, of course, limits the ability of the troops to rest.

When the situation is tense and the local population is hostile, it may be best to quarter the troops as complete units. In such situations, the officers remain with their platoons and the men remain fully dressed with weapons and equipment at hand. Horses must be bridled, saddled or harnessed, and picketed and positioned outside the stables, or even out of the town.

694. Every man must know what to do in a surprise attack. He must keep his weapon and equipment ready and be able to move out in the shortest time.

If the enemy penetrates a town in a surprise attack, everyone defends in position.

695. The town or bivouac commander initiates the gas alarm. In sudden danger every officer and platoon leader is authorized to give the gas alarm.

Every man immediately puts on his gas mask, or moves as quickly as possible to a gasproof shelter. The town or bivouac commander will issue specific instructions concerning gas defense measures.

696. During the day, the patrol and warning system will signal the approach of enemy aircraft. Upon warning, all personnel seek concealment and all movement stops.

Patrols and the warning service also give the air attack alarm. Upon the alarm, all personnel immediately take cover.

Alarms normally are not sounded when aircraft are sighted during the night. The town or bivouac commander may deviate from this standard procedure, but he should issue such instructions immediately.

697. The alert and air attack alarms must be relayed immediately by all buglers.

The gas alarm is only given through acoustic means. It is never given by voice.

The stand-down signal, given on order of the town or bivouac commander, releases the command from the conditions imposed by the gas or air attack alerts.

698. The town or bivouac commander issues the necessary orders covering the state of readiness; reactions to a surprise attack; air attack warning; and gas and air attack alerts.

XIII

CAVALRY*

---

699. Army-level cavalry units consisting of mounted, horse-drawn, and motorized elements, can move more rapidly than infantry. Cavalry units have great cross-country mobility.

Their higher speed allows them to cover greater distances in a shorter period of time.† The mobility of cavalry units is especially significant on the battlefield.

Cavalry can be committed to action rapidly from distant positions. In a short period of time it can deploy its forces on a broad front or concentrate them at decisive points. After breaking contact it can quickly distance itself from the enemy.

Speed, maneuverability, and high rates of firepower makes the cavalry effective for various missions. These factors sometimes make it superior to a stronger but slower enemy.

Its commitment is partially limited by dependence on the capacity of the horses and by the problems of training replacements. After strenuous operations it must have the opportunity to recuperate its strength and its march capacity.

Cavalry's high vulnerability to air attack during marches, movement, and assembly requires the attachment of strong air defense forces, particularly antiaircraft artillery and air defense machine guns.

700. Cavalry requires a large zone of action to achieve full operational capability. No matter how deep its operations may be, it must not lose contact with the main force.

---

*This chapter almost exclusively covers mounted (horse) cavalry, as opposed to modern mechanized cavalry. The significance of mounted cavalry already was in steep decline when *Truppenführung* was published, and a German cavalry division of that time had many motorized elements (see Appendix B). The Germans did commit a cavalry brigade in the Polish Campaign, and a cavalry division in the French campaign. They also used mounted cavalry units of various sizes in Russia.

†[Original Footnote] "See Annex 2 for march speeds and march performances of the different arms." The information in Annex 2 is summarized in the footnote on p. 83.

Cavalry is committed primarily on an open flank or in a broad gap between two elements. When two main forces are far apart, the deployment of cavalry to the front becomes very important. As the area for its operations becomes too small, cavalry should be withdrawn. If this is not possible, its incorporation into the front must be planned and well prepared.

When there is no advantageous mission for the cavalry, it should be held in reserve in a suitable position.

701. Decisive operations require the formation of a cavalry corps with strong corps troops. Based on the mission, cavalry must be reinforced by other units.

702. Cavalry committed to a deep mission can seldom be directed from the rear. The mission, therefore, must assign a deep objective and give the commander freedom of action. The higher headquarters must keep the cavalry commander continuously informed of the developing situation and the intent of the higher commander.

Changing the direction of an attack or withdrawing the cavalry from a movement already begun results in a loss of momentum and time. Current reconnaissance elements must be pulled back and newly committed reconnaissance elements must have time to cover the distance to the new front.

703. On occasion the cavalry must operate away from Army rear services and execute its mission without regard to its own supply communications. The detachment of forces to secure its rear communications will weaken its fighting power. If cavalry is committed to deep missions, it must be equipped with ammunition, weapons, equipment, and gasoline sufficient to make the force independent. The horses should be newly shod and the force will live off the land.

704. The multiplicity of missions, their independent and rapid execution, and frequent and rapid changes in the situation require that the senior cavalry commander exhibits a high degree of intellectual flexibility, coolness, daring, physical energy, operational understanding, and the ability to make quick decisions and issue short but effective orders. Early on he must establish personal observation of the ground from a position well forward.

705. The cavalry corps commander initiates the orders for aerial reconnaissance. He assigns the ground reconnaissance objectives of the cavalry divisions, the boundaries between them, and if necessary, the routes of march. He assigns the missions to the divisions, and if necessary, he directs their movements. He controls the deployment of the air defense units. The corps troops come under his command. Through short, concise orders he coordinates his divisions in combat.

The cavalry division commanders issue the orders for ground reconnaissance. The principles that apply to the operations of an infantry division generally apply to a cavalry division.

Missions

706. Reconnaissance missions for cavalry are covered in Chapter II. Screening missions are covered in Chapter IV.

707. Combat is the cavalry's principal mission. Attack against the flank and rear of the enemy is the most effective form of maneuver.

Such an attack can be made before the main force of the enemy is engaged, or when the battle is already in progress. In the first case, such an attack can set the conditions for the attack by the friendly main force.

The commitment of the cavalry to a mission that is too deep takes it too far from the focal point of the battle and can cause its late commitment to the main action. Simultaneous operations against the enemy line of communications can be profitable, but should not cause the dispersal of friendly forces.

An attack against an enemy in position is not a good mission for cavalry. When it is necessary to fix an enemy force in position, however, such an attack may be necessary.

When cavalry is committed to a mission of flank security, it should execute that mission by attacking aggressively at every opportunity.

708. In the pursuit, cavalry exploits combat success and strikes at the enemy operationally. If the cavalry is not committed or can be withdrawn from combat, it must be prepared to execute the pursuit at the proper time and place, and under unified command. Motorized forces should be attached and it should be supplied with sufficient ammunition and chemical decontamination equipment, as required. Special instructions should be issued to coordinate its communications with other units committed to the pursuit, particularly with reconnaissance aircraft and other air forces units.

The most successful direction of a pursuit is against the enemy's flank and rear. Every effort must be made to encircle the enemy force.

After a successful breakthrough, the speed and mobility of the cavalry best suit it for the pursuit. The senior cavalry commander personally determines the situation at the breakthrough point. Those elements that must move along roads are assigned their routes of advance. The lines of communication of the cavalry force also must be secured. The direction of the pursuit is prescribed, but the start time may be left to the division commanders.

A disorganized enemy should be bypassed. Newly forming resistance must be broken by rapid surprise attack.

If the enemy withdraws with his combat power still intact, he must be hit from the flanks with surprise fire and attacked at every available opportunity. Key areas in the enemy's rear should be blocked.

709. Cavalry is especially capable of conducting delaying actions. Frequently, cavalry will be committed to screen and secure assembly areas

and movements; to defend temporarily broad streams; to delay superior forces; to hold the enemy at a distance from the battlefield; to fix the enemy at another location; to deceive him; to facilitate the breaking of contact; to cover a retreat; and especially to counterattack an encircling pursuit.

710. Cavalry can divert the enemy's attention by appearing at unexpected points. It can block his occupation key terrain. It can operate against his lines of communications. Such missions should be ordered only when they are more important than the presence of the cavalry at the decisive point, or if the outcome of the battle will not be jeopardized by the absence of the cavalry.

Characteristics of Cavalry Movement and Combat

711. The speed and mobility of cavalry must be used at every opportunity to surprise the enemy.

Surprise can be achieved by faster or longer marches.

712. In the assignment of routes and the distribution of units, consideration must be given to the march speeds and march capabilities of the various arms.

Mounted units can surge their speeds over short distances. In the case of a long march, they must move more slowly in order to maintain their march capacity. Long and rapid marches are the exception and should be made only in critical situations. The losses produced by such forced marches must be weighed against the results.

713. The cavalry division normally moves in several march columns composed of cavalry regiments or brigades with attached arms. Motorized forces follow as motorized echelons or march as a motorized column on another route.

The interval between the cavalry march columns should not be so large as to prevent the coordinated and unified commitment of the division in the case of a meeting engagement. The echelonment of the various columns depends on the situation.

Bicycle units normally are attached to cavalry march columns. If they are not deployed forward or are not in the advance guard, they follow the march columns or move along separate routes.

714. The situation, the terrain, and the visibility determine the interval between the advance guard and the main body. Because of the greater marching speed of cavalry, this distance generally is greater than for foot troops with an advance guard of equivalent strength.

The advance guard should not be overly organized into detailed elements. A main body and a point are generally sufficient for an advance guard of one or two troops.

If contact with the enemy is imminent, the advance guard moves by bounds. The closer the enemy is assumed to be, and the less the opportunity for observation, the shorter the bounds, and the more carefully the area must be reconnoitered. In some situations the advance guard should move forward deployed.

The advance guard generally deploys patrols for security at up to ten kilometers to the front and flanks.

The main body of the cavalry column provides its own immediate security by deploying a main body point, patrols to either flank, and a rear point.

The commander of the column determines the march sequence of the main body. He normally marches close behind the advance guard.

715. When the advance guard engages the enemy, the situation must be quickly clarified by all available means, so the commander of the entire column has a basis to decide upon the commitment of the whole force.

716. When the situation permits, the attack must be pushed through rapidly. The assignment of attack missions to the commanders of the mounted march columns will accelerate the initiation and execution of the attack. Whenever possible, the attack will be executed without assembly for preparation. Heavy weapons should be deployed toward the front. They must receive their orders first so that they can open fire early. Under cover of the heavy weapons and the security provided by the combat reconnaissance and close-in security elements, the mounted units ride as far forward as enemy fire permits. When a unit cannot continue mounted, it dismounts, mounting again when the situation permits. The close coordination of fire and forward movement will accelerate the advance.

An attack initiated on a wide front increases the opportunity to execute a surprise attack with the mass of the force at a decisive point. Where the situation permits, the attack should be directed against the flank or the rear of the enemy. Organization in depth may not be necessary if the immediate commitment of the whole force promises quick success. Otherwise, the attack should be organized in depth. Deep echelonment of the wing will provide an opportunity to renew the envelopment of the enemy flank. The continuation of reconnaissance and security of the flanks during combat is especially important against a mobile enemy.

A cavalry regiment's zone for an attack organized in depth is approximately that of an infantry battalion (Paragraph 326).

If an attack is apparently failing, it should be broken off and freedom of maneuver should be reestablished as quickly as possible. Breaking contact can be achieved more quickly when it has been possible to hold the horses close to the dismounted troops.

The location, the security, and the bringing forward of the led horses must be carefully controlled.

717. Cavalry is poorly suited for defense missions of long duration. It is better suited for a delaying defense.

When cavalry is committed to the defense, the led-horses should be held beyond the effective range of enemy artillery. Because of its speed and mobility, cavalry may be committed as a rapid reserve in certain situations.

In a delaying defense, small detachments must face the enemy at considerable distances from the main force. These detachments hold off and delay the enemy, and then withdraw by the flanks, or by routes not directly in the field of fire of the main line of resistance. This leaves the terrain to the front of the main line of resistance open for the effective fires. It also allows the cavalry to harass the enemy from the flanks. For limited periods, cavalry can execute a delaying defense on a broader front than can less mobile troops. It can more quickly form defensive lines and can more easily surprise the enemy with fire from various directions. On the other hand, cavalry must break contact from its delaying line sufficiently early to permit its units to mount and withdraw without being observed by the enemy.

A frontal delaying defense can be supported by surprise fire and limited objective surprise attacks against the enemy flank. Mounted units are especially valuable for these missions.

718. Mounted combat normally only occurs during a meeting engagement of two small units or when a weak enemy is surprised, particularly during reconnaissance. A mounted attack against a demoralized enemy can have a great psychological effect.

719. Horse artillery must be able to follow the cavalry units wherever they go. Motorized artillery should be able to follow the motorized elements. The better routes, therefore, should be assigned to the artillery. During the march, elements of the horse artillery should be sufficiently far forward that they can quickly execute their missions. Since occupying a firing position requires time and mounted units move rapidly, advancing mounted cavalry frequently must engage without the covering fire of the horse artillery in position. Such cover by the horse artillery often would result in loss of contact between the two elements. If the cavalry must cross terrain that restricts its maneuverability in close proximity to the enemy, covering fire should be provided by motorized artillery, because it can follow more quickly.

During deployment and during combat, the artillery should be well forward. Every effort must be made to decrease the distance between the observation positions and the firing positions. Exposed artillery requires security from the nearest units.

720. Motorized infantry reinforces the firepower of the cavalry. It is dependent on other arms for reconnaissance and march security. Mounted patrols temporarily loaded in trucks can be attached to the motorized infantry. Such elements are very vulnerable to air attack. They advance by

bounds and usually are committed only after the situation has been clarified. A lateral displacement of this force in close proximity to the enemy must be avoided by advancing from assembly positions well to the rear.

As long as the infantry is loaded in trucks it is confined to the roads. Unloading must take place beyond the range of the enemy's effective fires and in a concealed area.

The commitment of motorized infantry to battle requires more time if elements of the horses are not readily available. Motorized infantry can be committed to relieve cavalry units in a rear position, to cover the withdrawal of advanced cavalry units, or at decisive points.

721. Bicycle units move principally on the roads. The speed of their movement is a function of the condition of the roads, the terrain, the season, the weather, and time of day.

They march rapidly and are comparatively silent. They are well suited for executing surprise attacks. They also can be committed at night.

Independent reconnaissance and more important combat missions are assigned to bicycle units only in exceptional situations. On the other hand, they can be used to occupy important positions near the routes of movement. Normally they must receive support from the other arms to execute this mission.

Because of their speed in combat, they can be employed as an effective reserve.

Bicycle units can achieve greater independence in combat if they are transported forward by trucks.

722. Motorcycle units are used similarly to bicycle units. Over limited distances they are independent of roads. Their speed and their operating range are considerably greater than bicycle units. They are not well suited for operations at night. Their speed and ability to shift rapidly make them an effective reserve. Normally they are committed in conjunction with motorized units. When assigned independent missions, motorcycle units should be reinforced by other motorized elements.

723. The engineer squadron of a cavalry division is employed for water crossings, for demolition missions, and for emplacing and removing obstacles. It may be necessary to assign engineer squads or platoons to individual cavalry brigades or regiments.

All available engineer squadrons must be assembled to support crossing operations over broad rivers.

724. Communications between cavalry and the next higher commander are often only possible by radio and aircraft.

All available communications facilities should be used. Cavalry divisions and corps do not lay trunk lines.

Truppenführung, Part II: 1934

Chief of the Army High Command
Reference: TA Nr. 2200/34 T4   18 October 1934

I herewith approve the Chapters XIV to XXIII
and the Annexes to this manual.

Changes and supplements require my approval.
Freiherr von Fritsch

XIV

ARMORED COMBAT VEHICLES*

725. Armored combat vehicles (*gepanzerte Kampffahrzeuge*) include armored cars and tanks that carry weapons and ordnance. It is possible to maintain an unrestricted arc of fire while the vehicle is on the move, but observation is difficult and vibration affects the accuracy of fire. Armored vehicle operations under combat conditions are very tiring for the crews. Armored vehicles generally can cross terrain contaminated by chemical agents without significant risk to the crew, especially if they are wearing gas masks.

Annex 3 lists detailed information on armored combat vehicles.[†]

Armored Cars

726. Armored cars are capable of high road speeds and a wide operating range, but they have limited cross-country mobility. Consequently, their deployment normally requires a usable road network. In general, their armor affords protection against small arms fire and artillery and mortar fragments.

727. Armored cars are used principally for reconnaissance. They may be used to screen troop movements and for rear area communications. Additional tasks, executed independently or in combination with other

---

[*]At the time the manual was written, the German Army did not have a single tank. The PzKpfw-I was introduced in 1934, about the time Part II of the manual was being released. The PzKpfw-I weighed 6.5 tons and was armed with only two machine guns. The first real German tank, the PzKpfw-IV did not enter service until 1936. The Germans formed their first *Panzer* division in 1935. In 1935 and 1936, however, notional *Panzer* divisions were being played in exercises at the *Kriegsakademie*. See Appendix B.

[†]Annex 3 is not reproduced in this translation. It listed the technical data for two machine-gun-carrying armored cars, and the PzKpfw-I through PzKpfw-III. When Part II of the manual was published in 1934, the PzKpfw-I was just coming into service, and the -II and -III were still several years off.

types of fast vehicles, may include long-range thrusts against the enemy's flanks, rear, and rear communications. Occasionally, they are used for carrying important orders and messages (Paragraph 98).

Communications between armored vehicles and the passing of orders and messages to command headquarters can be accomplished visually or in writing, and carried by messenger vehicles. At greater distances, radio communications (telegraph or telephone) should be used. Chapter XVII has further information on communications.

Tanks

728. Tanks are more heavily armed and armored than armored cars. They have good cross-country mobility. Their road speed and operating range are less than those of armored cars. Tanks are used for direct combat, mainly in the attack.

729. The difference between tanks armed with machine guns and those armed with heavier guns is that the latter are bigger, heavier, and more heavily armored.

Tank units also have armored vehicles designed for special tasks, such as radio communications, bridging, and resupply.

730. Machine gun–armed tanks* should be used to attack exposed and unprotected targets. They also are effective for reconnaissance, communications, and security missions.

Tanks armed with larger guns[†] are used to suppress enemy antitank weapons and armored vehicles, clearing the way for machine gun–armed tanks to penetrate the enemy's positions.

731. Tank operations are affected by the type of terrain and visibility conditions. Open, undulating ground is ideal. Wide and deep streams, lakes, swamps, thick forests, deep ditches, rough terrain features, and built-up areas limit or prohibit their use. Darkness and fog slow their movements significantly.

732. Surprise is one of the most important conditions for the successful commitment of tanks. All operational preparations should be conducted under conditions of secrecy. Tank track marks can best be concealed from enemy aerial reconnaissance by using roads with firm surfaces. On soft ground, track marks can be wiped out over short distances using techniques like dragging. Vehicle noise can be cut down by reducing engine power, by

---

*The PzKpfw-I was armed with only machine guns.

[†]The PzKpfw-II had a 20mm main gun; the PzKpfw-III had a 37mm main gun; and the PzKpfw had a 75mm main gun.

using soft ground, and by favorable wind conditions. Tank engine noise can be masked by other sounds in certain situations.

733. Communications within tank units can be conducted by radio (telegraph or telephone), by dispatch riders and messengers, or by visual signals. In combat situations, orders may be transmitted by radio in the clear. Chapter XVII covers communications.

Communications with other units are covered in the last part of Paragraph 340.

734. The commander's intent, the situation, the anticipated strength of the enemy's defenses, and most significantly the terrain are all determining factors influencing the specific type of tank deployment.

735. Tanks conduct reconnaissance primarily to determine the positions of the enemy's antitank weapons and to evaluate the terrain conditions in the sector where tanks will be committed. The tank unit commander receives key information from other elements, particularly infantry, artillery, engineers, and aviation. He frequently will be limited to the study of maps and aerial photographs, combined with his own observations—especially when little time is available.

736. At the focal point of a battle, where all available forces should be concentrated, the commitment of a particular arm should correspond to its relevance to the decisive situation. In the initial phase of a battle, particularly during a meeting engagement, detached combat elements may sometimes be committed against the enemy's forward positions or against an enemy putting up a determined resistance. Such elements also may be committed to a counterattack through friendly positions.

737. In most situations tanks should be assembled for an attack. Whenever possible, tank assembly areas should be secure from enemy air and ground reconnaissance, be oriented to the direction of attack, and be as close to the forward positions as enemy artillery fire will allow.

Movement into the assembly area must be secure and concealed, thus facilitating surprise. Tank units often proceed to the assembly area by separate routes, in split groupings, or under cover of darkness or fog.

738. The attack order issued by the tank unit commander should state the mission and the details of time, direction, and objective. When necessary, the order also will establish flank limits and contain specific instructions for coordination with other forces, communications, smoke screens, and consolidation upon completion of the attack.

739. A tank attack advances in deeply echeloned formations. The tank units move toward their targets at the maximum speed permitted by the condition and type of terrain. Supporting units follow closely. Depending on the development of the situation, they reinforce leading elements, rapidly break unexpected resistance, and exploit successes. The tank unit's reserves generally follow from covered position to covered position.

The width of the attack is a function of the situation, the terrain, and available friendly forces. The standard width for a tank battalion is between 800 and 1,500 meters.

740. The objectives for tank attacks are primarily the enemy's infantry (especially his heavy weapons), artillery batteries with their observation posts, command posts, reserves, tanks, and rear services and their installations.

Every tank unit should be assigned an objective. Tanks operating in coordination with infantry should be assigned the same objectives (Paragraph 339). If tanks must execute multiple missions, those missions should be assigned on the basis of one per unit, or they should be executed in succession. Normally it is impossible during combat to assign new missions to a tank unit.

741. When an attack has been completed, tanks should assemble to replenish ammunition and fuel and replace personnel, in order to be ready as soon as possible for follow-on operations. In general, follow-on assembly areas can be determined only for limited objective attacks.

742. During pursuit operations, tanks are assigned aggressive missions and deep objectives. They should attempt to overtake the defeated enemy. Significant success can be achieved by breaking through the lines of the retreating enemy and attacking his artillery, reserves, command posts, and rear communications.

743. The use of tanks in the defense is covered in Paragraphs 467 and 501.

744. During retrograde operations, a tank attack can facilitate the breaking of contact. In difficult situations it may be the only alternative. Repeated attacks against a pursuing and overtaking enemy can slow him down and force him to advance with caution. Such attacks also can relieve the pressure on friendly units when disengaging. Tanks must attack pursuing enemy armored vehicles.

745. Stationary tanks will be used as artillery or machine-gun platforms only in exceptional situations.

746. One or more tank regiments can be grouped with other motorized units and support troops into a combined arms armored force. Such units must be trained and organized for joint operations in cross-country conditions.

747. The tank unit has an armored heavy gun capability that can be used effectively on the move or during halts. Because of its speed and wide operating range, a tank unit can conduct surprise attacks against deep objectives. Appropriate terrain for movement and fighting are the requirements for the effective use of armored forces.

748. In combat an armored unit should be committed against the flanks and rear of the enemy, or committed to breaking through the enemy lines.

749. Motorized infantry units, consisting of motorcycle troops and

infantry transported in vehicles with cross-country capability, can be combined with other motorized units (antitank, artillery, combat engineers, signal) and with the necessary support elements to form a light motorized group. Such groups can be attached to armored units to reinforce or to exploit their success. A light motorized group committed independently should be reinforced with armored vehicles.

Speed, wide operating range, limited cross-country capability, and the potential for transporting fresh troops into the battle make light motorized groups capable of executing various missions. They can rapidly and unexpectedly be brought up to remote battlefield locations. They can deploy their forces quickly to fight on a broad or a narrow front.

750. Armored units and their attached light motorized groups frequently will be required to operate out of contact with their rear communications. In such cases, they must be heavily equipped with ammunition and fuel and authorized to forage for supplies on the battlefield. Ammunition and fuel supplies must be assured and future support requirements must be anticipated and planned for.

Defense Against Armored Vehicles

751. The appearance of enemy armored vehicles must be anticipated at all times. Headquarters, combat units, and rear support elements must be prepared to defend against armored attacks. All personnel must be able to identify enemy vehicles by type, capability, possible employment, and identification markings.

All reconnaissance patrols must immediately inform the commanders of threatened units as soon as the enemy armored vehicles are identified.

752. Defense against armored vehicles depends primarily on the terrain. Efficient surveying and mapping will indicate areas where the operation of enemy armored vehicles is probable, possible, or impossible. Terrain favoring the defense against armored vehicles must be exploited to maximum advantage.

753. Obstacles should be emplaced when the situation permits. Obstacles on roads and trails are used primarily against armored cars. Obstacles against tanks generally require a great deal of time, personnel, and material. For additional information see Chapter XX and Annex 3.*

754. Friendly armored forces with anti-armor weapons constitute the

---

*Annex 3 is not reproduced in this translation. A minefield 300 meters wide and 10 meters deep required 800 mines. One combat engineer company could emplace such a minefield in one to four hours, depending on the terrain. A heavy tree barrier, 100 meters wide and 50 meters deep and interspersed with mines, could be erected in six hours by a combat engineer platoon equipped with power saws.

primary defense against enemy armored vehicles. They can be augmented by antitank guns and field artillery.

755. Defense against an armored attack while on the march or in bivouac will be organized as described in Chapters IV and XII.

756. In combat the enemy normally will deploy his armored vehicles in great numbers and with the advantage of surprise. Defenses, therefore, must be prepared as strongly as possible at all points where enemy attack is probable.

757. Artillery must engage enemy armored vehicles when they are preparing for attack, approaching, or in the process of attacking. The fire of multiple batteries should be massed whenever possible. Artillery fire should be registered-in to cover the zones where enemy armored attack is most likely.

When infantry antitank guns are committed, their function is to destroy enemy armored vehicles before they succeed in breaking through to the main infantry positions. Antitank guns should be deployed in concealed firing positions that provide mutual supporting fire. The positions should be covered by the lay of the land, or by obstacles that will prevent them from being overrun. In certain situations, antitank guns should be positioned to the rear of threatened positions.

Elements of the artillery and infantry heavy weapons should be given the primary mission of attacking the enemy tanks, their supporting infantry, and the observation posts that support the enemy armored attack.

Light infantry units must avoid tank fire as far as their mission—which is the engagement of follow-on enemy infantry—permits.

758. Enemy tanks that break through are engaged by antitank guns deployed in depth and by the reserve. The preparation of a defense against such an attack is the responsibility of the divisional antitank battalion commander, based on the guidance of the division commander.

If the division commander retains direct control of the antitank battalion, he must have secure communications with its commander, who frequently will have to act independently when attacked. The entire divisional antitank battalion should concentrate its fire at the point of the main effort of the enemy armored attack. The antitank battalion may be placed under the control of the commander of the threatened sector, as the situation requires.*

Selected individual guns and artillery platoons should engage with direct-fire enemy tanks that break in. Rapidly emplaced obstacles (mines, wire entanglements, etc.), and in exceptional situations antiaircraft gunfire, also can be used to halt the advance of enemy tanks.

---

*Generally, the regimental antitank companies protected their respective regiments, while the division commander held control of the antitank battalion as a mobile reserve. The Germans tried never to commit single guns, except in the most extreme situations. [*Wedemeyer Report*, p. 25]

XV

AIR FORCES*

759. The success of large-scale military ground operations requires the establishment of air superiority (*Luftüberlegenheit*) at the operational focal point. To accomplish this, available air units must concentrate in a timely manner. If necessary, air units must be drawn in from other sectors.

Close coordination between air and ground units, and especially air defense units, is a necessary condition for success. Such coordination is the responsibility of the overall commander.

760. Units with dedicated air support will achieve the highest effectiveness in ground combat operations. Commanders and staffs of such units must have a good knowledge of aircraft types and capabilities and the capabilities of the aircrews.

Aircraft performance capabilities are listed in Annex 3.†

761. Headquarters with multiple air units under their control will have an air forces commander as an adviser, who will exercise functional authority over all air units within the sector or under the command.

762. The deployment and operations of air units depend on the weather. The weather forecasting services provide vital planning information.

Fog, heavy rain, hail, snowfall, low clouds, and heavily overcast skies seriously restrict air operations, particularly in mountainous terrain.

The wind influences an aircraft's speed and its force is a primary factor in long-distance flights. Direct sunshine reduces visibility in the air, especially when looking toward the sun. Mist and smoke on the ground and

---

*The original German title of this chapter was *Luftstreitkräfte*. The German Air Force, the *Luftwaffe*, did not exist when this manual was published. On 1 October 1934, Hitler ordered the creation of the *Luftwaffe*, along with the secret expansion of the Army and Navy—all in violation of the Versailles Treaty. The first military aircraft also entered production that year.

†Annex 3 is not reproduced in this translation. It listed six basic types of aircraft. The two reconnaissance planes had an operating radius of 700 to 800 kilometers. The two fighter aircraft had flight duration times of 2 to 2.5 hours. The light bomber carried a bomb load of 250 kilograms out to 1,000 kilometers, and the heavy bomber carried up to 1,200 kilograms to a range of 1,600 kilometers.

high humidity in the air make orientation more difficult and create difficulties for photographic reconnaissance and target identification.

Weather conditions affect night air operations more than day operations. Flying is easier in moonlight.

Short flights, such as combat aerial reconnaissance and low-level battlefield attacks, generally can be executed in almost any weather conditions. Weather conditions become more important in direct proportion to the distance to the target.

Reconnaissance Aircraft

763. Reconnaissance squadrons (*Aufklärungsstaffeln*) normally consist of nine aircraft.

Special squadrons with enhanced performance aircraft conduct operational reconnaissance missions.

Reconnaissance squadrons normally operate under the control of commands down to the corps level, but may be attached temporarily to infantry or cavalry divisions, armored forces, and light motorized groups.

764. Apart from aerial reconnaissance missions, reconnaissance aircraft can be used for liaison missions, and for surveillance of friendly forces to evaluate their camouflage. If properly equipped, they can lay light smoke screens or deliver light ordnance during reconnaissance missions.

Artillery aerial observer planes are reconnaissance aircraft deployed to acquire and mark targets for the artillery and to observe and adjust the fall of shot.

Fighter Aircraft

765. Fighter aircraft operate in wings (*Jagdgeschwader*) and regiments (*Jagdregimenter*). A fighter regiment consists of two or three wings. A wing consists of three squadrons of nine aircraft each. Three aircraft form a flight (*Kette*).

In normal situations fighter units operate under the control of an army.

766. The commander of a fighter unit must maintain direct communications with the command to which his unit is attached. Within the scope of his mission, he should have freedom of action.

767. The basic elements of a fighter's combat effectiveness are the aircraft's performance and the efficiency of its crew. The maximum duration of an operational mission should be two hours, including time to and from station.

Fighters may fly two or three daylight sorties if there are periods of complete rest between the sorties. Aircraft equipped for night operations normally fly one sortie per night. Two sorties per day normally are the absolute maximum for low-level attacks.

768. A fighter mission normally begins from its air base. Generally, the dispersal of fighters to advanced landing fields—especially when those fields are distant from the main air bases—can only be justified in exceptional situations, such as when high sortie rates are required.

769. Fighters fly in wings, squadrons, or flights during daylight operations. Single aircraft generally fly night operations.

Aerial combat takes place at close ranges.

Friendly ground forces must be notified if the airspace over their areas will be used for night operations.

770. Fighters support the ground forces best by attacking enemy aircraft. They also can be used to provide cover for aerial reconnaissance missions over enemy positions, to attack enemy aerial reconnaissance, and to protect friendly units and vital rear installations from enemy air attack.

Fighters should not be used to form an air defensive line in their air sector. Assigned missions should define the time and space in which a fighter unit operates. A fighter wing can be assigned to an operating airspace of about 20 square kilometers. Larger patrol areas should clearly designate the directional emphasis of the attack.

Air superiority may be impossible to achieve, even against a weaker enemy. It is possible, however, to achieve limited air superiority in time and space.

771. Ground attack is an additional fighter mission, if sufficient forces are available. Ground attack can be especially effective in combination with operations by ground forces.

Ground attack targets for fighter aircraft generally lie beyond the range of artillery observation. Fighters primarily are committed against enemy troop concentrations, enemy columns on the march, and troops crossing rivers or confined in narrow spaces.

Heavy aircraft losses must be anticipated when the enemy is prepared for such attacks. Justification for the losses must be clearly established when fighters are committed to ground attack missions.

772. Ground attack missions normally are flown only in daylight and by formations of not less than a wing. The greater the number of fighters making a simultaneous surprise attack, the greater the effect and the greater the difficulty for the enemy defenses.

During an attack, fighter formations normally fly at the lowest level possible, dropping small fragmentation bombs and firing machine guns. They avoid aerial combat during the approach flight. If aerial combat cannot be avoided, it usually means that the ground attack mission must be abandoned.

773. Other important targets for fighters include enemy artillery aerial observer planes and captive balloons. These normally are targets of opportunity.

The weather, the situation, and the enemy's state of alert all influence the timing and targets for attack. The optimal time for attack is in the early morning and evening. Captive balloons provide very restricted reconnaissance coverage. Attempts to attack such targets often will result in their withdrawal.

774. The destruction of enemy aircraft in the air is a common mission for fighters and air defense units. They achieve the best results when they work in close coordination. Maximum coordination can be achieved only during daylight operations. A shortfall in fighter and air defense units may require the assignment of separate missions to each arm.

Fighters must know the positions and ranges of their own air defense units. The air defense units must know where and when the fighters will be operating and their numbers. The overall commander ensures this coordination. Good communications between the commander, the fighters, and the air defense units is essential.

Immediate attack by fighters is the best form of defense, provided that friendly fighters are capable of reaching the enemy in time. The aircraft warning service (*Flugmeldedienst*) must provide timely information on the number, course, altitude, and type of enemy aircraft. The service also guides the fighters in the direction of the enemy by radio or ground markers. Firing from antiaircraft guns in the direction of the enemy also can direct friendly fighters.

The scattering of enemy aircraft formations over friendly territory by air defense artillery may create favorable conditions for the fighters to attack. Air defense artillery units must prevent the enemy from committing reinforcements during aerial combat.

It is difficult to locate enemy aircraft during darkness. When night aerial combat occurs over friendly territory, air defense searchlight batteries must identify enemy aircraft so they can be attacked by fighters.

Bomber Aircraft

775. Bombers are organized in bomber wings (*Bombengeschwader*). Each wing consists of three squadrons of nine aircraft.

Bomber forces normally are controlled by the High Command. Based on the situation, that control can be passed to armies or army groups.

776. The commander of the bomber unit maintains direct communications with the headquarters to which his unit is attached. Within the limits of his orders, he retains discretion in the execution of his mission. If some

or all the aircraft cannot reach their primary targets, the commander may order them to attack alternate targets.

777. Wings normally conduct daylight bomber attacks. Bombers attack at night singly or in small groups in sequence, separated by short time intervals.*

If the targets are not too distant,† bombers may fly two missions in one day. The same applies to night missions during periods of long nights.

778. Missions in support of ground units must coordinated with those units regarding the extent and direction of the attack. Bombing attacks cause both physical damage and produce a demoralizing effect, which can be more significant. The attacks are directed primarily against targets beyond the range of friendly artillery.

779. The types of bombing attacks include high-level, low-level, and dive-bombing.

During a daylight high-level attack, ordnance is delivered from high altitude. At night, the attack level is lower. High-level attacks are directed mainly against large targets, such as troop concentrations, built-up areas, bivouacs, loading and unloading operations, ammunition dumps, rear installations, large march columns, and rail and motor transport.

During low-level attacks, ordnance is delivered from the lowest possible altitudes, generally after making a low-level approach to ensure surprise. The low-level approach improves the odds of the strike and avoids much of the enemy's air defenses. Low-level bomber attacks generally are directed against targets similar to those assigned to fighters.

During a dive-bombing attack the aircraft descends on the target from a high altitude with maximum speed and releases its ordnance from less than 1,000 meters. Such attacks are directed against smaller targets, including bridges, locks, and similar installations.

Communications and Ground Installations

780. The coordination between the air forces and the other arms requires efficient and secure communications among service elements with the joint command staff.

781. Air forces units generally depend on the Army's wire net. Their own telephone equipment provides them with only short-range connectivity to an existing wire net, and with connectivity within wings and squadrons.

782. Radio communications between air forces and other arms are con-

---

*5- to 10-minute intervals. [*Wedemeyer Report*, p. 129]
†400 kilometers or less. [*Wedemeyer Report*, p. 122]

trolled by the joint command. Internal radio communications, including radio navigation (*Funkortung*), are controlled by the air forces.

783. Voice communication capability between aircraft is planned for fighter and bomber units in close formation daylight operations.*

784. If aircraft are equipped with radio sets, radio is the fastest method of air-ground communications. An aviation unit's command set normally is located in the radio station of the air base or forward airfield. Only artillery aerial observers and aircraft conducting special missions communicate with other ground stations.

Radio stations of command headquarters and other ground units monitor the aviation nets. In situations where aircraft communications are exposed to enemy signals intercept, or where encoding radio messages is not feasible, pre-established special abbreviations and radio codes can be used. Normally aircraft should transmit by radio only those messages that are time sensitive.

Communications for artillery observation are the exception. Annex 3 lists additional information on aircraft radio equipment and their ranges.†

785. Messages, orders, maps, and photographs can be transmitted and exchanged by message drop or by aircraft retrieval hook. Hook pickup should be used only for the most important messages, when no other alternative is possible.

Message drop zones should be established in advance by the responsible unit commander, or upon request from the aircraft to the nearest commander.

Messages should be dropped from an altitude of about 50 meters, with the aircraft flying into the wind.

The message drop zone will be marked by a cloth cross panel laid out on the ground. The following areas and obstacles should be avoided for message drop zones; cornfields, lakes, forests, high or single trees, buildings, and telephone wires. All of these are dangerous to the aircraft and can delay the finding of the dispatch cases. The message drop zone also should not be too near a headquarters or a troop concentration.

Hook pickup zones are established on order of the unit commander who has access to the necessary equipment.

---

*The manual anticipated a technological advance in air-to-air radio communications. This was still a weakness for the *Luftwaffe* as late as the Battle of Britain in 1940. Royal Air Force fighters had clearly superior radios.

†Annex 3 is not reproduced in this translation. Radios in tactical reconnaissance aircraft had a maximum range of 150 kilometers; those in operational reconnaissance aircraft had a range of 300 kilometers. Bomber radios had a range of 600 kilometers. Only lead fighters carried radios, with a maximum range of 50 kilometers.

The hook pickup zone must be marked on the ground with an arrow indicating the direction of the wind. The pickup of the message bag is made by an aircraft equipped with a special hooking rod, flying at an altitude of about 5 meters. Safety considerations require that the terrain in front of and behind the zone is clear of obstacles and that there is an emergency landing area in the direction of departure.

786. At the request of friendly aircraft, ground units use ground signals, flares, and smaller ground panels to indicate the trace of the front line.

Large ground panels mark command posts, drop zones, and hook pick-up zones. They also communicate specific messages to aircraft as established in special orders. The signal panels are deployed at the request of the aircraft.

Ground units and aircraft also communicate through the use of signal flares and aircraft signal cartridges. The meanings of such signals must be established in advance and should be revised periodically.

Improvised signals generally serve only to attract the attention of friendly aircraft to a particular point. Such improvised signals include reflecting metal, signal flares, tracers fired into the ground, panel signals, or flags.

787. The task force air commander establishes the manner in which aircraft will transmit their messages. The options include radio, message drop, or post-mission delivery upon return to base or an advanced airfield.

788. The locations and condition of airbases determine the effectiveness of air units. The choice of location depends on terrain and the tactical situation.

The characteristics of the ground, its surface, and its load-carrying capability become more critical with the size of the aircraft, its takeoff and landing speed, and its payload capacity.

High-tension pylons, telephone lines, towers, and chimneys require particular attention during takeoffs and landings. These hazards can disrupt air traffic, especially during periods of darkness and poor visibility. Good access roads, billeting facilities, water, electricity, telephone connections, and a rail connection all facilitate the establishment of an air base. Good camouflage potential also is important.

789. The timely establishment and preparation of required air bases is an important factor in military operations. It is especially critical during advance and withdrawal operations. A lack of airfields can greatly degrade combat effectiveness.

790. Airfield construction units and specially designated personnel prepare air bases. Aircraft, depending on their type, can either be parked in tents or in the open.

791. Air bases are the locations where air units are established and

have their facilities. Annex 3 contains information on air base size requirements.*

792. Forward landing fields generally measure 500 by 500 meters. They are established close to a command headquarters and are used to facilitate the transmission of orders and to shorten flight distances.

Forward landing fields are indispensable for aerial reconnaissance operations. Fighters and bombers use forward landing fields only in exceptional situations.

793. Dispersal airfields are an effective means of avoiding the effects of a surprise attack by enemy bombers. Such fields also serve as an emergency runway if the main air base is damaged. Air bases of adjacent units may be designated for use as dispersal airfields.

794. Dummy airfields can deceive the enemy, but they are only effective in conjunction with simulated air traffic.

795. Every air base must be secured against air and ground attack.

The air unit itself is primarily responsible for such security. Defense against air attack is augmented by antiaircraft guns and machine guns from the area command in which the air base is located.

If cavalry, armored, and light motorized forces deploy reconnaissance elements, the air bases may have to displace far to the rear or to the flanks, under the cover of the main forces. In such situations, radio communications with air bases become especially important and aircraft missions flown from advanced airstrips become a priority.

796. The displacement from one air base to another depends on the tactical situation. It usually becomes necessary when direct communications become difficult between the senior commander and his supporting air unit commander. Enemy air attacks also may dictate a move.

The displacement of an air base must be preceded by reconnaissance. An advance party conducts the initial occupation, followed by the main body in trucks, or by train at greater distances. The aircraft displace by air. Communication facilities at the new base must be established before the move.

Aviation motorized columns travel 150 to 200 kilometers per day. With adequate preparation, an air base can be torn down in three to five hours. The provisional establishment of an air base requires four to seven hours. A hasty displacement of an air base increases these times.

Airfield operations should suffer the least possible interruption during the displacement.

---

*Annex 3 is not reproduced in this translation. Fighter aircraft and light bombers required a landing field 750 meters square; heavy bombers required 1,000 square meters.

797. Night-lighting systems assist aircraft to find their course and guide them for the return to base. Often, the lighting will be established with additional means provided by the air defense units. The lighting must be established in accordance with standardized procedures that limit the sources of visible lights—including from antiaircraft guns, rockets, blinker lights, and revolving beacons.

The air unit is responsible for air base recognition signals and runway lighting.

XVI

AIR DEFENSE UNITS*

798. The enemy will extend his aerial reconnaissance and attack operations to the range limits of his aircraft. All units must be prepared at all times for enemy air operations. The threat of air attack increases in daylight and under favorable flying conditions. Air defense is most important in the decisive operational sector.

In addition to their normal mission, enemy reconnaissance aircraft may direct immediate attacks against targets of opportunity. In exceptional situations, reconnaissance aircraft might even deliver single bombs against especially lucrative targets.

In most situations, enemy fighter and bomber attacks are executed with surprise and with great speed. Sometimes, such attacks can be anticipated if enemy reconnaissance aircraft are observed preceding fighters and bombers in order to identify targets.

799. The early detection and friend-or-foe identification of enemy aircraft is critical to effective and timely air defense.

The type of aircraft, their engine sound, numbers, altitude, and attitude are all indicators of identification and probable intent. High altitude and extreme ranges complicate identification.

Friendly aircraft use various signals to identify themselves to ground forces.

800. Air defense is the responsibility of the headquarters that deploy the attached air defense units.

801. Air defense units operate independently or in coordination with fighter aircraft to prevent enemy aerial reconnaissance and artillery aerial observation. Air defense units also defend ground installations against air attack, and provide support to friendly aircraft. The aircraft warning service must detect enemy aircraft in a timely manner and notify all threatened units.

---

*Air defense units were Air Force organizations, attached to Army units as operational requirements dictated. Air defense units included light and heavy air defense battalions, and searchlight battalions.

Requirements for the commitment of air defense units include correct judgement of the air situation and knowledge of the enemy's principles of aircraft attack tactics.

Air defense units must be maintained at the highest levels of training and equipment readiness. Their morale and equipment serviceability are essential.

802. The objective of air defense is the destruction of enemy aircraft. At a minimum, the enemy must be forced to break off his attack, or be prevented from fully accomplishing his mission.

803. In many situations, air defense weapons may be required to fire directly above friendly forces, which may result in friendly casualties.

804. Air defense units are armed with antiaircraft guns (*Flak*), automatic antiaircraft guns (*M. Flak*), antiaircraft machine guns (*Fla. M.G.*), air defense searchlights (*Fla. Schw.*) and aerial obstruction devices.

Aircraft warning companies also are assigned to air defense units.

805. The antiaircraft gun is the principal element of air defense. It moves by road or rail. A good and dense road network facilitates the deployment of motorized antiaircraft guns. Railway-mounted antiaircraft guns can move quickly over long distances, but they are tied to the rail net.

Camouflage of air defense batteries is difficult, which makes them vulnerable to attack. It is necessary, therefore, to shift their firing positions regularly when within the range of enemy artillery.

The most profitable targets for antiaircraft guns are multiple enemy aircraft in tight daylight formation, flying in a constant direction and altitude. Individual aircraft flying at medium or low altitude also make good targets. Enemy fighters, especially in small numbers and at high altitudes, are not good targets. The situation, however, may require engaging them. Antiaircraft machine guns rather than antiaircraft artillery should engage aircraft at altitudes lower than 1,000 meters.

806. Antiaircraft machine guns are mounted on trains or motor vehicles. They are especially effective at engaging low-level, short-range aerial targets.

Antiaircraft machine guns, therefore, can be used to protect troop concentrations, units in the line of march, and rear installations (airfields, ammunition dumps, etc.) against low-level air attack. On the battlefield they augment the fires of antiaircraft guns. They are deployed in forward areas only in exceptional situations. In coordination with searchlights, they are effective for defense against night air attacks.

807. Air defense searchlights* are mounted on trains or motor vehicles.

---

*A searchlight battalion had three batteries, each with nine 1,500mm searchlights and six sound detectors. The 1,500mm searchlight had a range of approximately 10,000 meters. The battalion was completely motorized. [*Wedemeyer Report*, p. 138]

Their mission is to illuminate enemy aerial targets, holding them in a cone of light so they can be engaged by antiaircraft weapons or by fighter aircraft. Searchlights also blind enemy aircrews, disorienting them and disrupting their ability to deliver their ordnance. Ground fog and low cloud cover limit the effectiveness of air defense searchlights.

808. Aerial obstruction devices (barrage balloons or kites) augment air defenses. Their deployment depends on the wind speed. During night operations or in periods of poor visibility, aerial obstructions can reduce the number of air defense weapons required. Balloons and kites cannot be used effectively to block large areas. Enemy awareness of aerial obstructions may cause him to fly at higher altitudes or to abandon the attack.

809. If the situation permits, air defense units can be attached temporarily to infantry, cavalry, armored units, and light motorized groups when their missions require such support.

810. It is impossible to provide air defense coverage everywhere. Any attempt to do so will only disperse combat power.

Orders, therefore, must define where the air defense effort has priority. In general, the priority of coverage should go to ground operations, based on the nature of the enemy air threat. Priority, however, may be given to support of friendly air operations and to the attack of enemy aircraft. Thus, air defense priority does not always have to correspond directly to the ground combat action. In some situations, units can be held in reserve in positions back from the forward area.

811. The fire of antiaircraft weapons will attract enemy attention to the area being defended. Ordering units to withhold firing and illuminating operations can moderate this effect. Conversely, heavy firing and illuminating can be used to deceive the enemy in a certain area. Only exceptional situations, however, can justify the resulting high expenditure of ammunition.

812. The use of antiaircraft weapons in ground operations reduces their effectiveness in their primary role and should be limited to exceptional situations. This use is justified only for defensive fire against combat vehicles at close ranges.

813. The army-level air defense commander, or the senior air defense unit commander, is the advisor to the army commander in all matters concerning air defense. He is in charge of the deployment, re-equipment, and ammunition resupply of all air defense units under his control. He directs the regional aircraft warning service and ensures their reports are delivered through the communications system to adjacent units, the rear areas, and air units.

When strong air defense units are attached to a corps, that headquarters also may be assigned an air defense commander.

814. The air defense commander is responsible for coordination with friendly air forces units.

The battle for air superiority requires good communications between the air defense commander and the air forces commander. It also requires the fast and reliable operation of the aircraft warning service. The rapid evaluation of information and its continuous exchange must enable air forces and air defense units to engage rapidly and to modify orders in response to the changing air situation.

815. The commander of the air defense artillery battalion* normally directs the operations of all the air defense units in the corps, in accordance with the orders of the corps commander.

He issues the orders to the units, indicates the areas to be covered, supervises the entire air defense deployment within the corps area, and ensures the coordination of all air defense units with adjacent units and air units deployed in the area.

In coordination with the corps signal officer, he also is responsible for the effectiveness of communications within his unit. He directs the aircraft warning service in his zone and ensures that important reports are delivered immediately to adjacent units and to rear areas.

He is responsible for ensuring ammunition resupply for all corps air defense units.

He must remain continuously abreast of the situation and the intent of the corps commander.

He maintains close—and if possible personal—contact with the corps commander, both on the move and in position. During combat his command post should be located close to the corps command post. The most important factor is effective command and control of the air defense units. The battalion commander may leave his command post to visit batteries, to check the effectiveness of the air defenses, and to familiarize himself with the air situation.

816. Synchronized engagement by air defense units is essential.

---

*Wedemeyer reported two different types of air defense battalions. The completely motorized heavy battalion had four batteries, each with two 20mm antiaircraft machine guns and four 88mm antiaircraft guns. This outstanding weapon, first introduced in 1918, underwent several modifications throughout World War II, serving in a wide variety of roles and missions. The battalion also had four automatic gun direction devices. The light air defense battalion had three batteries, each with twelve 20mm antiaircraft machine guns and four 600mm searchlights. A fourth battery was armed with nine motorized 37mm antiaircraft guns, and four 600mm searchlights. During the exercises at the *Kriegsakademie* in 1937 and 1938, infantry divisions normally had an attached light battalion. [*Wedemeyer Report*, pp. 24, 136–138]

A deployment is effective when the covering ranges of the batteries overlap. If multiple and widely dispersed points require simultaneous cover, the standard solution is to deploy the batteries and air defense searchlights at the most critical point and to cover other areas with antiaircraft machine guns.

817. Air defense batteries should not be positioned close to field artillery firing positions. The air defense batteries may be affected by field artillery firing, it is difficult to camouflage them well, and they will attract enemy fire to the field artillery batteries. The selection of firing positions for air defense batteries must be coordinated with the field artillery commanders.

If the terrain and enemy fire permits, it may be possible to position single air defense batteries in forward areas, from which they can engage aircraft beyond friendly forward lines.

The effective engagement of enemy aircraft and observation requires the deployment in strength of air defense forces in the forward area.

818. Changing the firing positions of air defense batteries will degrade their effectiveness. Conversely, frequent shifts of battery positions restrict the effectiveness of enemy reconnaissance. Shifts may become necessary to avoid losses when positions have been identified and have come under enemy attack that could paralyze operations.

Air defense searchlight batteries should be held as far back as possible during the day, and then moved up into position at dusk.

819. The effectiveness of the aircraft warning service is essential to the entire air defense system. The service can provide important indicators of the enemy's intent (Paragraph 184).

The speed of air operations places great demands on the reliability and rapidity of this service.

820. The aircraft warning service ensures the timely commitment of air defense units and fighter aircraft; informs ground commands and air units of the air situation; warns ground units and rear services of impending attack; and provides time to initiate defensive measures before the arrival of the enemy. It also identifies any message-dropping activities and enemy aircraft landings in friendly territory.

821. The aircraft warning service of the field army consists of the air guard observers of the air defense units and the air observation posts of the air warning companies.

The air warning company is deployed as a unit—or by platoon where air defense units are under strength—and augments communications in the air defense battalions. It also is responsible for the establishment or the completion of the aircraft warning net behind the front lines, and from the area of operations to the rear.

822. The commander of an air warning company establishes the air

information center in coordination with the air defense commander. The company commander is responsible for efficient communications and for maintaining surveillance of the airspace—especially on the flanks and in gaps in the front lines. He serves as the chief of the air information center of the command to which his company is attached.

823. The aircraft warning service requires good communications. The air warning company, therefore, will use the area communications net of the command to which it is assigned.

Priority should be given to wire communications. Unless radio silence has been imposed, radio communications may be used between air defense units, air observation posts, air warning companies, and the air information centers.

Reports from friendly aircraft must be exploited fully.

824. Air information centers are very vulnerable because of their high level of communications traffic. They should be situated beyond the range of enemy artillery and away from prominent landmarks, built-up areas, and main roads.

XVII

COMMUNICATIONS

825. Signals corps units and unit communications platoons establish and maintain signal traffic between command headquarters and units, as well as within units.*

The signal corps also operates the communications net to the rear services. It assists in the collection of intelligence, the maintenance of information security, and deception and counterintelligence measures.

826. Wire and radio are the primary means of communications from signal units. Other technical communications may be used, including carrier pigeons and messenger dogs in special cases.

827. The methods of signal communications must complement each other. Any single method can fail at various times and places because of enemy action, terrain, weather, or other difficulties.

The means that produce the fastest and most secure communications should always be the first choice.

Priority communications should be reinforced by the use of multiple means.

In friendly territory, permanent installations form the foundation of the communications net.

828. Wire is the essential element of signal communications. It is used for both for telephone and telegraph. Overland cables are vulnerable to external effects. The installation and reconstruction of lines are greatly affected by the terrain. The installation of permanent cables is time consuming.

---

*The divisional signal battalion had a fully motorized radio company and a partially motorized telephone company. The radio company had fourteen smaller 5- and 2-watt radios, and four 100-watt radios with a voice or Morse code range up to 300 kilometers. The telephone company had four switchboard sections; six horse-drawn line sections; ten motorized line sections; and two connecting sections for short hookups in the headquarters area, Each motorized line section carried 12 kilometers of wire; the horse-drawn sections carried 8 kilometers; and the connecting sections carried 3 kilometers. [*Hartness Report*, p. 45]

The telephone is used for the oral exchange of information, orders, and messages, and for direct discussions.

High-speed telegraph and teletype systems can transmit large amounts of data in words in a rapid and secure mode. Normally, only senior headquarters use both systems.

829. Radio communications can be put into operation quickly and can transmit information over great distances. Transmission can be either by telegraph or voice. Radio communications are not greatly affected by weather, terrain, or enemy weapons. They are, however, sensitive to strong electrical disturbances. Any radio message can be intercepted and the position of the transmission station can be located through radio direction finding. Radio is a valuable supplement to the telephone, and frequently is the only substitute for wire communications. In the field, radio is used principally for the transmission of command communications traffic. Radio also is important for communications between ground units and aircraft, and between aircraft.

Radio traffic must operate on a well-defined schedule to avoid interference between stations.

Transmissions must be brief. The network will become overloaded by long messages, which also provide an exploitable signal intelligence opportunity to the enemy.

830. Signal lamp communications are not affected by terrain. Their effectiveness is degraded by poor weather conditions (rain, snow, fog, mist). The nature of the terrain may make it difficult to establish effective signal lamp positions.

In combat, signal lamps are an indispensable backup for wire and radio. Over short distances signal lamps also augment wire and radio.*

831. Pyrotechnic and light signaling equipment generally transmit preestablished signals. Their effectiveness depends on visibility conditions. They are easy to carry and to operate. Confusion with enemy signals and false transmissions by the enemy are potential risks. They can be useful for communications between combat units, especially between infantry and artillery and between other ground units and observation balloons. Paragraph 786 covers their use in communications between aircraft and ground units.

Sound alarm equipment can be used to alert against air or gas attacks.

832. Carrier pigeons and messenger dogs can transport messages, orders, and sketches.

---

*Signal lamps were a very slow means of communicating. Under combat conditions, a 20-word message could take up to 10 minutes to transmit. [*Wedemeyer Report*, p. 63]

Carrier pigeon operations require extensive preparations. Head winds, rain, fog, snow, and especially thunderstorms will reduce their effectiveness. In many situations they cannot be used at all. Pigeons do not fly in darkness.*

If properly handled, messenger dogs are reliable over short distances. They are used in frontline areas.†

833. Near the battlefront, telephone conversations, radio messages, and signal lamp messages all can be intercepted by the enemy. Security must be established though special procedures. Enemy intelligence gathering must be countered by technical means. Violations of communications security procedures can result in serious consequences for friendly units.

Duplicate and heavily insulated wire lines may be required in sectors where there is a threat of the enemy tapping into them (generally within 3 kilometers of the front line).††

Radio messages must be encoded. Signal lamp messages must be encoded only if the possibility of enemy interception exists. In situations of imminent danger, a commander is authorized to transmit in clear text radio and signal lamp messages that the enemy has the capability to intercept. Aircraft communications are covered in Paragraph 784, and armored vehicles in Paragraph 733.

The contents of a radio message can be transmitted using standard code charts. Frontline reconnaissance elements can send their messages in this manner if they believe their presence is known to the enemy, or if the message will not compromise their unit. Fire orders and fire direction information of immediate effect, and artillery observation and reconnaissance information that does not have tactical implications may be transmitted in the same way. Names of persons, unit designations, and locations must be masked.

Radio voice transmission can be used to send messages from front-line reconnaissance elements and artillery observation and reconnaissance information that does not have tactical information useful to the enemy. In other situations, radio voice transmission will only be used in situations of imminent danger, or on the order of unit commanders. The messages will

---

*Carrier pigeons took at least three days to orient. They also had difficulty navigating in snow. They flew at a speed of about one kilometer per minute. [*Wedemeyer Report*, p. 64]

†Messenger dogs could remember and locate positions on a battlefield within a 2 kilometer radius. They could follow an established scent trail up to 6 kilometers. [*Wedemeyer Report*, p. 64]

††As early as 1914, the German Army had the capability to read enemy phone traffic using induction techniques, which do not require physically tapping into a line.

be constructed in such a way that the enemy cannot make immediate use of them.

834. Every sector must evaluate the threat of enemy interception and determine the requirement to limit signal communications in time and space, or even to prohibit them.

835. The responsible staff determines the requirements for radio silence and establishes the priorities, time of commencement, and duration. Radio silence ends at the start of an operation unless instructions otherwise are in force. In certain situations, reconnaissance units not in enemy contact may be required to send their messages to radio stations assumed known to the enemy. Every officer has the authority to break radio silence on his own initiative if the situation requires the immediate and timely transmission of a message, and no alternative means are available.

836. Deception through signal communications requires careful tactical and technical preparation and focused leadership. The deceptive traffic must be coordinated with other deception tactics, such as dummy transportation, false troop movements, and feints.

837. Headquarters at the army level and above can order the jamming of enemy radio traffic.

838. Public radio stations can be used to broadcast official Army communiqués to inform, explain, and warn the general population, and to counter enemy propaganda. The use of public radio services for military purposes is directed, controlled and managed by the Army High Command.

839. The army headquarters manages radio traffic down to the division level. The division commander is responsible for monitoring radio traffic to the subordinate echelons.

The senior commander retains final authority for radio traffic.

840. The signal officer is the communications adviser to the division commander. He simultaneously may be the commander of the divisional signal battalion. In accordance with the commander's intent, he directs signal corps operations and supervises coordination between signal units. He also is responsible for reinforcement and replacement of personnel and equipment.

The unit signal officer runs the information service of his unit and maintains contact with the divisional signal units.

841. Signal commanders and unit communications officers must keep their commanders continuously informed of the current situation. They also must maintain their own awareness of the situation and the intent of the command. They make recommendations concerning communications operations.

Paragraph 106 covers the responsibilities for establishing communications between senior and subordinate staffs and adjacent units.

842. The commitment of signal units is determined by the situation.

The primary operational direction and the point of the main effort require secure and reliable communications. Communications are especially important to an open flank that is isolated and threatened.

No signal officer should hesitate to commit all the personnel resources at his disposal to execute any urgent task required by the situation.

The use of salvaged communications equipment saves time and personnel. Such equipment, however, must be inspected thoroughly before being put back in service. In general, only signal units should use such equipment.

843. Changes in the situation may require a reorganization of communications. Reserve signal elements should be established and held available for this purpose.

Signal units must not be moved or relieved when such action would interfere with friendly communications traffic.

844. All commanders must consider the requirements of signal units when siting their headquarters and observation posts. The establishment of a communication network will be easier when the senior commander designates the locations of the subordinate headquarters.

Paragraph 109 covers the locations of senior commanders on the march and in combat.

845. While on the move, radio communications between command headquarters are maintained on standby and wire connections are held in readiness.

846. The signal units of an army headquarters establish communications with adjacent army headquarters, making maximum use of permanent telegraph, telephone, and radio facilities. They also communicate forward to corps headquarters and rearward to the senior command and to home territory. Wire connections are established as permanent field telephone lines or with field trunk lines.

847. The corps signal battalion establishes a communications net in coordination with the signal units of the army headquarters—or when in home territory, with the postal authorities. The corps communications net connects the divisions with the corps headquarters. On order, the divisions tie their own communications into the corps net. If the integrated net cannot be established within a reasonable period of time, the corps signal battalion assists in establishing it. If the corps controls a large number of divisions, two lines should be laid along the corps' line of march. The corps headquarters directs the establishment of forward telephone stations, to which the divisions connect during extended halts.

848. The divisional signal battalion establishes communications between the division headquarters and the subordinate units. This is an especially critical mission in combat. It also connects the artillery commander to his subordinate commanders.

During an advance, the battalion lays the divisional trunk line along the route of march, connecting it with the corps' communications. An infantry division will not establish a separate divisional trunk line if a corps signal battalion is laying a cable to the most forward units through its sector. If necessary, however, the divisional signal battalion can be tasked to support or to complete the construction of that line. In such situations the divisional signal officer is responsible for the establishment of the wire connections in the division area.

The greater part of the divisional signal battalion must be available to accomplish its mission on the battlefield. When contact with the enemy is imminent, the division must be freed from maintaining unnecessary communications to the rear. The higher echelons should assume that function.

849. The unit signal platoon establishes communications between the unit commander and his subordinate commanders.

850. Radio is the backup to the communications provided by the divisional trunk lines. When an infantry division's trunk line fails, radio and signal lamp communications are used.

Several measures can be taken to improve the efficiency of wire communications to the rear and to avoid extremely long lines. Before an operation starts, the corps signal battalion and army signal units can extend the divisional trunk lines, improve their operational readiness, and install lateral communications links.

851. The use of communication units is covered also in Chapters IV to XII. The principal information is in Paragraphs 90 to 119, 259, 291, and 346 to 348.

Chapter XIII covers communications between cavalry and its higher headquarters. Chapter III covers communications between motorized reconnaissance units and their higher headquarters.

XVIII

CHEMICAL WARFARE*

852. Chemical weapons include irritant, blistering, and asphyxiating gases.† They temporarily or permanently disable unprotected or insufficiently protected troops. They also affect animals and well protected troops during field operations. Because they expand in a given space, the standard means of protection against other weapons are ineffective against chemicals. Motorized units with troops wearing gas masks can cross contaminated terrain. Otherwise, such ground cannot be crossed without the use of specialized units and techniques.

Chemical agents are often more effective than conventional weapons because of their duration and ability to expand in space. They also produce important psychological effects, particularly among inexperienced or poorly protected troops.

853. The effect of chemical agents is a function of their level of toxicity. Their effectiveness increases with the density of the agents in the air or on the ground and with their persistency. The larger the affected surface, the greater the effect.

Air agents only have a limited persistency. Ground agents can remain effective for days or weeks.

854. The potential effectiveness of chemical agents depends on the weather conditions and on the time of day. The wind and its direction are

---

*Although the 1925 Geneva Protocols prohibited the first use of chemical weapons in warfare, *Truppenführung* nonetheless devoted an entire chapter to chemical warfare. This entire chapter undoubtedly was influenced by the German successes with chemicals in World War I, particularly under the direction of Colonel Georg Bruchmüller during the 1918 Ludendorff Offensives. Neither the 1941 nor the 1944 editions of the U.S. Army's *FM 100-5* have chapters devoted to chemical warfare. Any discussion of chemicals in those two manuals is devoted largely to defensive measures.

†Specifically not mentioned here are nerve agents. By World War II the Germans had developed the world's first nerve agents, Sarin and Tabun. They assumed, incorrectly, that the Allies also had developed nerve agents.

key factors, and become more important as the target is closer to friendly units.

Strong wind can disperse most agents, making them ineffective. Heat from the sun makes them rise and accelerates evaporation on the ground. Cool weather prolongs their effects, but extreme cold can completely destroy the efficacy of most agents. Light fog and light rain favor air agents and mask their presence. Strong rain will precipitate air agents and neutralize ground agents. Heavy snowfall clears the air but does not neutralize ground agents. An agent may be preserved under the snow, re-emerging during trenching operations or when establishing emplacements.

The most effective times for the use of gas are at night, early morning, or dusk.

Ongoing weather observation by units augments the observations of the meteorological service, whose forecasts are transmitted to units on a timely basis.

855. Terrain characteristics influence the effectiveness of chemical agents. Everything that facilitates cover and camouflage enhances the effectiveness of chemicals. Hollows, valleys, ravines, and areas sheltered from the wind increase the duration of chemicals. Wet ground and marshy areas tend to dissipate chemicals.

856. Maximum effectiveness can only be achieved by the use of large quantities of chemical agents simultaneously. However, the repetitive use of smaller quantities also can achieve good effect and produces a considerable psychological impact on the targeted enemy troops.

857. The effect of chemical agents is enhanced if they are delivered by surprise attack or if the method of delivery misleads the enemy into reacting incorrectly and taking the wrong countermeasures. Surprise and deception can be achieved through selection of the time, place, and method of delivery; by the amount and nature of the agents; by extending or irregularly interrupting attacks; and by combining chemicals with smoke.

The use of chemical agents is a command decision. They can create surprise in a way that facilitates the rapid exploitation of their effects.

858. The methods of delivering chemical agents include artillery and mortar rounds, release from canisters, chemical projectors, spraying, bombs, and dispersal from close support aircraft.

859. Artillery and mortar rounds are the most frequent methods of chemical delivery. When attacking targets close to friendly units, the enemy must be downwind. Delivery by artillery and mortar rounds is less affected by wind direction than other methods. Large quantities of chemical ammunition are required, but no other special preparations are necessary. Surprise, therefore, is most easily achieved by artillery and mortar attack.

The categories of chemical fire include surprise gas attack, neutralizing fire, defensive fire, and gas combined with high explosive.

A surprise gas attack requires the rapid build up of a dense gas cloud over an unprotected enemy unit. Neutralizing fire should produce and maintain such a high density of chemical agents in the air over the enemy that the combat effectiveness of even a protected unit is degraded—at least for the duration of the barrage. Defensive fire lays down sufficient quantities of ground contaminating agents that forces moving through the area suffer losses and lose much time because of the necessity to detour or decontaminate.

Safety distances between the friendly front line and the target can vary based on wind direction and speed, the type of terrain, and the types of chemical agents.

860. Containers installed in the ground or carried on special vehicles are used for the release of air chemical agents. Specialized chemical warfare units operate this equipment. The release of the gas produces a high-density cloud, and requires clear terrain and a low wind speed in the direction of the enemy.

A chemical projector* attack delivers multiple gas projectiles, launched from banks of ground-mounted tubes. Wind direction is less important because the gas cloud is produced inside enemy-held terrain. This type of attack produces the most intense gas cloud. When well prepared, it has the greatest surprise effect.

The gas release and chemical projector methods are rarely used in mobile warfare.

861. Spraying chemical agents is the most effective means of contaminating terrain. Special chemical units are necessary for spraying larger areas. Localized ground contamination can be executed by combat engineers or by artillery or mortar fire. Aircraft delivered chemical bombs can be used to contaminate terrain beyond artillery range, but are ineffective for larger areas. Low-flying aircraft can spray large areas, but not with a great degree of precision.

Defiles, forested and broken terrain, low-lying land with intersecting water courses, and mountains make effective areas for contamination. Ground contamination is particularly effective on irregular terrain, at specific points, and in areas of great width and depth. Such contaminated areas can augment obstacles and other barriers.

862. The wind direction is the key factor in the protection of friendly units when using chemical close combat weapons (gas hand grenades and toxic smoke candles).

Burning toxic smoke candles in the front lines requires the same conditions as the release of gas from canisters.

---

*Similar to the Livens Projector system used by the British in World War I. By the start of World War II, this system was considered obsolete.

863. Large quantities of chemical agents generally will not be available during rapidly moving engagements. In such situations it will only be possible to neutralize a small number of targets through artillery or mortar chemical fire.

If larger quantities are available, enemy artillery is the primary target for chemical attack. Additional targets include breakthrough points in the enemy lines and surprise gas attacks on troop concentrations, reserves, etc. (Paragraph 344).

864. Aircraft-delivered chemical agents are particularly effective in pursuit operations. Men and animals are vulnerable to ground contamination agents delivered by low-level attack.

865. Chemical agents are easier to deploy during defensive operations, particularly when conducting a fixed defense. Defensive measures can be reinforced by establishing chemical obstacles in front of emplacements, by artillery and mortar chemical fire, and the use of close combat chemical weapons to counter enemy penetrations. The use of chemicals in a delaying defense is covered in Paragraph 502.*

866. When disengaging or withdrawing, barriers can be created by chemical shelling, by using chemical units to contaminate larger areas, or by contaminating obstacles.

867. Command directed measures must ensure the chemical protection of every soldier. Those measures must take into consideration the characteristics and types of the enemy's chemical agents.

868. Timely knowledge of the enemy's equipment, types of chemical agents, and their methods of employment is extremely important.

869. The weaknesses of enemy chemical agents must be fully exploited for the protection of friendly forces.

870. An enemy with large quantities of chemical agents can likewise make only limited use of them in unfavorable weather. This is exploitable in some situations.

871. Good use must always be made of the terrain to degrade the effects of the enemy's chemical agents. When occupying a position for extended periods, it may be necessary to abandon individual points and firing positions that are not gasproof, even if those points are well camouflaged.

Elements echeloned in depth or widely dispersed can reduce the chemical threat with frequent movements and dummy positions. Such measures restrict the enemy's target acquisition and his ability to focus his chemical assets on lucrative targets.

---

*This paragraph is especially interesting because the experiences of World War I offered very few examples of successful use of chemicals in the defense. Almost all the successes (Riga, the Ludendorff Offensives) came in offensive operations.

872. When the weather is unfavorable for chemical operations, units still must remain on the alert and continually observe enemy positions. A unit not on gas alert can suffer severe damage if hit, even by chemical agents degraded by unfavorable weather.

Gas alert can be ordered when air attacks are imminent or when units come within range of enemy medium or light artillery.

873. If enemy chemical weapons are detected, an immediate gas alarm is raised (Paragraphs 695 and 697). False alarms will disrupt the troops and over time will cause complacency. Nonetheless, a late gas alarm can have serious consequences.

874. Chemical detectors can provide early warning. They must be deployed as soon as the use of enemy chemical weapons is anticipated— especially ground contamination. Chemical detectors may be especially useful for reconnaissance and terrain survey elements.

875. Timely detection of the enemy's preparations will produce the most effective measures against his chemical weapons. Successful defensive measures include the destruction of his chemical weapons by fire, and the neutralization of enemy artillery and mortars.

Units cannot rely solely on the wind to avoid chemical attack.

XIX

SMOKE[*]

876. Smoke assists the concealment of units and installations from enemy reconnaissance, deceives the enemy, restricts his battlefield operations, and reduces the effectiveness of his fires.

877. The premature lifting of a smoke screen requires agile and determined performance by units.

878. Enemy ground reconnaissance can be restricted by laying down a smoke screen, either around his units, or by smoke screening friendly units (*Selbstverneblung*). This can be achieved with either a smoke screen (*Nebelwand*) or a smoke zone (*Nebelzone*) if the wind direction is perpendicular to the axis of enemy observation. For all other wind directions only a smoke zone will create the required effect.

Enemy aerial observation can only be partially restricted by establishing a smoke zone around friendly units. It is almost impossible to conceal important installations or a bridge construction for a long period by this method.

879. The concealing of friendly units with smoke will attract enemy attention and fire. The smoke coverage, therefore, must be extended much farther than the unit or the installation that is to be concealed.

Laying smoke on the enemy will reduce the effectiveness of his fires more than will smoking friendly forces. It will impose on the enemy the disadvantages of moving and fighting in smoke, and often requires much less smoke equipment than would be needed to conceal friendly forces. Laying smoke on the enemy, therefore, is generally the best option.

880. A deceptive smoke screen can mislead and distract the enemy, attract his fire, and reduce his state of alert. Such a technique only works when the enemy does not recognize it as a deceptive measure.

881. The dimension and density of a smoke screen and its duration depend on the weather and wind, on the distance from the source of the smoke to the target area, on the terrain, and on the quantity and type of

---

[*]*Künstlicher Nebel*, literally, artificial fog.

smoke devices. These include dispensers, munitions, and other smoke generating devices (smoke candles, smoke hand and rifle grenades, and smoke bombs).

Higher levels of air humidity will produce thick and long-lasting smoke. Cool weather and a cloudy sky produce better results than hot weather or frost. Strong sunshine will lift the smoke, heavy rain will precipitate it. A steady, light wind from a constant direction is the best condition for employing smoke screens.

Based on weather conditions, the concealing effect of smoke decreases faster or slower in relation to the distance from the smoke source. A smoke screen seldom remains opaque when farther than 500 meters from its source; a smoke zone, 1,000 meters. The obscuring of visibility often has a much wider effect.

Mountainous, heavily rolling, or forested terrain is unfavorable for the uninterrupted expansion of smoke. Open terrain with high ground moisture is the most favorable for smoke effect.

882. Smoke devices should only be used when secured by friendly units. When firing artillery or mortar smoke rounds, or delivering smoke by aircraft (by generation or bombing), the smoke source should be positioned over or projected into enemy territory.

Smoke generating, smoke shelling, or smoke release by aircraft varies based on wind and terrain.

Smoke generation is effective at wind speeds of 2 to 10 meters per second for screening friendly areas in all wind conditions and terrain; but not for screening the front line in the case of a head wind. It also is effective for obscuring the enemy, but only with the wind blowing in his direction, at short distances, and in favorable terrain.

Smoke rounds and delivery by aircraft are effective for obscuring the enemy in almost any weather, with wind speeds up to 8 meters per second, and in any terrain. The screening of the friendly front line is possible in head-wind conditions.

Annex 3 has additional information on smoke generation, smoke shelling, and release by aircraft.*

883. Smoke screens can be used to obscure sections of the battlefield and to restrict observation. When the wind blows diagonally or perpendicularly to friendly lines, adjacent units may be affected by the smoke. The employment of smoke screens, therefore, must be closely coordinated. All

---

*Annex 3 is not reproduced in this translation. A smoke-generating platoon could smoke one square kilometer for 40 minutes. A battery of light field howitzers could produce a smokescreen 150 meters long. It took between 8 and 16 rounds per gun to establish the screen, and four to six rounds per minute to sustain it.

unit commanders are authorized to use their smoke equipment on their own authority only if they can confirm that the weather and wind conditions will not cause the smoke to affect adversely their own combat effectiveness, or that of other units not under their command. Otherwise, prior authorization from higher echelons must be obtained. If possible, adjacent units should be informed in advance of the use of smoke.

884. If drastic weather changes that will affect combat effectiveness occur between the issuing of a smoke order and the execution of that order, it is often better to cancel the order. The responsible commander must clearly understand the consequences of canceling a planned smoke operation.

885. The means of smoke generation available to units are designed to produce small and local screens of short duration. In certain situations, the commander may centrally control the use of smoke or assemble the generating equipment of multiple units in one position.

Armored vehicles may use their own equipment to screen themselves at any time.

886. The commander of an army or a corps allocates chemical units and smoke munitions to the subordinate units, or he withholds them for special missions.

The division commander controls the commitment of the chemical units and their equipment allocated to him. He coordinates their operations with the fire and movement of his own units.

Smoke units and equipment should be concentrated where the operations plan, the terrain, and the weather conditions indicate the optimal effect. Every use of smoke, its purpose, effect, duration, and type must be controlled and coordinated with adjacent units.

887. The commander of a smoke generation unit is the adviser to the commander to whom he has been attached. He must remain constantly aware of the commander's intent and the combat situation. Based on his observations, he conducts an estimate of the situation and makes recommendations for the commitment of his unit.

888. In order to synchronize smoke effects with the combat action, the overall commander may place the smoke unit under the operational control of the unit to be concealed, or he may instruct both to cooperate. A condition of subordination only occurs when the required smoke effect covers only a single unit.

If a smoke screen is to be produced by the combined action of artillery, infantry mortars, and smoke generation units, the artillery commander should exercise overall control.

The synchronization of smoke with fire and movement is most effective when controlled by a schedule.

889. If a smoke screen is required only when a certain phase of the battle has been reached, the commander will either release the smoke under his own initiative or leave the decision to the unit to be screened.

890. Combat and movement in smoke are affected as much as in natural fog. Natural fog differs from smoke insofar as the latter occurs by surprise, is denser close to the smoke source, and only lasts for a short period.

Away from clearly marked routes, a compass is the most reliable means to maintain direction in smoke or fog. In some situations, the wind direction identifiable by the movement of the smoke or fog can indicate direction.

Advancing by sections through smoke or fog is an effective method of maintaining the cohesion of a unit.

891. When attacking a smoke-screened enemy, the attacking force, even when entering the smoke, has the advantage over the defenders—despite the difficulty in maintaining direction.

892. Defenders must maintain the effectiveness of their fire in a smoke screen.

Hasty counterattacks in smoke screens produce decisive results in close combat. Units, therefore, must be held close to the threatened points.

Deliberate counterattacks are executed generally after a smoke screen has lifted.

893. The enemy may attempt to attract fire against a smoke screen that appears at the same time they do. The temptation to fire must be resisted. All engaged units are authorized to fire independently only at smoke screens directly in front of their own positions.

894. All efforts should be made to conduct aerial reconnaissance to determine enemy actions behind a smoke screen.

895. Smoke can be mixed with chemical agents. When friendly forces are smoke-screened by the enemy, gas masks must be worn and kept on until confirmation that the smoke is not toxic.

XX

OBSTACLES

896. Obstacles (*Sperrungen*) on roads, paths, and terrain restrict the enemy and channelize his movement in specific directions. Obstacles and barriers (*Hindernisse*) are important means of controlling a battle, especially in the defense. They supplement security, either when units are stationary or on the move. They also facilitate smoke operations and contribute to the deception of the enemy.

The obstruction of transport routes (railways, waterways, motor roads, and permanent lines of communication) restrict enemy traffic and operations.

897. The key considerations for the extension of obstacles and the types deployed include the commander's intent, the situation, the time required to emplace the obstacle, the available forces and means, and the terrain.

Annex 3 has additional information on obstacles and barriers.[*]

Paragraphs 861, 865, and 866 cover the use of chemical warfare agents as obstacles.

898. The obstruction of roads, paths, terrain, and traffic routes is more effective in proportion to the depth of the obstruction. The obstruction of terrain also is more effective in proportion to the width of the obstruction. The effectiveness of obstacles is increased if they are covered by friendly fire; if the enemy is surprised by their presence; if he is forced to deploy special methods and personnel to clear them; or if he is forced to fight under unfavorable conditions to clear them.

The effect of obstacles is increased by employing different types and by using dummy and concealed obstacles.

Obstacles that incorporate mines[†] or chemical warfare agents can inflict losses on the enemy, even if not covered by friendly fire.

---

[*]Annex 3 is not reproduced in this translation. See the footnote on p. 195.

[†]The Germans used two basic types of mines. S-mines (*Schützenminen*) were antipersonnel. T-mines (*Tellerminen*) were anti-vehicle. The latter got their somewhat colorful name because they were the shape and general diameter of a dinner plate (*Teller*).

In many situations natural obstacles, such as waterways, lakes, swamps, forests, and hilly terrain, can be used as obstructions and reinforced in their effect.

Obstacles can be used to increase the effect of friendly defensive fire.

899. Roads, paths, and terrain are obstructed by the reinforcement of natural obstacles and by the creation of artificial obstacles, such as minefields, dams, demolitions, and the use of high-tension electricity. Paragraphs 901 and 902 cover roads that cross obstructed terrain.

900. The long-term obstruction of lines of communication is accomplished through permanent disruptions (*gründliche Unterbrechungen*); short-term obstructions through temporary disruptions (*leichtere Unterbrechungen*).

901. Permanent disruptions of lines of communication can only be authorized by the High Command, the commander of an army or army group, or the independent commanders of army and cavalry corps and divisions.

The permanent disruption of railways, waterways, and motor roads generally requires the large-scale destruction of principal buildings and installations.

The permanent disruptions of fixed communications requires the destruction of above-ground and underground cables over long distances, or the destruction of the technical installations of telephone exchanges, telegraph centers, telegraph relay stations, and radio stations.

902. The temporary disruption of lines of communication and the obstruction of roads, paths, and terrain can be executed independently by any unit commander unless, in exceptional situations, the senior commander has contrary requirements. The commanders issuing the orders are responsible for everything that happens or fails to happen.

The temporary disruption of lines of communication and the obstruction of roads, paths, and terrain are essential where unit security demands it. On the other hand, such measures should be avoided during an advance through a friendly operational sector; are optional when at standstill; are imperative during a withdrawal; and always should be attempted inside an enemy operational sector.

903. Unit commanders may have combat engineers and specialists attached to their commands to execute complex and extensive obstructions. Engineers, alone or reinforced by other units, may be directed to establish such obstructions.*

---

*The corps engineer battalion had four motorized companies. Each company carried 260 T-mines; 104 S-mines; 60 K-Rolls (concertina wire); 16 rolls of barbed wire; and 667 2.5-kilogram explosive charges. The German Army also had obstacle columns (*Sperrkolonne*), consisting of two platoons of twenty 3-ton trucks each. Each platoon carried 1,800 mines, 135 K-rolls, and 1,500 kilograms of explosives. [*Hartness Report*, p. 43]

All arms must be capable of establishing simple obstructions with the means at their disposal.

904. Reconnaissance to detect obstacle opportunities must be conducted in a timely manner. Initial indicators often come from map inspection. The reconnaissance of more extensive obstacle tasks will be based on aerial photographs and data from higher headquarters.

905. Local commanders must report the time, place, and category of obstructions of lines of communications to their higher headquarters. Commanders also must report any possibility of the disruption of friendly traffic.

906. The order to permanently disrupt lines of communication must be issued as a formal order, generally in writing. If the order is transmitted by technical communications means, it must be confirmed in writing immediately.

When destroying important structures, the responsible commander decides the timing of the demolition, especially during a withdrawal. The untimely issuance of destruction orders can have serious consequences.

907. The orders to establish major obstacles should include: the purpose, degree, and extent of the obstacle; the required means; the scheduling and security of the construction; the requirement for and location of gaps; the authority to close gaps; and the communications requirements during the construction period. If necessary, the order also will specify how and by whom the finished obstacle will be used for security and other tactical purposes.

Removal of Obstacles

908. The removal of enemy obstacles may require extensive preparations, which must be initiated in a timely manner.

In some situations, bypassing obstacles may be the best course of action, especially when the enemy can be expected to use them in his defense.

909. Aerial and ground reconnaissance can determine the position, type, and extent of an enemy obstacle; any gaps; and any possibility of bypassing it. A survey should be made to locate any hidden booby traps or mines.

Often, obstacles are only detected for the first time during combat operations. Combat engineer officers, equipped as necessary, should be attached to reconnaissance elements and sent forward to survey obstacles.

910. Based on the survey, the necessary forces and equipment can be committed to remove the obstacle.

Infantry, cavalry, artillery, and motorized units alone generally can remove simple obstacles. When required, combat engineers, signal troops,

or other technical units can be committed. Combat engineers also can operate independently to remove obstacles.

Combat engineers, construction troops, or other specialist units may be
required to clear minefields, high-voltage obstacles, and dammed-up areas;
or to reconstruct destroyed installations or construct new ones.

In some situations, obstacles can be destroyed by shelling or bombing,
or can be removed by tanks.

911. The removal of extensive obstacles may require considerable
forces and means, as well as specific security arrangements.

XXI

ARMORED TRAINS

912. An armored train (*Panzerzug*) can cover long distances in a short time. But because it is confined to rails, which are easy to destroy, its effectiveness is limited. It can achieve considerable psychological effect when appearing by surprise and confronting inferior forces.

Armored trains are not effective for long-term combat operations or against an enemy who has artillery.

913. In addition to the locomotive, an armored train generally consists of eight to ten rail cars that serve as carriages for weapons and protective equipment, living quarters, and mess facilities. Normally, the locomotive with its tender is positioned in the middle of the train. The security cars, loaded with equipment or sand, are located at the front and rear.

The vital elements of the locomotive and the weapons cars are armored against small-arms fire and shell fragments.

The weapons cars are equipped with mortars, machine guns, and rapid-firing cannon. Each carries its own combat crew.

Armored trains are equipped with communications systems for the transmission of orders and fire control and for external communications.

The quarters and mess cars are dropped off as soon as combat is anticipated.

914. The complement of an armored train consists of the combat unit, the train crew, and a railway construction unit. One element of the combat unit operates the train's armament. The other element consists of infantry, up to company strength, to be deployed outside the train. As the situation requires, combat engineers and their equipment can be included.

915. A train with improvised armor is equipped similarly to an armored train, but its combat power is inferior.

916. An armored train on alert status can be ready to move in about 30 minutes; otherwise in about three hours.

Parking the train in separate sections on different tracks is the preferred technique to confound enemy aerial reconnaissance.

The speed of an armored train is normally 20 to 30 kilometers per hour.

917. Armored trains can be attached temporarily to an army or corps headquarters.

The staff transportation officer supervises the train's operation in coordination with the railway authorities.

918. Armored train missions must be planned carefully and kept secret. The commander of the armored train must know the general situation. He also must be familiar with the track system or have access to the necessary aerial photographs.

Armored trains are not used at night, in forested areas, or in areas that are difficult to keep under surveillance.

919. Armored trains are used to ensure the security of rail traffic operations, troop loading and detraining, railway demolitions and repair work, supply and evacuation operations, retrograde movements, and for mopping-up operations in unsecured areas. They can also be used as a rapidly deployed reserve.

920. Whenever possible, armored trains are deployed in pairs, particularly when operating in enemy-held areas. They move either following each other, or if double-tracking is available, echeloned side by side. They communicate by whistle or light signals and by radio.

Reconnaissance patrols may be used to screen armored trains. Equipped with machine guns, they can be deployed on locomotives, or on hand-powered or motorized railway trucks. They should be supplied with equipment necessary to repair light damage.

When on the move, machine guns must be in the air defense firing position.

921. When conducting operations into the enemy-held areas, all necessary means should be employed to maintain communications with the rear. The locomotives themselves can be used for this purpose.

922. Railway stations and other installations must be checked before they are passed.

When an armored train halts, it must be protected against unmanned trains or locomotives. Security obstructions, therefore, must be established on the tracks.

923. Ammunition economy is essential. As the situation requires, supplies can be transferred from other trains.

924. The commander of an armored train must know when and how the track and its wire connections will be dismantled.

925. Weak enemy resistance will generally be broken by fire from the train's onboard weapons and the simultaneous advance of the infantry. Closely following trains are also an effective means of support.

If an armored train meets an enemy with superior artillery, the train will withdraw under the concealment of smoke.

926. When armored trains engage each other, the most important target

is the enemy locomotive. The infantry will attack the enemy train under cover of the fire from all available weapons. They will try to cut off the enemy train's retreat. Precautions also must be taken against the approach of other enemy trains or units. At the appropriate moment, the train will advance to the attack.

To avoid attack by an enemy armored train, a friendly train can lay a smoke screen, push rail cars in the other train's direction, and drop obstacles to block the track.

927. When friendly units anticipate an attack by enemy armored trains, the tracks should be disrupted if possible (Paragraphs 896 to 907).

Hidden obstacles can be used to derail a train. Visible obstacles are intended to make it stop at a position where it can be engaged with fire.

Fire engagement areas should be prepared at places where poor visibility forces the enemy to proceed at slow speeds.

The timely commencement of fire requires the earliest possible report of the approach of an enemy armored train.

If adequate forces are available, an immobilized enemy train should be attacked. Security against other enemy armored trains or follow-on units should not be ignored.

XXII

TRANSPORTATION

928. Transportation of units and their equipment takes place by rail, road, and ship. In the absence of specific orders from the High Command, the means of transportation will be determined by the major command. Transportation officers are responsible for the management of movements.

Railways make it possible to move units of any size quickly and safely over great distances and to supply elements of large armies.

Motor vehicles reduce the burden on and complement the railway. They are used primarily for shorter distances and their carrying capacity is considerably smaller. The use of motor vehicles depends on road conditions.

Waterways take advantage of the large capacity of ships. This, however, it is a slower and more uncertain means of movement. Ships effectively can carry mass consumption supplies and return sick and wounded personnel or enemy prisoners.

Special manuals cover the movement of units by coastal and high seas shipping.

Railways

929. Railways are decisively important for the management of war. They are critical for mobilization, strategic concentration, and the maintenance of the Army's combat readiness. During operations they make possible the movement of major commands of the Army.

The High Command controls the use of the railways for military purposes. The railway authorities are required to comply with military directives.

The transportation officers of the command headquarters issue the military orders to the railway authorities in their sector. Together, they oversee the execution of the orders and monitor progress.

Railway station officers are assigned to key stations to coordinate traffic between the transportation commander and the railway officials. They issue any military orders necessary to maintain discipline and order in the station. They operate under the command of the responsible transportation officer.

The military use of requisitioned and newly built railways in enemy territory is managed jointly by the High Command and the railway authorities.

930. The efficiency of a standard gauge track for military purposes is a function of the number of military trains it can handle daily in either direction. A number of 24 indicates the number of trains that can go in both directions in a 24-hour period.

Based on their composition, the speed of military trains generally corresponds to that of public trains. The average travel speed is 30 kilometers per hour.

931. The capacity of a railway station (*Bahnhofsleistung*) is a function of the number of military trains that can be loaded and unloaded in a 24-hour period. It can be increased by special measures, such as the construction of auxiliary platforms. In general, the loading and unloading of twelve trains per day is a good station capacity.

932. The preparation of empty trains for the movement of units, the management of the movement, and the preparation of loading and unloading points all require time. Before the first train can leave, approximately three days are necessary for the preparation of high-volume transport ordered without prior warning to the railway authorities. If standard preparations are already in place, this period can be reduced to a few hours for movements requiring only a few trains.

933. The establishment of standard trains or alert trains will facilitate movement.

Standard trains (*Einheitszüge*) are based on the fully authorized strength of the units of the various arms. Alert trains (*Bereitschaftszüge*) are established corresponding to the movement strength of the unit to be moved.

934. The duration of a movement is a function of the total number of trains, their daily availability, the distance of the move, and the travel speed.

935. When moved by train, the time required for units to be ready for deployment on arrival is a function of the preparation time, the duration of the movement, the time required to march to the loading station, and the time required for assembly after unloading.

The readiness of units for deployment can be accelerated by either transporting the marching units by rail and moving the mounted and motorized units under their own means; or transporting the marching units by motor vehicle and the mounted and motorized units by rail. The disadvantage is that the units are separated and they lose their mobility until reassembly.

In some situations a foot march will result in a faster arrival at the objective, especially over short distances.

936. Movement orders clearly indicate the overall intent of the command. All measures, therefore, must be taken to ensure the security of such orders.

937. The senior commander determines the earliest loading time in coordination with the transportation officer. The transportation officer will make all efforts to accommodate special requirements to modify the sequence of movement or arrival, or even the method and execution of the movement.

938. The dispatching office advises the transportation officer of all movements.

939. The movement order normally includes the loading table; general indications concerning the composition and priority of the move; loading and departure; the timetable, stops for food supply and water; and arrival.

940. Advance parties move forward by public rail, special trains, motor vehicles, or air. They make all the necessary preparations for unloading, quarters, and food supply for the units in the unloading and assembly areas. Rear detachments follow after having completed their tasks.

941. The dispatching office appoints a transportation officer for every movement. He issues the military orders for loading, travel, unloading, security, and the internal control of the movement. Loading officers may be assigned as augmentation. The transportation officer and his movement must adhere to the railway operating procedures.

Any interference with the railway service is forbidden.

942. Units are responsible for their own messing during movement, unless other arrangements have been made.

943. Transport movements rarely can be hidden from enemy aerial reconnaissance. The more traffic increases beyond the normal, the easier it is to recognize. Movements can be conducted solely at night only in rare situations. If the situation permits, a unit should unload away from the sector where it will deploy, and then advance by night march.

944. During loading and unloading operations, all units are responsible for their own security against aerial reconnaissance and air attack, even when air defense units are available.

Assemblies of troops on the loading ramps, access roads, and close to railway stations must be avoided. Approach and departure marches should be conducted in sections as small as possible, on different roads, and out of the sight of aircraft. Assembly points should be designated close to the loading and unloading areas, but concealed from aircraft observation. Defilades close to and at the railway stations should be identified and marked. Units divided into loading groups should be able to approach the ramps and load immediately, and unloading troops should leave the station area immediately. These measures must be established in coordination with the station officer or the responsible railway authority.

During movement, units will mount machine guns in air defense firing positions on open railway coaches. Such weapons should be distributed effectively over the length of the train.

Loading and unloading operations must be secured against ground attack. In some situations, units should make all preparations for immediate readiness for action during the movement. When the situation is uncertain, an officer may travel on the locomotive, with the concurrence of the railway authorities.

945. Railway installations should be secured against ground attack by local details and patrols along the tracks.

Air defense coverage is essential for railway stations with important operational or military facilities, intersections, power plants, and major rail bridges. Air defense units, fighter aircraft, and smoke screens provide coverage by day, supplemented by blackouts at night.

946. Deception movements can only be made if the rail network and the required rail missions permit. They only are useful if they are not recognized as such. If such movements are made with empty trains, enemy aerial reconnaissance may be deceived, but not generally enemy intelligence.

Motor Vehicles

947. Specially organized motor vehicle units can transport supplies, units with their horses and their vehicles, or elements of the horses and vehicles.

948. Movement by motor vehicle is more flexible than by train. The march speed of motor vehicles is high when road conditions are favorable. The loading and unloading of troops, however, depends on many variables and is highly subject to friction. These difficulties will grow with the size of the transported unit.

949. Units of reinforced infantry regiment size and larger can be transported efficiently by motor vehicles over distances of at least 60 kilometers. The transport of smaller units and supplies over shorter distances might also prove effective.

950. In exceptional situations army-level columns, divisional supply columns, or columns constituted on an auxiliary basis from public sector motor vehicles from can be used to transport units.*

---

*This paragraph recalls the French use of Paris taxicabs to rush reinforcements to their lines during the Battle of the Marne in 1914.

951. Important movements by motor vehicles can only be executed on roads that are in good condition.

Before initiating the movement, the road conditions must be surveyed (Paragraph 275). If this is impossible, the survey must be accomplished during the move.

Distributing engineers with their equipment along the line of march or incorporating them in the march column are effective options.

952. The motor column's average speed is a function of the gradient, the type and condition of the roads, the time, the season and weather, and the type and condition of the vehicles.

The establishment of a fixed march speed is generally unfeasible. Every motor vehicle column moves at the speed of the slowest vehicle. Consequently, the distances between the columns will vary, as well as the distances between the vehicles. The faster the progress, the greater the intervals. Cohesion within the different march columns, however, must not be lost. A closed march column also is impractical.

Motor vehicles with similar capability should be grouped in one march column or in one of its sections.

953. Normally, the fastest motor vehicles are put at the head of the column so all sections can move at their maximum speed. If units are to arrive as a closed formation, or if elements will have longer rest halts, the slower sections should be put at the head, with the faster ones to proceed later.

954. March capacity is a function of the same factors as average speed.

Generally, a driver should not drive more than 10 hours, including short stops, during a 24-hour period. March capacity can be nearly doubled by relieving drivers periodically. Commanders and drivers who cannot be relieved, as well as troops transported with their equipment, will face a greater challenge.

955. Rest days are vital for personnel. Equipment must be checked after every movement and at every rest halt. A daily minimum of two hours must be scheduled for servicing the equipment and refueling.

For more important maintenance, motor vehicle units generally need one day per week.

956. The senior headquarters establishes the priorities for movement. The troop commanders, generally the commanders of the units to be transported, are responsible for the execution of the movements. The motor transport unit commanders are their technical advisers. Close coordination between all these commanders is essential before and during the movement.

957. For all motor movements the controlling headquarters will designate times of departure and arrival, routes, march objectives, daily objectives (if necessary) and rest halts, priorities at intersections and when over-

taking, supply for refueling, repair of roads, and disposition of empty vehicle columns.

Details are coordinated directly between the commander of the motor transport unit and the commander of the transported unit.

958. Wide roads and motor parks that are not situated on or immediately before slopes are optimal for rapid loading and unloading operations. The essential conditions for rapid loading and unloading include: security against aerial reconnaissance and air attack; short approaches for the units to and from the site; and favorable entry and exit roads for the motor columns. The calculation of the necessary road lengths should be based on 300 to 500 meters for a motor vehicle column at the halt.

Loading or unloading all units at the same time is rarely efficient. Normally, loading and unloading will be conducted at different places and sequenced in time.

If a unit is tightly assembled, or if it will be tightly assembled after unloading, it should be loaded or unloaded at one specially designated place on the line. For loading, the units and the motor columns are brought to the line by sections, one after the other. For unloading, the columns are brought in sequentially. Every group of motor columns or every single column will leave as soon as it is loaded or unloaded. This procedure facilitates air defense measures, and also facilitates the loading and unloading of line handling equipment and the equipping of the loading parties.

959. The loading of a motor column takes about 30 minutes, if sufficient handling equipment is available. Unloading takes 15 minutes, but an untrained loading unit requires more time.

960. A closed, tactically organized column, as described in Paragraph 198, is generally not effective for motor vehicles.

If combat is anticipated shortly after unloading, the sequence of a motor column should be organized in such a way that the units ready for immediate commitment arrive at the unloading point first.

If motor columns that have been loaded at different points are to proceed along the same route from a certain position, their arrival at that position must be carefully sequenced and controlled.

In most cases the movement of larger units will require multiple roads. When allocating the routes to the march columns, all efforts should be made to maintain unit integrity. Generally not more than one reinforced regiment should be assigned to one road.

961. The senior commander should be the first to arrive at the unloading area. The march column commanders and the corresponding motor column commanders will position themselves where messages and orders can reach them easily. All other troop commanders will accompany their units in transit.

962. The execution of a motor march requires special procedures. In certain situations the different motor columns will proceed directly to the day's objective, or to the unloading point; or the total march column might move forward in large bounds. In other situations it may be necessary to require the motor column to halt and report at control points, only proceeding on specific orders.

Within a moving column, the commander of every element and every vehicle must know the route and the objective.

Messages and orders are transmitted within the column by motor cyclists or other messengers.

963. Traffic control is essential, especially when there is the possibility of encountering other units along the route. In such situations, the overall commanders will establish the relative priorities.

Traffic control agencies will place route markers—arrows at the side of the road, for example—at difficult points. During darkness, soldiers must be posted as traffic guides, especially at unsupervised positions.

964. Night marches are frequent requirements. Large-scale movements over long march distances and during short nights often start or end during the day. The deception of enemy aerial reconnaissance may dictate sending all or part of the column in a false direction during daylight. The size of the resulting detour must be taken into consideration.

The loading and unloading of larger units in darkness is difficult and requires special procedures. Processing larger units also takes more time by day.

Driving without lights is a method to confound enemy aerial reconnaissance. On clear nights driving is possible at reduced speeds. In total darkness only low speeds are possible.

The planning factors for night marches are generally the same as for day marches.

965. If enemy action is anticipated during a motor movement, other units should provide screening against ground attacks until unloading has been completed.

The senior command will allocate antiaircraft units to provide air defense for loading and unloading larger units, as well as for threatened points on the line of march.

The effects of enemy aerial reconnaissance and air attack can be reduced by splitting up a motor movement. Unit air defense requirements are the same as for foot marches. On the air attack alarm (Paragraph 241), the weapons designated for defense against low-level attack will be ordered to engage, while the motor column continues the march.

966. Required longer rest halts are designated before the start of the march (Paragraph 957). During each rest halt, technical and tactical adjustments are made as necessary.

Commanders may order as needed short halts that will not disrupt the total movement.

Paragraphs 254 and 304 cover the requirements for rest halts. The route of mach must be kept clear, local conditions permitting.

967. During a motor movement, bivouacs are generally established along the route of march. Motor column troops quarter together with the transported units. The vehicles generally remain loaded.

968. Fuel and equipment supply follow the general procedures outlined in Chapter XXIII. Elements of the fuel and lubricant supply columns may be incorporated into the march column; elements may be sent forward to designated resupply points; or they may bring up the rear.

Equipment repair is accomplished by motor vehicle repair shop elements. Such elements will either precede the column and establish repair points along the routes, or be positioned in the unloading area. They also may provide coverage in the loading area. Elements also should be incorporated into the march columns to tow damaged vehicles. Depending on the road network and available repair shops, the damaged vehicles will be taken to specifically designated points.

969. Rations are prepared in field kitchens during the march and distributed during rest halts.

Units generally carry their rations for the march. In addition to the ration supply train, all vehicles of a motorized unit will be used for this purpose.

Rations planning must recognize the fact that immediately after unloading, units may not have immediate access to the horse-drawn ration supply train.

The movement of larger units by motor vehicle over greater distances requires special procedures for ration supplies.

970. During a motor movement, the transported units' medical officers provide medical services, including to the transportation unit.

971. Horse-drawn elements moving by rail or road, and assigned to units being transported by motor vehicle, will be sent forward in advance or will follow. Since such units are only of limited use until they are reunited with their horse-drawn elements, some motor vehicles should be left with them until their own vehicles come up. The headquarters ordering the motor movement determines the number of motor vehicles to be left.

972. The transmission of orders and messages between units transported by motor vehicle and their horse-drawn elements must be maintained continuously.

XXIII

LOGISTICAL SUPPORT IN THE AREA OF OPERATIONS

973. In order to maintain combat readiness, units must be supplied continuously with all their requirements. They must be relieved of concerns that could affect their operational efficiency.

974. Supplies, well timed and in sufficient quantity, are one of the most important requirements for the success of military operations. The importance but also the difficulties of supply operations will grow with the size of the units to be supplied and with the escalating tension of the combat situation. Because of varied and often quickly changing requirements, supply forecasting must be managed with strong and coherent leadership.

The supply requirements peculiar to cavalry are covered in Paragraph 703; armored units and light units are covered in Paragraph 750.

975. The chief of staff is responsible for the management of logistics in accordance with the commander's intent. At the army level he is assisted by a deputy chief of staff for logistics; at the corps level by a quartermaster general staff officer. The division staff also has a general staff officer in charge of logistics. At the various levels of command, the logistics general staff officer must understand the commander's intent and the current situation. He is responsible for issuing timely orders to the officers and officials (*Beamten*)* who operate the various supply systems.

At the lower echelons, logistics are managed in a similar manner. Supply officers manage the supply services in accordance with the orders of the unit commanders. A paymaster (*Zahlmeister*)† may be assigned in support. The situation will dictate whether specialized supply management elements, such as ammunition resupply, will be attached on a temporary or permanent basis.

---

*German staffs generally included civilian military officials (*Wehrmachtbeamten*) who wore uniforms and held nominal rank. In some cases, they were classified as combatants.

†Paymasters were civilian officials who generally held the nominal rank of 2nd lieutenant. They were responsible for pay and allowances, rations and messing, clothing accounts, and unit finances.

All commanders must ensure that no more manpower than is absolutely necessary is committed to the supply services.

976. Supply matériel are assembled and prepared for shipment in munitions plants, ration depots, and ordnance offices in home territory.

From there, supplies are moved by ammunition, ration, or other trains, or as individual shipments. In most cases the public rail system is used. The shipments go to forwarding stations where they are redistributed or reorganized into individual shipments as necessary. Supplies also may be transported directly to supply unloading stations, where the matériel is taken over by the army, corps, or division.

Shipments from home territory also can be made by motor columns directly to depots, dumps, or distribution points.

Shipment by water is only used for large quantities of mass consumption supplies or for the evacuation of the sick and wounded and the return of empty containers.

977. The army headquarters establishes supply unloading stations (*Ausladebahnhöfe für Nachschub*). The army transportation officer also will establish unloading stations based on requests from the corps or divisions. The threat of enemy air operations will dictate the maximum efforts to establish a supply unloading station for every division. In many situations, however, the corps or multiple divisions will have to use a single unloading station.

Unloading stations should be situated as close behind the front lines as the rail net and the situation allow. Because of traffic congestion and enemy air threat, stocks of supplies and groupings of vehicles around the stations should be avoided.

978. The army deposits the bulk of the supplies in depots and dumps. It also may keep part of the supplies mobile in supply trains and columns.

When the distance between the unloading station and the front line becomes too great, the army headquarters will establish branch depots (*Zweiglager*) and dumps farther forward, or it will move the supplies to breakdown or distribution points. At the breakdown points established by the army, the supplies are transferred to corps or division supply columns for shipment to the units at the distribution points (*Ausgabebestellen*).

The corps and the division either keep the supplies mobile in their supply columns or issue them directly to the units. Stocks of supplies are maintained only in rare situations.

979. The army headquarters controls the rear services of all the supply branches as well the security and military police forces.

980. The army can augment the corps with rear services on a temporary basis to supply the corps' subordinate divisions (Paragraph 23).

A cavalry corps has sufficient supply columns to carry the ammunition and rations provisions for its divisions. The cavalry corps also controls a number of motorized ambulance platoons; veterinary motorized ambulance columns; a fuel and lubricant supply column; and a motor maintenance shop platoon.

981. Infantry and cavalry divisions have the rear services necessary to supply their units. When the transportation assets prove insufficient, the army provides the primary augmentation.*

The divisional supply columns generally carry part of the initial issue of ammunition and one day's rations. These supplies cover the gap between the supply unloading station, the army's rear installations (depots, dumps, breakdown points), and the divisional distribution points.

982. The contents of the divisional supply columns should be stored at the distribution points in such a way that units can be resupplied quickly and easily. The loading criteria for supply columns are very different than those for light columns and ration supply trains. Only in exceptional situations, therefore, will supplies be transferred from supply columns to light columns and ration supply trains by transloading from vehicle to vehicle.

983. The light columns (*leichten Kolonnen*)† carry ammunition, equipment, and other combat matériel for their units. The artillery will draw men and horses from the light columns to replace any initial combat losses.

984. On the march, the light columns are normally incorporated into the same march column as their supported unit. The unit commander may deviate from this practice in certain situations. The incorporation of the light columns and their quartering is the responsibility of the commander in charge of the march. The position of the light columns in the march column is covered in Paragraphs 288 and 289.

Under march conditions the column commander will designate the position of the light artillery (based on the advice of its commander), the advance of the light columns, and the preliminary march objectives. If the march conditions change, new positions for the light artillery will be designated by the artillery commander, with the approval of the unit commander. The light columns will also receive their orders from him. Subordinate commanders must immediately establish contact with their light columns. They determine the points for the distribution of ammunition and other

---

*The trains of an infantry division consisted of eight truck columns, each with ten 5-ton trucks. Columns number 7 and 8 usually carried ammunition. [*Wedemeyer Report*, p. 40]

†Infantry light columns (one per infantry regiment) had 39 wagons with a carrying capacity of 19 tons. Both signal and engineer light columns (one per battalion) had ten 1.5 ton trucks. [*Wedemeyer Report*, p. 41]

combat supplies based in the situation, the terrain, and the closeness of the combat trains. These factors also determine the further position and actions of the light columns.

985. Trains consist of combat trains (*Gefechtstross*), ration supply trains (*Verpflegungstross*), and baggage trains (*Gepäckstross*).*

Officers and senior noncommissioned officers must limit any additions to the trains to absolute necessities and ensure that the road space of the combat unit does not increase.

With command approval, a train may be enlarged temporarily by increasing the number of supply vehicles. An increase also may be made by adding vehicles to transport barrage or personnel unable to march. The unit commander making such a decision on his own initiative must report his action to his higher headquarters.

986. The combat train carries essential supplies, including arms and ammunition, spare parts, tools for small repairs, medical and veterinary equipment, daily rations, and emergency rations for the field kitchens. Its detailed composition and loading are based on the table of organization and the table of equipment.

The combat train remains continuously with its unit, led by a noncommissioned officer who is designated by the unit commander.

987. The position of a combat train in a march column is covered in Paragraph 290.

On the battlefield the combat train is kept under cover and as close as possible to the combat units. It can be divided in several sections or combined under a single leader, and positioned with the combat vehicles, limbers, ammunition sections, and other vehicles.

988. The ration supply train of nonmotorized units consists of both horse-drawn and motor vehicles. The horse-drawn vehicles of the ration supply train are grouped as ration supply train No. 1. The motor vehicles are grouped as ration supply train No. 2.

Ration supply trains No. 1 and No. 2 each carry ration allocations for one day.

Ration supply train No. 1 usually is the link between the field kitchens and ration supply train No. 2, which generally receives the rations from the ration distribution point.

A motorized unit's ration supply train consists of motor vehicles that

---

*At the company level, the combat trains consisted of three wagons (one for each platoon) and the field kitchen. The combat trains primarily hauled ammunition. The company baggage trains consisted of one wagon. In nonmotorized units, company ration supply trains consisted of one wagon per company, and one truck for every two companies. [*Wedemeyer Report*, p. 41]

carry ration allocations for two days. The motor vehicles are not organized as ration supply trains No. 1 and No. 2.

989. If the march is organized in elements of a single arm (Paragraph 278), ration supply train No. 1 will normally follow the combat train of its unit. In all other situations it will follow the combat units in the ordered march sequence, and will maintain the required distance. This also applies during the march of a division on multiple routes. During a withdrawal, ration supply train No. 1 will take precedence and march to the flank on the side away from the enemy.

Cavalry units may elect to add to their train supply vehicles carrying a part of the daily rations for the horses.

The ration supply train of a motorized unit will march with its unit. When moving to or from ration loading points, it may be combined with another unit's ration supply train No. 2.

990. Ration supply train No. 2, after loading at a distribution point, will be taken by its commander to the positions designated by the division. From there, the rations will be drawn by the units and by the commanders of the billeting groups. Only the ration supply train commander can authorize the early withdrawal of vehicles.

The vehicles of ration supply train No. 2 will advance as far as their units, if the situation and road conditions permit. Otherwise, they transfer the rations to the vehicles of ration supply train No. 1 at points designated by the unit commanders.

991. The vehicles of ration supply train No. 1 normally remain with their units. Once the vehicles of ration supply train No. 2 have issued the rations to their units, they remain in place, situation permitting, until those units move forward. They also can return to the rear for another issue. In all other situations, the division determines the quartering of ration supply trains No. 1 and No. 2.

The consolidation of the ration supply train vehicles remaining with the units must be planned and managed carefully. The ration supply trains must not delay or restrict the movement of the units. The ration supply train vehicles normally consolidate only after their units move forward.

992. The baggage train, which usually is motorized, transports baggage, clothing, and other equipment not used in combat.

If the march is organized in elements of a single arm (Paragraph 278), the commander of the entire column may allow the baggage trains to move with the units. Otherwise, they will follow the combat units at an appropriate distance, in the designated sequence, and organized by sections that correspond to the march columns. The march commander designates the sequence of the sections.

Units must have access to their baggage trains as often as possible. If the baggage train does not march with its unit, it should be positioned at designated points for access by the units.

The baggage train normally assembles only after the departure of the unit. It then proceeds in the designated direction of the march.

993. The ration supply and baggage trains of mounted and motorized units in the front lines must not restrict the movements of their own or follow-on units. If security or other factors require, the trains will be left in whole or part with the main body, to follow later. The overall commander will make the necessary determinations.

Ammunition Resupply

994. Commanders of all ranks must ensure economy of ammunition and manage its timely resupply.

All measures must be taken to resupply combat units with the ammunition required to maintain their volume of fire. Victory or defeat depends on these efforts.

995. Portions of the division's basic load of ammunition are carried by each man, combat vehicle, and limber. The light columns carry another portion. The remainder is held under the control of the division commander in the divisional supply columns.

During combat, ammunition resupply initially takes place from the combat vehicles. They replace their basic loads from the light columns, which in turn draw from the ammunition distribution points.

996. The ammunition distribution points are stocked from the supply columns. One division generally requires multiple ammunition distribution points. They should be established not too far to the rear, but beyond the range of enemy artillery fire. They must be camouflaged and organized and positioned along solid roads to permit as many vehicles as possible to load simultaneously. The ammunition distribution points should be stocked with the ammunition for the types of weapons in that sector of the area of operations. Otherwise they should be stocked with all possible types of ammunition, to prevent forcing the light columns to make detours and cross the battlefield.

High explosive,* smoke, and chemical ammunition must be stored separately. Paragraphs 1049, 1056, and 1057 contain additional information.

---

*Prior to World War I, high explosive and shrapnel were separate types of ammunition. Shrapnel rounds exploded in flight, projecting forward hundreds of steel balls. High explosive rounds produced a blast effect, but no significant fragmentation effect. By the end of World War I, all sides had perfected the chemical and metallurgical formulas necessary for an artillery round with both significant blast and fragmentation effects. From that point on, shrapnel ammunition disappeared. During World War II the Allies called the new type of round high explosive. The Germans called it *Splitter*—literally, fragmentation. Essentially, it was the same round.

The army normally directly resupplies the ammunition for the air defense units. As the situation requires, antiaircraft ammunition may be stocked in the divisional distribution points.

997. The division determines the timing, location, and scale of ammunition distribution.

998. Regular and reliable inventory reports submitted by the units form the basis for the computation of ammunition requirements. Ammunition resupply is centrally managed at division headquarters. If necessary, specially assigned officers can assist in the management of this function at the lower echelons.

999. Shell casings, misfired ammunition, and dunnage must be turned in when drawing new ammunition.

Ammunition must be removed from dead and wounded soldiers. The wounded will, however, keep a few rounds for self-defense.

Ration Supply

1000. Every commander is responsible for the continuous and adequate ration supply of his unit. The administrative officials assigned to command headquarters must plan all necessary measures well in advance. In the event of ration supply problems, units must be supplied at a minimum with their bread ration.

1001. Ration supply sources within the area of operations must be exploited to the maximum extent possible. Rations can be acquired through purchases and requisitions with local shopkeepers. Shortfalls are made up from transported supplies or from stocks outside the area of operations.

The senior headquarters normally manages ration procurement.

1002. Subsistence payments in field quarters will be available only on a limited basis and only for senior organizations.

1003. Administrative officials normally make the ration purchases. The senior headquarters will determine whether and to what extent unit ration supply officers will be allowed to make purchases in occupied areas. The senior headquarters also establishes price limits and methods of payment.

1004. The confiscation of supplies in home territory is authorized only in accordance with existing law, and only insofar as the requirements cannot be met otherwise.

In allied countries, specially negotiated treaties establish the procedures.

1005. Requisitioning is the best way to procure subsistence supplies in enemy territory. Although primarily managed by the administrative officials of the senior headquarters, units also may requisition their immediate requirements in their own areas.

Requisitions normally are made by the authority of an officer. There are exceptions, however, such as reconnaissance patrols. All efforts should be made to obtain the cooperation of the local authorities or leading inhabitants. A requisition normally must be authorized by a troop commander.* Only in emergency situations can a requisition be authorized on the order of a subordinate commander, who must command at least at the battalion level. In such a case, the place and time of the requisition, the type and quantity of the requisitioned rations, and the method of payment must be reported in writing to the troop commander.

In all cases, the type and quantity of the rations and the area in which the requisition was made must be recorded in writing.

Administrative officials make requisitions to establish and maintain well-balanced stocks in the theater of war.

1006. Stocks of rations that have been located and seized make units less dependent on the resupply system. Such stocks located to the front or flanks of larger units can be especially valuable for cavalry and motorized units. Stocks exceeding their own requirements must be reported by all units to their higher headquarters. Units may be required to guard seized stocks until they can be turned over to the administrative authorities.

1007. Stocks of rations may be destroyed only on order of the senior headquarters. During a withdrawal, all leaders must prevent stocks from falling into enemy hands.

1008. In the field, every man and horse is provided with a field ration, the composition of which is specified in the ration standards.

1009. The field kitchen carries the field ration. Soldiers carry their bread ration in their bread bags. The oats for horse field rations are carried by the horse or on vehicles. The ration supply vehicles carry the food stock for current consumption, generally one to two portions (*Portionen*)† and rations (*Rationen*).†† Rough fodder normally is procured locally.

The mount horses of the divisional reconnaissance battalion and the cavalry units carry 1/3 of a ration for current consumption, which must be replaced immediately upon use.

1010. Units carry two iron rations (*eiserne Portion*)§ per soldier as a permanent ration stock. The soldiers carry one shortened ration (biscuits

---

*See Paragraph 26 for the definition of a troop commander.
†Human rations.
††Animal rations.
§An iron ration consisted of biscuits (250 grams), cold meat (200 grams), preserved vegetables (150 grams), coffee (25 grams), and salt (25 grams).

and canned meat) in their rucksacks or saddlebags, and the field kitchen carries one complete ration (biscuits, canned meat, canned vegetables, coffee, and salt). For every horse, except for the mount horses of the divisional reconnaissance battalion and the cavalry units, an emergency ration is carried by the horse or in vehicles.

The iron rations and portions may be consumed only on the explicit order of a commander down to battalion level. In emergency situations, independent commanders of smaller units are authorized to give such an order. Consumed iron rations and portions must be replaced as soon as possible.

1011. The procurement and transportation of food for dogs and carrier pigeons requires special management.

1012. If units cannot replace the rations taken from the supply vehicles through purchase or requisitions, they will be resupplied at the ration distribution points. Issue normally takes place by regiment and battalion. Perishable supplies, especially fresh meat, must be distributed to the field kitchens on the first day of issue.

Mess officers generally manage the further breakdown of rations to the companies.

1013. Bakery companies, using mobile ovens or civilian ovens in the area of operations, supply the units with bread. Maximum efficiency requires leaving a bakery company in one position for as long as possible. The bakery company normally brings the bread to the ration distribution points.

1014. The butchery platoon processes animals procured from the countryside, or forwarded by cattle trains. If possible, the butchering should be done in slaughterhouses in the area of operations to ensure the delivery of fresh meat to the ration distribution points. In exceptional situations, units may be required to do their own slaughtering.

If freshly slaughtered meat must be cooked before it cools, adequate cutting and pounding will render it edible.

Fatally wounded or dead horses may be used as rations, but they must be butchered as soon as possible.

1015. Stationery and other comfort items are supplied as required from the ration distribution points and sold to the troops.

Uniform and Equipment Replacement

1016. The advanced ration supply depots maintain a laundry and small quantities of the most important uniform and field gear items, mainly jackets, trousers, and boots. These items are issued to units at the request of the division during ration distributions. Immediate requirements are reported through the chain of command, and the items are sent directly to the units from home territory by the military clothing offices.

Medical Service

1017. The medical service (*Sanitätsdienst*) is responsible for health care and medical treatment, the quartering and evacuation of the sick and wounded; and the medical supply system.

1018. The medical officer is the adviser to the commander for all medical and health issues. The division surgeon simultaneously is the unit commander of the division's medical units. He makes recommendations for their deployment.

1019. On the march and in field quarters, the medical company or the divisional surgical hospital (*Feldlazarett der Division*) will establish one or more easy-to-reach collecting stations (*Krankensammelpunkte*), to which units evacuate the sick and wounded. When necessary, motor ambulances support the collecting stations.

As soon as the sick and wounded have been treated, the collecting station personnel must rejoin their own medical unit or be transferred to other medical service stations.

1020. During field quartering of longer duration, the medical service will be organized in a manner similar to that in a garrison. Units will establish field dispensaries and major units will establish field infirmaries. Both may operate in conjunction with local hospitals. The medical units provide the personnel and the equipment for these installations.

When movement resumes, the field infirmaries will stand down or be transferred to follow-on medical units.

In a bivouac, the medical service is organized in the same way.

1021. In combat, unit medical officers establish aid stations (*Truppenverbandplätze*), usually at the battalion level. Unit litter bearers or auxiliary litter bearers bring the wounded to the aid stations. Often, aid stations develop from smaller aid posts. Closely situated aid stations should be consolidated.

The aid station should be concealed from observation and covered from at least small-arms fire. It should be located as close as possible to the front line and easily reachable. A close water source is essential.

The infantry litter bearers assemble with the medical vehicle when combat is imminent. They drop their packs at the aid station and advance with the stretchers and aid bags. Auxiliary litter bearers are designated by the unit commander and function the same as litter bearers.

1022. Serious attention must be given to preventing a reduction in a unit's combat power under the pretext of taking care of the wounded.

Minor casualties, capable of walking, should go back to the aid station alone. They leave their ammunition in the front line, keeping a few rounds for self-defense. They keep their weapons. Soldiers who are not designated litter bearers will not carry the wounded back without the authorization of an officer. Soldiers who have been ordered to carry the wounded to the rear will return immediately and report to their units.

1023. The clearing station (*Hauptverbandplatz*) provides more extensive medical assistance than the aid stations. It is established on the order of the division commander and positioned by the medical company. In exceptional situations, two clearing stations can be established in a divisional sector. The criteria for the clearing station are the same as for the aid stations. It must be marked with the insignia of the medical service (generally a red cross on a white background). The national flag also may be raised next to the clearing station.

The ambulances of the medical company should advance as far forward as possible to transport the wounded to the clearing stations or to other locations for the evacuation of the wounded.

1024. The medical company may establish a nearby collecting station for walking wounded, to relieve congestion at the aid stations and the clearing station.

1025. In the event of large numbers of wounded, the division surgical hospital should be established close by, but preferably beyond the range of enemy artillery fire. It handles only those cases too serious to survive further transportation.

1026. As the battle progresses and the clearing station and the field hospital move or are transferred to the medical elements of other units, the medical company and the surgical hospital can be brought forward, in whole or by platoons.

1027. During a withdrawal, the sick and wounded who cannot be moved should be put under the care of local civilian doctors. Otherwise, they will be left behind with the necessary medical personnel, under the protection of the Geneva Convention on the Wounded of 27 July 1929.

1028. The motor ambulance platoons evacuate the sick and wounded from the clearing stations to the divisional surgical hospital, or farther to the rear to the collecting stations or to the army hospitals. Columns of empty vehicles also may be used to bring back the wounded and the sick not suffering from contagious diseases, so long as they are not required to make long detours.

1029. The army ambulance battalion establishes collecting stations along railroads, roads, or waterways where a heavy flow of sick and wounded can be anticipated. They remain at the collecting station only until they can be transported on hospital trains, hospital trains for minor cases, hospital ships, or hospital ships for minor cases to base hospitals for either category, or to home territory.

1030. If necessary, hospitals may be established for gas contamination cases or for contagious disease.

1031. After a battle every unit must search the battlefield to collect the wounded and to protect the dead and wounded against plundering and looting by mobs, especially at night. Units also must bury their dead. The senior commander is responsible for assuring the accomplishment of these tasks.

1032. Unit medical equipment is provided from the stocks of the surgical hospital medical company or from the divisional surgeon's medical resupply vehicle. The medical units draw their equipment from the divisional or the army-level surgeon's resupply vehicle or from the army-level medical depot, which also can deploy advanced branch depots as necessary.

Veterinary Service

1033. The veterinary service provides for the health care of military animals; the prevention and treatment of contagious diseases; treatment, care, and evacuation of sick animals; horseshoeing; fodder inspection; livestock and meat inspection; horse knackering and the utilization of animal corpses; and supply of veterinary equipment.

The veterinary officer is the adviser to the unit commander on veterinary service matters. The division veterinary officer is simultaneously the commander of the divisional veterinary troops. He makes recommendations for their deployment.

1034. The unit veterinary officer and his assistants provide primary care for wounded and sick horses.*

Only horses that are ambulatory and fit for service and without contagious disease remain with their units. All others are transferred to the horse hospital. Incurable cases are sold or slaughtered.

1035. On the march and in field quarters, the divisional horse hospital establishes one or several easy-to-reach veterinary collecting points, to which units bring sick and wounded horses that can walk. Those unable to walk are collected by the units and moved on horse transport vehicles.

During combat, units establish veterinary aid stations close to their combat trains. The aid stations should be concealed from observation, covered from fire if possible, and positioned near a road. Access to farms and a source of water are highly desirable. The divisional horse hospital establishes one or multiple veterinary collecting stations, farther back but within easy reach.

---

*[Original Footnote] "The term 'horses' applies to all kinds of working animals in military service."

Veterinary personnel bring the sick and wounded animals back from the veterinary aid stations to the veterinary collecting station, if they cannot be brought back by their units. The sick and wounded horses are transferred from the collecting stations to the divisional horse hospital, positioned farther to the rear, on or close to the main march route.

1036. In order to keep the divisional horse hospitals cleared for action, horses that require more extensive treatment will be brought by veterinary motor ambulances to the army-level horse hospitals, which normally are set up near railroads. If the distance between the divisional and the army-level horse hospitals is too great, the latter can advance one or multiple army-level veterinary collecting stations.

If required, an army-level veterinary hospital can be established as a hospital for contagious diseases.

1037. Horses that are permanently disabled and those whose recovery will take a long time will be transferred by rail from the army-level veterinary hospital to a hospital in home territory.

1038. Remounts are supplied from the divisional remount depot. It is supplied with fit-for-duty horses from the divisional veterinary hospital and horses from the army-level remount depot.

The divisional remount depot generally is established near the veterinary hospital and moves with it.

1039. Requisitioned and captured horses must be inspected immediately by a veterinary officer and then transferred to the veterinary hospital. Because of the threat of contagious disease, they may be used by troops only in critical situations and on the responsibility of the unit commander. They must be kept separate from the other horses in the units.

1040. Army-level mobile test stations conduct animal blood tests.

1041. Veterinary officers draw equipment from the army-level depot, and in critical situations from the divisional veterinary supply vehicle. Branch depots can be advanced to the divisions, and are supplied by the army-level depot.

1042. The veterinary depot supplies horseshoeing equipment, field forges, and smithy coal, if such items cannot be requisitioned or purchased locally.

Motor Maintenance and Supplies

1043. Fuel, lubricants, and tires are the principal requirements for motor vehicle operations. The difficulties of procuring these items dictate economy and strict management.

Captured or found stocks must be reported and fully exploited.

1044. Divisional motorized units and individual motor vehicles carry fuel and lubricants for 750 kilometers, either onboard the vehicle or on trucks in the fuel supply columns.

1045. Unit vehicles and those belonging to headquarters draw their support for fuel, lubricants, and tires from fuel points. The fuel and lubricant supply columns of the motorized units establish the fuel points at appropriate locations.

The fuel points and the fuel supply trucks draw from the fuel and lubricant supply column.

The supply columns fill up at fuelling railheads, where they also draw tires. Supplies from home territory are distributed from army-level combined parks and railheads.

1046. Motor transport equipment is maintained in army-level vehicle parks. Units hold a small stock of spare parts and tools for minor repairs. The division and the army have assigned motor maintenance repair shop platoons. These shops should remain in operation in one position for as long as possible to make maximum use of their capacity. If possible, they should operate in conjunction with existing motor repair shops in the area of operations. Major repairs must be performed at maintenance facilities in home territory, to which motor vehicles are evacuated via the army-level motor park.

Repair and Replacement of Weapons and Equipment

1047. Weapons and equipment are difficult to replace and must be maintained carefully. Weapons and equipment that have been dropped, damaged, or captured should be collected.

Weapons requiring repair must be sent to the rear immediately. Extra weapons and equipment are carried in only small quantities by trains and light columns or stocked in depots. Most weapon and equipment replacements for units, therefore, must come from home territory.

The tables of equipment and the tables of organization establish the types of requisitions.

1048. Unit armorers make minor repairs. The light signal supply column of the divisional signal battalion maintains all the division's communications equipment. With the exception of motor, medical, and veterinary equipment, units turn in equipment requiring major maintenance to the divisional ordnance collecting point. From there, weapons, animal-drawn vehicles, and bicycles are sent to the army-level field workshop. All other equipment is evacuated via the army-level ordnance collecting point, either to depots or back to home territory.

Units are authorized to request replacements only for equipment turned in to the ordnance collecting points.

Supply Battalions and Companies, and Ammunition Administration and Ration Supply Offices

1049. The divisional supply companies and the army-level supply battalions have specialized personnel to load and unload rail trains and supply columns and to man the depots, dumps, and distribution and transloading points. Supply companies also may be committed to clear a battlefield and to set up collecting points for salvaged equipment and captured material. They also can be used for other labor services.

At the army level, ammunition administration offices come under the supply battalion. In the division they are subordinate to the supply commander (*Nachschubführer*). The ammunition administration offices establish ammunition depots and distribution points and manage the stocks.

A senior administrative official (*Intendant*)* oversees the ration supply offices, which manage the ration stocks and the distribution points. The ration supply offices also purchase rations.

The ammunition administration and ration supply offices control inbound supplies and manage existing stocks and the distribution and transloading points. They are assisted in these functions by the commanders of the receiving columns and trains and by mess officers.

The administrative organizations and specialists must be committed in sufficient time to prevent the weakening of the combat units through levies for labor details.

Trains and Rear Services Movements

1050. The commanders of the ration supply trains, baggage trains, and rear services must keep current with the situation in order to accomplish their missions. Subordinate commanders also must remain abreast of the situation, the march route, and the objective, so elements that fall behind can regain contact.

All support commanders must maintain constant contact with their higher headquarters. Priority should be given to maintaining wire connections. Commanders also must ensure their units reach their assigned objectives by the designated time, and are ready to provide support to the combat units. All efforts must be made to supply the combat units at the right time. This requires the maintenance of the most stringent personnel and march discipline.

---

*A civilian official in the administrative services, usually with the nominal rank of colonel.

1051. The trains and rear services can be divided into elements for movement and quartering, if they are not temporarily assigned or deployed elsewhere. The exact composition of an element is a function of the commander's intent, the situation, the load and the means of movement, and the security and quartering of the column. If no one has been designated specifically to command a column element, the senior person assumes command. Special orders will designate the column's checkpoints and the quartering area.

The element commander controls the element's movement and rest halts. Movement along roads wired for communications will facilitate the maintenance of contact with the chief of supply services and the unit commander, and between elements.

If combat is imminent, elements of the ammunition column and the field hospital (if they are horse-drawn) can be combined with a combat train echelon. This train must be kept as close to the battlefield as the situation and the road and cover conditions allow. Ammunition resupply of the light columns from the combat train must be done quickly and in secure conditions. If the situation requires, individual vehicles can be sent forward to the combat units.

1052. The movements of the supply trains, baggage trains, and rear services must be coordinated carefully with each other and with the unit movements, in order to avoid congestion on roads and at intersections.

During a withdrawal, trains and rear services must pull back as far as necessary to avoid interfering with the combat units.

1053. Movement orders for supply trains, baggage trains, and rear services should be planned in such a way that if at all possible, they require no additional security coverage.

In general, a point and a rear point are adequate for independent march columns and rear services. Increased security and reconnaissance screening will be required when the civil population is hostile, or if rapid and mobile enemy threats are anticipated. In a particularly unsecure situation, special escorts might be necessary. Trains and rear services are only lightly armed and are not capable of serious fighting.

1054. The smooth flow of all movements requires the careful control of those roads with heavy traffic. Choke points and built-up areas, particularly with narrow streets, require extra control measures. The situation may require the assignment of traffic control officers and workmen to repair roads and traffic signal equipment. Military police can be attached to the traffic control officers.

1055. Traffic at distribution points must be controlled in such a way that arriving and departing vehicles use separate routes. Only the exact number of vehicles that can load and unload simultaneously should be at the distribution point at any given time. Inbound columns and supply trains should know this number in advance. Waiting vehicles must be able to halt under cover, close to the distribution point and off the road. Traffic in transit must not be blocked.

1056. Distribution points should not be established at crossroads. If they are within the range of enemy fire, they should not be located at points easily identified on a map that will make them easy targets for enemy artillery.

1057. Distribution points, depots, dumps, railway stations where supplies unload, and other important rear service installations should be covered by air defense units and the air warning service, especially during the hours of heaviest traffic. This, of course, is dependent on the situation and the forces available. Critical rear service installations also must be camouflaged against enemy aerial reconnaissance.

Military Police Services

1058. Area headquarters and guard units are attached to the army. Military police (*Feldgendarmerie*) units are attached to divisional and higher headquarters. Military police may be reinforced by troops from combat units only in the most exceptional situations.

1059. Guard troops secure depots, dumps, and other such installations. They also assume custody of prisoners to transfer them out of the combat area.

Guard troops will not be used for screening missions against the enemy.

1060. Area headquarters are established at key points—such as road junctions—outside the area of operations of the combat units. The area headquarters provide local traffic control and provide security in their area and for the quartering of march units in transit. Frequently, they also establish information centers and collecting points for stragglers and prisoners. Guard troops and military policemen may be attached to the area headquarters to support these functions.

1061. Military police units operate the police service in the rear area of the army. In certain situations they also may be used to augment the guard and security services. The army commander also may attach a few military policemen to his staff.

Military police missions include the maintenance of order and traffic control at distribution points, depots, dumps, rail stations, and along routes. They also are responsible for collecting and forwarding stragglers; the prevention of looting and unauthorized requisitions; the supervision of the civilian population, as well as their protection against atrocities; and the enforcement of police measures to control contagious diseases.

1062. Military policemen in uniform and wearing on their left arm the green brassard marked "Military Police" while on duty must be considered military guards. When off duty, they exercise only those privileges due their rank.

Military policemen must be circumspect in their dealings with officers and officials holding officer rank. Infractions of regulations and military police instructions must be pointed out. If necessary, the military policeman will request the name and unit of the concerned officer, in order to file a complaint against him.

Military policemen are not authorized to take action against combined troop detachments. They report any problems with such units to their own commander.

1063. All members of the Army must support the military police when requested.

1064. With the exception of officers in the military police chain of command and senior commanders to whom the military police may be attached, only field grade officers and above are authorized to reprimand military policemen who have committed irregularities.

Military policemen on duty can be arrested only on the order of their own superiors or any general officer.

LIST OF ORIGINAL ANNEXES

ANNEX 8:
GUIDELINES FOR WRITTEN COMMUNICATIONS, COMBAT REPORTS, AND WAR DIARIES

Written Communications

1 Keep written communications as simple as possible.

2. Check written communications repeatedly. Read back any message being written down by dictation, in order to avoid misunderstandings and errors.

3. Always check which command posts are to receive an order, report, or excerpt. Multiple orders or reports sent to the same recipient should be numbered.

4. Directions like right, left, in front of, behind, this side of, beyond, above, and beneath, should be used with caution. If there is any possibility of confusion, they should be replaced with azimuth bearings.

Indications like right and left flank or wing and flank security are determined by their position with reference to the enemy. March columns and detached units should be named after their commander, unless a simple name based on an order of battle symbol is more suitable. The front and rear of march columns are designated based on the direction of march.

5. The front-to-rear space between columns is called distance (*Abstand*), and the lateral space between units is called interval (*Zwischenraum*).

An echeloned unit has both distance and interval. The forward spacing is measured from the head of the column, and the rearward spacing is measured from the rear of the column to the next following echelon.

6. Abbreviate day, month, and year either as 20.9.33 or as 20.Sept.33.

In order to avoid doubt, a night should be indicated by noting both days separated by a forward slash; [Night 20./21.6 or 20./21.June].

Indicate time in hours and minutes, using the following formats.

Handwritten and printed; [9^{05} Hours or 18^{00} Hours]

Typed; [9,05 Hours or 18,00 Hours]

Teletype in four-digit numbers without adding hours; [0905 or 1800]

Indicate midnight as 24 or 0^{00} Hours, depending on whether the duty period starts or ends at that point in time; [15. May 24 Hours or 16.5.0^{00} Hours].

Depending on the situation, terms like yesterday, today, and tomorrow require clarification.

7. Place names must be written in the Latin alphabet* and copied from the map with clarity and accuracy. If the same name appears more than once in the same region, include additional information to avoid any doubt; [Neuhof 3km east of Öls]. The same notation should be used for places that are difficult to find on the map. Places with double names or suffixes should be marked with their full names; [Ottstedt a. Berge]. The position of a place where the name is unknown must be indicated by special notation to eliminate any possibility of misunderstanding; [Group of houses on the east edge of the woods between Siegsdorf and Holzen]. Transliterate the pronunciation of a foreign place name, noting it behind the original; [Plsn (Pilsen), Breszeczany (Bjechany)].

8. Roads normally are named after the two places at either end; [Road Hohentann–Barnau]. Roads, junctions, crossroads, and exits must be identified carefully. In most cases they should not be indicated with azimuth bearings.

9. The identification of a point by its elevation always requires an additional designator; [Point 328, 2.5 km west of Giersdorf].

10. Indicate lines such as combat sectors and boundaries by at least two points; [Church Jähnsdorf–windmill 1 km northwest of Dahlewitz]. It may be necessary to insert "including" or "excluding." Generally, a schematic drawing on a map is better than a complicated description.

11. Designate unit positions and terrain sectors and areas in sequence from the friendly right or from the enemy's left in a counterclockwise direction.

12. Places and other points frequently can be identified more easily by map grid references, but only if the recipient is on the same grid. This method should be used if the enemy has the capability to intercept communications.

13. Orders indicating terrain references generally should include map references too, even if the recipient does not have such a map. Likewise, any designations that can only be understood by use of a map reference

---

*Written or printed in the Latin alphabet as opposed to the Old German, or *Fraktur* alphabet. *Truppenführung* was printed in *Fraktur*. Contrary to popular belief, rather than encourage the use of *Fraktur*, the Third Reich abandoned its use in printed German in 1940.

must be restricted to cases where the recipient is likely to have the same map. Always note the map reference number as well.[*]

14. Abbreviations of headquarters and unit names must comply with the correspondence and communications regulations.

15. Write all correspondence with sufficient clarity so that it can be read in poor light conditions. Do not use writing media that can be smudged by rain or snow.

16. Prior to filing documents written in pencil, the recipient must coat the documents with some sort of protective solution, such as milk or diluted rubber solution.[†]

17. The following guidelines apply to the use of the standard message forms:[††]

The Originating Post block indicates the headquarters, the division, or the current mission of the unit. Do not note the name of the individual originating the report; [2.K.D.;[§] Picket Detail Schulze 9./I.R.8;[¶] Reconnaissance Patrol 2./R.R.8[#] above Gunthersleben at Ohrdruf; Observation Post Book-B].

Keep the address brief; [To I.R.10;[‖] To the Advance Guard Commander].

The Signature block should contain the clearly written name of the sender. Indicate the point of origin and the time of dispatch on the envelope. The recipient acknowledges receipt on the envelope.

The narrow strip on the side of the form is used for punching or gluing and should not be written upon on either side.

The envelope may be sealed only if the message is confidential or of a personal nature. In the latter case the notation "Personal" must be made.

Message forms should be printed on firm paper, allowing one carbon copy.

---

[*]In the late 1930s the German Army had three basic types of maps. The 1:25,000 map was used almost exclusively by the artillery. It was the most detailed and accurate. Terrain elevations were indicated by contour lines. The 1:100,000 was the primary tactical map. Both of these maps were issued in black and white. The 1:300,000 was the primary operational map. It was printed in six colors. [*Hartness Report*, pp. 13–14]

[†]Anyone who has ever worked with World War I or early World War II documents in the German Military Archives (*Bundesarchiv/Militärarchiv*) fully appreciates the value of this procedure.

[††]The original manual reproduced examples of two standard forms. One was in C6 format (114x162mm), the other in A5 format (148x210mm).

[§]2nd Cavalry Division.

[¶]9th Company, 8th Infantry Regiment.

[#]2nd Squadron, 8th Cavalry Regiment (*Reiterregiment*).

[‖]10th Infantry Regiment.

Senior headquarters and staffs are not required to use the standard message form. They generally use notepads and carbon copies.

Combat Reports[*]

The start of a combat report (*Gefechtsbericht*) indicates the positions on the battlefield and the unit deployments, followed by the strength of individual units and the overall state of the command.

The description of the action must include accurate times, the opening situation, the orders issued, decisions with a short description of the reasons, movements before and after the action, and the situation at the end of the battle. Summarize the main influences on the course of the action.

If possible, record verbatim the key orders issued in writing or by wire. Note the lesser important and verbal orders, indicating the time and place of transmission or receipt.

Document sent or received messages and other information the same way as orders.

Note precise information on the method and means of order and message transmission.

All orders and messages attached to a combat report should be attached on separate sheets in chronological order, and in such a way that they can be unfolded to the right for reading.[†]

Supplement a combat report with indicators of future intent; evaluations of the enemy's actions and his future intent; information on enemy units and their losses; friendly losses of troops, horses, weapons, and equipment; friendly ammunition consumption; an inventory of captured materiel; and information on the battlefield and the weather. Attached marked-up maps, schematics, and simple terrain sketches all contribute to clarity.

Conclude a combat report with the author's signature, rank, and unit.

Combat reports for minor actions can be recorded on a standard message form.

War Diaries

A war diary (*Kriegstagebuch*) is a primary record of the entire range of a unit's actions, either in the field, during frontier defense, or in situations of civil unrest. In conjunction with combat reports, war diaries are the basic

---

[*]In modern parlance these would be called After Action Reports.

[†]This is another practice greatly appreciated by historians working in the archives.

documents for conducting after-action analyses. They also form the core of the historical archives.*

All headquarters and units down to battalion level (including cavalry units) maintain war diaries. Smaller units maintain war diaries when their actions are not included in the war diary of the next-higher echelon. In case of doubt, the next-higher commander makes the decision.

An appropriate officer is assigned to maintain the war diary.† The daily entries must contain accurate time notations. There is no standard format for recording events.

The commander confirms on a monthly basis the completeness and accuracy of the entries.

Every war diary must begin with a statement of its purpose and maintenance.

---

*To a greater extent than most armies, the German Army was especially disciplined and conscientious in maintaining thorough and accurate war diaries. After World War I they became the primary sources for the analyses that preceded the von Seeckt reforms of the 1920s. Historians today consider those war diaries that have survived as extremely valuable sources.

†At corps and below, the operations section (Ia) generally maintained the war diary. At army level and above, many of the principal staff sections maintained their own war diaries, with the operations section maintaining the overall war diary.

ANNEX 9: GUIDELINES FOR SCHEMATICS, SKETCH MAPS, PANORAMIC SKETCHES, AND SITUATION MAPS

The primary requirements for any military drawing are clarity, legibility even in low light, and clear emphasis on the key features.

Schematics*

Schematics clarify written descriptions and even can replace complicated written descriptions.

If time is short, use a few pencil lines to depict the terrain and indicate friendly units. In most cases such schematics are drawn by eye. Key distances and measurements, such as the width of a waterway at a certain point, should be indicated in figures. Entering such information directly on the drawing eliminates the need for detailed descriptions.

If sufficient time is available and if the basic measurements can be transferred from the map, the illustrator indicates the terrain's surface conditions and the key lines of direction, aiming beyond the edge of the drawing sheet. Estimate distances, or if necessary, measure them by pacing, riding, or driving. Note elevations. The form of the terrain can be indicated with contour lines, hill edge-lines, or shading.

Sketch Maps

Sketch maps complement the main map. They are based on reconnaissance information or are used as a rough draft for terrain organization.

Sketch maps should closely resemble the main map. If necessary they should be supplemented with an overview sketch.

---

*In current NATO practice, most operations orders include a schematic drawing of the scheme of maneuver for each phase of an operation. U.S. soldiers sometimes call this schematic, "the cartoon."

Sketch maps usually have a 1:25,000 scale. Use the 1:12,500 scale for key details, and 1:50,000 or even smaller for larger terrain sections. Always indicate the scale on a sketch map.

Orient all sketch maps to north.

Define specific combat situations by plotting units or through special drawings and text notes. Certain situations may require attached foldouts or an accompanying terrain map.

Begin a sketch map with the transfer of the grid from the main map, enlarged as necessary. Enter the road network first, followed by waterways, place names, and open areas and woods. These entries use the same symbols as in the main map. Arrows indicate the flow direction of rivers. Indicate the origins or end points of railways and routes as [From (to) A ... ... x km].

The primary drawing indicates the shape of the terrain. Enter the elevation lines first, followed by the hill and contour lines. Shading the slopes will enhance the visual conception of the terrain. Light, medium, and heavy shading indicates the terrain's suitability for driving, walking, or climbing.

Plot friendly and enemy positions last, in different colors and identified with abbreviations.

The sketch map should have a legend that explains any abbreviations and, if necessary, indicates the positions of units. The legend also should include all other necessary information, and especially any information on the nature of the terrain not indicated on the sketch map proper.

The illustrator of the sketch map notes his name, rank, and unit in the bottom right corner.

Map extracts of the same scale can substitute for sketch maps.

Panoramic Sketches

Panoramic sketches depict the terrain from the perspective of the illustrator and are especially useful for outposts and observers.

Begin a panoramic sketch on a sheet of paper with a profile of the observed terrain. Then enter the key points and lines of the landscape with soft, dark pencil lines. Mark the background with soft, light pencil lines, and the foreground with stronger lines. Enter place names above or below the picture, and indicate and explain unit positions. A panoramic sketch must note the position of the illustrator and his azimuth of observation.

Situation Maps

A situation map depicts the positions of friendly or enemy units, or both. It also can be used to indicate the positions of one or more types of arms, or only the base and rear service positions at the designated point in time.

The method of drawing, including different colors, shading, solid and broken lines, or light and heavy lines, can be used to distinguish different situations at different times. As necessary, add notes to clarify abbreviations, unit designations, and other symbols.

APPENDIX A: GERMAN INFANTRY DIVISION, 1937–1938

By the late 1930s the German infantry division was a modern combined arms organization. Based on their World War I experience, the Germans eliminated the brigade as a command echelon and adopted the triangular organization. The following structure was reported by Captain Albert C. Wedemeyer, who attended the *Kriegsakademie* as an American exchange officer from 1936 to 1938. [*Wedemeyer Report*, pp. 35–40]

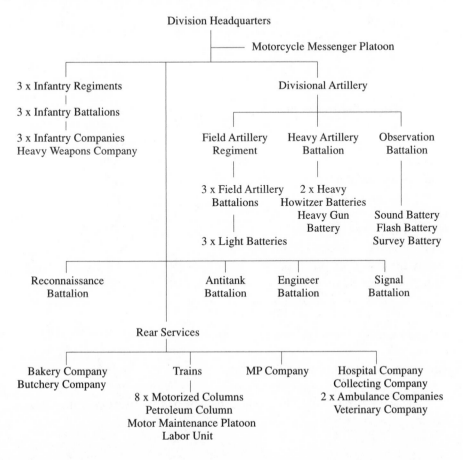

Division Headquarters

Motorcycle Messenger Platoon

3 x Infantry Regiments
3 x Infantry Battalions
3 x Infantry Companies
Heavy Weapons Company

Divisional Artillery

Field Artillery Regiment
Heavy Artillery Battalion
Observation Battalion

3 x Field Artillery Battalions
3 x Light Batteries

2 x Heavy Howitzer Batteries
Heavy Gun Battery

Sound Battery
Flash Battery
Survey Battery

Reconnaissance Battalion
Antitank Battalion
Engineer Battalion
Signal Battalion

Rear Services

Bakery Company
Butchery Company

Trains
8 x Motorized Columns
Petroleum Column
Motor Maintenance Platoon
Labor Unit

MP Company

Hospital Company
Collecting Company
2 x Ambulance Companies
Veterinary Company

Infantry Division Strength

Element	Men	Horses
Division Headquarters	207	10
Infantry Regiment (x 3)	3,051	657
Artillery Headquarters	38	19
Light Howitzer Regiment	2,362	1,163
Heavy Battalion	899	571
Observation Battalion	619	Motorized
Reconnaissance Battalion	587	316
Antitank Battalion	618	Motorized
Signal Battalion	441	58
Engineer Battalion	883	52
Combat Strength	15,701	4,160
Rear Services and Supply	1,562	305
Total Strength	17,263	4,465

Infantry Division Armament

Rifles	13,500
Pistols	3,000
Light Machine Guns	355
Heavy Machine Guns	133
Light Mortars (50mm)	37
Heavy Mortars (81mm)	54
Light Infantry Cannon (75mm)	20
Heavy Infantry Cannon (150mm)	6
Antitank Guns (37mm)	75
Light Artillery Howitzers (105mm)	36
Heavy Artillery Howitzers (150mm)	8
Artillery Guns (105mm)	4
Antiaircraft Machine Guns (20mm)	16*

*The Air Defense Battalion was attached to the division from the Air Force.

APPENDIX B:
NOTATIONAL GERMAN *PANZER* DIVISION, 1935–1937

The first real German tank, the PzKpfw-IV, did not appear until 1936. The first *Panzer* divisions were formed in the fall of 1935 but were not fully operational until later in 1937. The students at the *Kriegsakademie* were using a notional *Panzer* division in their exercises and war games up through the end of 1937. The following structure was reported by Captain Harlan Hartness, who attended the *Kriegsakademie* as an American exchange officer from 1935 to 1937. [*Hartness Report*, pp. 48–50] This is virtually identical to the structure of the 1st *Panzer* Division as of 15 October 1935.

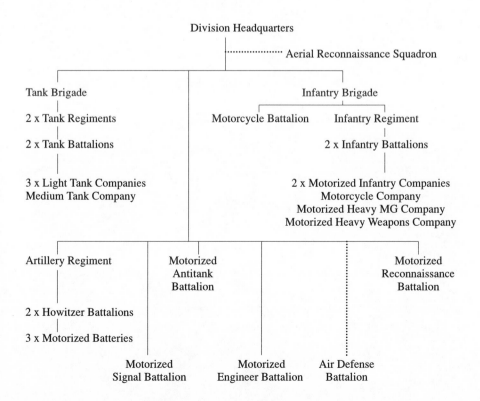

Armaments	
Tank Brigade	All Other Divisional Elements
416 Tanks	48 Heavy Machine Guns
748 Light Machine Guns	224 Light Machine Guns
153 20mm Machine Guns	22 20mm Machine Guns
6 37mm Guns 48	37mm Antitank Guns
52 75mm Guns	36 37mm AAA Guns*
	24 105mm Howitzers
	9 Reconnaissance Aircraft*

*Attached from the Air Force

APPENDIX C:
GERMAN DIVISIONAL STAFF, 1937–1938

Operations Division	Supply Division	Administrative Division
Ia, Operations Section	**Ib, Supply Section**	**IIa, Personnel Section**
1st General Staff Officer 1st *Ordonnanz* Officer Map Office	2nd General Staff Officer 2nd *Ordonnanz* Officer Infantry & Artillery Equipment Officer Ammunition Office Supply Trains Commander Baggage Train Commander Postmaster	Adjutant Assistant Adjutant*
Ic, Intelligence Section	**IVa, Administration Section**	**III, Legal Section**
Intelligence Officer 3rd *Ordonnanz* Officer Interpreters (2)*	*Intendant** Paymasters (2)* Ration Office Accounting Office	Judge Advocate* Legal Document Clerk
Advisors	**IVb, Medical Section**	**V, Chaplain Section**
Artillery Commander Engineer Commander Signal Commander Antitank Commander Air Defense Commander**	Division Surgeon Assistant Surgeon	Catholic Chaplain Protestant Chaplain
	IVc, Veterinary Section	**Headquarters Section**
	Veterinarian Assistant Veterinarian	HQ Commandant HQ Guard Commander Motorcycle Messenger Platoon

* *Beamter*
** When attached

At the divisional level the operations officer (Ia) usually was "dual hatted" as the chief of staff. Above the divisional level the two positions were separate. In the late 1930s a division normally had only two fully qualified general staff officers, the Ia and Ib. Sometimes the Ic also was a qualified general staff officer. The *Ordonannz* officers were senior staff officers, but not general-staff qualified. In some cases, they even might have completed the course of instruction at the *Kriegsakademie*, but yet failed to qualify for appointment at the end of their probationary period. The functional advisors in the Operations Division had command authority over their respective units. German military staffs also had a number of civil servants (*Beamter*) in key positions. The senior of these was the *Intendant*, who was the head of the IVa section.

APPENDIX D:
CONTENTS OF U.S. ARMY *FM 100-5*
FIELD SERVICE REGULATIONS:
OPERATIONS (1940)

Contents

APPENDIX E:
GERMAN ANALYSIS OF U.S. FIELD SERVICE REGULATIONS

Preface

The following study was undertaken by the Historical Division, Headquarters USAREUR, as a Department of the Army assignment. Its purpose was to secure from a panel of German experts a critical analysis and evaluation of the United States Army basic tactical doctrine as contained in the *Field Service Regulations (FM 100-5)* on Operations. The project was taken on by *Generaloberst* Franz Halder who in 1939–1942 was the Chief of the General Staff of the German Army. General Halder selected as his panel six distinguished members of the former German General Staff who had extensive expertise in the preparation of training literature, particularly that dealing with tactical doctrine, and who had proved their worth as commanders in combat. The panel freely consulted other general officers of the former German Army who were specialists in various fields such as armor, artillery, engineers, logistics, signal communications, airborne tactics, air forces, partisan warfare, and so on.

The methods generally employed by the panel included individual study of the manual in general, group discussions, assigned individual analysis of specific topics, further group conferences, and final decisions by *Generaloberst* Halder in doubtful cases. The report itself was prepared by General von Bechtelsheim under *Generaloberst* Halder's supervision; and although it incorporates much written material prepared by other members of the panel, the overall document must be credited generally to General Halder. The English translation was checked by General von Bechtelsheim, who, as a graduate of the U.S. Artillery School at Fort Sill and former German attaché in London, is bilingual and familiar with American military terminology.

Finally, after editing and review in the Historical Division, the study was submitted for comment to Brigadier General Einar Gjelsteen, Chief of Staff, Seventh Army, who when a member of the faculty at the Command

and General Staff School was associated with the preparation of a number of volumes of training literature, including FM 100-5. It was also reviewed by Brigadier General Douglas V. Johnson, G3 Headquarters USAREUR who has had extensive experience in the G3 field.

The end product, it is felt, is an exceptionally valuable document. The reader will appreciate that it is an event unique in military history when key members of the military forces of a recent antagonist assist the United States by furnishing freely their most carefully considered advice based on lessons learned in war against the next-most-probable enemy of the United States.

As an overall evaluation, *Generaloberst* Halder states that our manual is sound and well written, and that it will "stand up." The German panel was greatly impressed, but not surprised by the fact that FM 100-5 coincides closely with German doctrine. The reason for this is, of course, that both are based on the unchanging principles of war as enunciated by the great masters of the art. The reader will note, however, that the detailed criticism follows an up-to-date trend, discards outworn ideas freely, and in many respects is a complete denial of what many Americans have been thought to believe are "German" concepts. Whether the U.S. reader agrees with all that *Generaloberst* Halder and his panel assert, he must admit that their report is most stimulating and thought-provoking.

Foreword

In accordance with the suggestion made by the Chief of Military History, U.S. Government, on 28 February 1952, the U.S. Manual *Field Service Regulations: Operations,* Department of the Army *FM 100-5* has been subjected to a critical analysis by the undersigned German officers. As their standard of reference, they adopted the tactical views prevailing in the German General Staff until its dissolution in 1945, and the experience gained in World War II, particularly on the Eastern front.

Chapters 4 to 12 of the manual have been separately studied by each of the officers. Their findings were analyzed and thoroughly discussed during a series of conferences at which all the participants were present. The results were then coordinated. The resulting joint work appears in the following pages. It is presented as a single study because the interdependence of the individual chapters of the manual prevents separate consideration.

In appending their signatures, the officers certify that the study fully and accurately renders the substance of their ideas and they declare themselves in agreement with submission of the report in this form.

Frankfurt (Main), April 1953

Franz Halder,
Colonel General (ret)

Otto Stapf,
General of Infantry (ret)

Edgar Roehricht,
General of Infantry (ret)

Anton Freiherr von
Bechtelsheim
General of Artillery
(ret)

Alfred Kretschmer,
Lieutenant General (ret)
General Staff

Albert Zerbel,
Colonel (ret)

Hellmuth Schultz,
Colonel (ret)
General Staff

Part One: General Analysis

The manual represents a successful attempt to formulate the practical experience of World War II in clear, generally valid, rules. It provides a comprehensive survey of tactical problems in the conduct of operations, which may arise in a future war and furnishes practical guidance for solving them.

Since combat experience is often gained in differing circumstances, the general validity of the lessons to be drawn will frequently differ and may result in differences of opinion and suggestions for changes. Additionally, the contributions to 100-5, particularly those bearing on special fields, have been written by different authors and vary in quality. Consequently, this study will, itself, be somewhat uneven. Neither of these circumstances detracts from our overall impression, especially since the U.S. Army's superiority and worldwide experience in some technical fields must be unconditionally acknowledged.

In the following pages, when conflicting viewpoints are presented, they are accompanied by carefully reasoned suggestions for the practical solution of the problem in accordance with the purpose of this analysis. In the main, our experiences were gained in combat against an opponent who also deserves close attention with reference to the future. It is therefore believed that the lessons drawn from these experiences constitute a useful contribution.

Chapter 1: General Principles

In addition to providing practical principles and views on command and combat, an army manual has an important training task. This training aspect has been consciously given precedence here.

For the German command the main objectives of leadership training were as follows:

a. A great capacity for independent action on all levels of command.
b. Adherence to the mission: that is, a moral obligation to act at all times in the spirit of the assigned mission.
c. Avoidance of a fixed pattern of action.
d. The ability to make "complete," that is clear and unambiguous decisions and, in carrying them out, to establish a definite point of main effort.
e. A constant concern for the welfare of the men and the conservation of their combat efficiency.

I. Basic Ideas

1. One the most important tasks of a manual on operations is the training of all grades of officers to be willing to accept responsibility and to act independently.

2. Uniformity of doctrine is a prerequisite of independent action within the overall operational framework. If, however, doctrine is uniform and a subordinate commander has, accordingly, been given freedom to act in the spirit of his mission, then any additional instructions hamper his initiative. The manual frequently attempts to foresee or forestall possible developments in a combat situation by the use of an order and to arrange details in advance. This tendency cramps the initiative of a commander who, being on the spot, has a better chance of assessing the situation. Thus, it robs the troops of one of the major prerequisites of success. For instance, to make every single decision to withdraw from a sector of the front dependent on permission from the immediate superior is unjustifiable and conducive to irresolution.

According to our experience, the method of assigning broad missions is the best, provided a trained officer corps is available. According to this method, clear and unambiguous missions are assigned, but their execution is the responsibility of the subordinate commander. As a result it may be said that "Orders should confine themselves to what is necessary to achieve their objective."

3. In the past, successful leadership required personalities of outstand-

ing competence and strength of character. Today, however, in accordance with the character of modern warfare, the circle of those entrusted with responsibility has been widened appreciably. Aside from the responsibility of the commander, there is now the responsibility of the individual combatant. In former times, the combatant's lack of assurance could be overcome through drills in association with others, but today he has to depend exclusively upon himself and on his own skill in critical moments. For that reason, the manual should stress, in pertinent sections that even in peacetime, the development of individual combatants, able to cope with the situations of modern warfare, should be one of the major objectives of training. In spite of all the advances of technology, the value of the individual combatant is still the decisive factor.

4. In the consequences of superiority in matériel, the manual often presents the solution of difficult problems as being too simple. It should be pointed out that the conditions which favored the U.S. Army during the final phase of the war in Europe, the influence of which is apparent in the manual, cannot be taken as a norm for the future. It may therefore be wise to train all officers, down to company commander, with regard to situations in which they cannot draw freely on resources. The manual should take this into account. Moreover, war is full of imponderables and surprises. Only a commander who can depend on his own ingenuity and that of his men will be able to make the improvisations dictated by the moment and master situations not described in the manuals. True, in order to do this, he will have to know exactly what it is he wants to do.

Although the following principle is mentioned in the text, it should be brought out more strongly, and at the beginning of the manual:

"Every individual from the highest commander to the lowest private must always remember that inaction and neglect of opportunities will warrant more severe censure than an error of judgement in the action taken." This principle deserves more emphasis.

5. The attempt to find a solution for every single situation, which may confront the lower echelons, occasionally results in a cut-and-dried "recipe" which is far more detailed than needed.

An example of this is the requirement that attacks be divided in principle into main and secondary attacks. Thoroughly worked-out fire plans secure a maximum effect: they are, accordingly, of the highest importance in both attack and defense. Nevertheless, the tendency to have them prepared in advance for the next phase in the battle prevents the independent decision making which is necessary to take quick advantage of an unexpected opportunity. The same applies to "security requirements," which are often exaggerated and frequently cause adherence to a plan which takes priority over the accomplishment of the mission. The principle to be stressed here is that any sort of cut-and-dried planning inhibits initiative.

6. The understandable effort to obtain as complete as possible a picture of the enemy and his intentions must not impair the ability to act boldly in situations which have not been clarified. What matters is the mission and the will to carry it out successfully. Flexibility in the selection of means and in execution is often necessary.

II. Principles of Command

1. A conspicuous feature of the manual is its overrating of the offensive as a form of combat, even in situations where this does not appear wholly justified.

The incentive for attack lies in the psychological advantage of gaining the initiative. This is one of the secrets of military success and has always been stressed by the German General Staff, as it is in this manual. Nevertheless we are opposed to elevating the offensive to the level of a dogma and to any exaggeration which teaches "attack at any price." We do not underestimate daring and boldness in action, but we do not want an officer who is uncertain about his next move to be misled into taking refuge in attack just because attack is "more soldierly."

2. According to the manual, the defensive is justified only when it permits attack elsewhere. This concept, though not overvaluing the attack, underestimates the defensive as a form of combat: although in a larger context the defensive may well be an end in itself. The manual regards the defensive as a passive form of combat, in contrast to the active form. In our opinion this is not a sound distinction. The defensive imposes one's will on the enemy indirectly, preventing him from carrying out his intentions. According to Clausewitz, it has the advantage of being the stronger form of combat. True, depending on the current status of the continual contest between defensive and offensive weapons, this concept will not always seem so impressive. It will, nevertheless, remain valid for the foreseeable future, especially if we bring out more sharply in our manuals the hitherto unstressed difference between a systematically prepared defense and defense ad hoc, which often results involuntarily from the clash of two forces. This argument does not invalidate the German view: that the defensive leads to decisive success only if it ends in an attack.

3. In both forms of combat—the attack and the defensive—depth is in most cases a prerequisite of success. As long as it is present the commander has freedom of action.

4. Nowhere in the manual is the concept of tying down the enemy given enough prominence. In many cases, however, ability to contain the enemy with weak forces is the prerequisite to a decisive blow.

5. As an army manual, *FM 100-5,* just as did our own prewar service

regulations, overlooks the presence of a civilian population inhabiting the combat area. It contents itself to consideration of buildings, traffic installations, etc. In these days of widespread philosophical divergences, however, the population of an area touched by war, be they friendly or hostile, will create problems not only for the higher command but also for the combat force, and which may even affect the tactical level of command. They must be prepared for this. Aside from such hindrances as the mass flight of civilians, problems of supply, and similar considerations, the main problem is that of coping with partisan warfare. Today, a service manual must cover this aspect in full. The exposition under "Special Operations" is too restricted, and touches only surface matters. In no way does it do justice to the importance of the problem.

6. The psychological aspect of operations is not everywhere given its due. This applies not only to sections like that in Chapter 10 where, in the discussion of withdrawal, a special "psychological paragraph" is deemed necessary. We believe that a manual on operations should include specific psychological operations. For instance, in spite of all technological progress, the physical and combative demands made on the infantry today are among the heaviest and most difficult to satisfy. (An example is the individual soldier fighting a tank, at close range, with a bazooka.) Accordingly, on psychological grounds, an operations manual designed particularly for the infantry should arouse the pride of the infantry by stressing their importance and the nature of their contribution.

Psychological warfare is not actually a part of the mission of combat forces. Yet with respect to the civilian population of a theater of operations it may have importance for frontline troops. Mistakes in the treatment of the inhabitants of such a region may have far-reaching repercussions involving the troops, especially in conjunction with a partisan problem.

Chapter 2: Tactics

I. In the future, more than up to now, marches and movements of all types will be undertaken mainly at night. This has not been made clear enough in the manual. On the other hand, night combat, especially by infantry, has certain limitations, which can be circumvented to some extent by intensive training but which cannot be altogether set aside. We feel that the paragraphs of the manual dealing with night attacks substantially overestimate the actual possibilities of such combat and success by compact units.

II. It seems to us that the importance given in the manual to relief while an action is still under way is out of all proportion to the part it actually plays. The impetus derived from rested troops cannot be denied, but the *timing* of relief requires careful consideration. Relief is best executed at the end of a phase of the fighting: during attack, after the capture of an objective. Experience shows that premature relief paralyzes aggressiveness.

During a pitched battle, the familiarity of troops with the enemy and the terrain often outweighs, in importance, the increase in strength that fresh forces would represent. A firm attitude with respect to a desire to be relieved sometimes pays.

III. The manual should not assume that the enemy will fight according to the principles prevailing on the friendly side. In this connection some suggestions concerning combat against the Russians have been appended to individual chapters. These suggestions include large-scale infiltration on weak fronts; instances where the defender's infantry allows itself to be overrun during a tank attack; selection, for decisive action, of an unaccustomed time of day and a terrain which the enemy is unfamiliar; shelling by artillery and bombing by ground-attack aircraft, especially on the area occupied by the enemy infantry; and separation of enemy assault infantry from its accompanying tanks as a condition of successful defense against combined attacks.

IV. There are passages in the manual which give the impression that the infantry division is underestimated as an attack force, even when it is effectively supported by artillery, organic armor, and air forces. Apparently, according to the manual, even an attack against a well-organized, strongly defended battle position should be conducted only by armor. We feel that against a position of this sort, with its minefields and tank obstacles, the attack should in general employ infantry divisions, at least at first.

V. A weakness for pattern-type planning is shown by the tendency to retain the outworn concepts of an outpost system regulated in every detail (an idea one hundred years old) and march security. Both concepts are obsolete and have been made so by extensive motorization, aircraft, and radio. Adaptation to the given situation is necessary.

VI. Throughout the manual, two concepts of close cooperation are presented: "teamwork," in small actions, and "coordination" in large-scale operations.

In stressing "teamwork," that is, the importance of a group which has practiced working as a unit, the value of training the individual should not be overlooked, since the individual is the key to every team.

"Coordination" is a duty that devolves upon all commanders who are to carry out a task jointly. In places the manual gives the impression that the initiative for this coordination is left to the subordinate agencies themselves, working together. On the contrary, except in routine missions, it must be the order issued by the superior commander that first sets forth the extent and limitations of coordination.

VII. In discussions of attack and defense, not enough importance is given to shifting the point of main effort as a means for flexible conduct of operations.

The concept and employment of "ammunition tactics" is missing. This concept involves increasing the allocation of ammunition to assist in establishing a center of gravity and to restore the balance of forces, for example, on a front weakened in men and weapons.

Chapter 3: Field Service Regulations—Technical

I. A manual should avoid anything that may be misinterpreted. It is impossible to overestimate the importance of a fixed standard nomenclature and terminology, and of clearly defined and universally understood concepts always used in an identical sense.

It is our impression that the list of expressions currently in use in the U.S. Army needs considerable expansion in order to achieve clear-cut differentiation between tactical concepts which are similar but not identical.

Examples follow:

War of movement (*Bewegungskrieg*)	Static front (*erstarrte Front*)
The defensive (*Abwehr*)	The defense (*Verteidigung*) *
Delaying action (*hinhaltendes Gefecht*)	Delaying defense (*hinhaltender Widerstand*)
Wings (*Flügel*)	Flanks (*Flanke*)
Envelopment (*Umfassung*)	Outflanking (U*mgehung*)
Counterthrust (*Gegenstoss*)	Counterattack (*Gegenangriff*)
Unit (*Einheit*)	Unit (*Verband*) †

II. The manual is concerned almost wholly with command and combat of the infantry division as "the basis of organization of the ground field forces." To aid understanding, it would be desirable for this statement, together with a justification, to be placed at the beginning of the manual rather than in the final chapter.

III. Understanding of the manual is made more difficult by the fact

---

* [Original Footnote]According to German concepts the defensive includes defense and delaying action. The latter includes delaying defense and delaying attack.
† [Original Footnote]The German term *Einheit* refers to companies and batteries. *Verband* refers to battalions, regiments and divisions.

that its paragraphs jump, without transition and without definite indication, from discussions of large-scale actions to discussions of small engagements.

IV. In many instances the text could be shortened by continuing a train of thought through a number of paragraphs, making subsequent repetition unnecessary.

V. The manual discuss "delaying action" (which uses space as a weapon and thereby attempts to weaken the enemy with all the means available) very briefly and only as a adjunct of defense, although additional references are distributed over other chapters. In conformity with the importance of delaying action it would be more appropriate for a special chapter to be devoted to it as a distinct form of combat.

VI. A basic service manual on operations should avoid making reference in the text to other manuals. It must express what it has to say itself so that it can be understood without other manuals. If reference to a more complete discussion in another manual is necessary, a footnote should be used.

VII. From the German viewpoint the appendix titled "Lessons of the Pearl Harbor Attack" does not properly belong in *FM 100-5.*

SELECTED BIBLIOGRAPHY

Balck, Hermann, *Ordnung im Chaos*, (Osnabrück, Germany: 1981).

Beck, Ludwig, *Studien*, Hans Speidel, ed., (Frankfurt, Germany: 1956).

Behrehdt, Hans, *Rommel's Intelligence in the Desert Campaign*, (London: 1985).

Blumentritt, Guenther, V*on Rundstet, The Soldier and the Man*, (London: 1952).

Citino, Robert M., *The Path to Blitzkrieg: Doctrine and Training in the German Army, 1920–1939*, (Boulder, Colo.: 1999).

Clausewitz, Carl von, *On War*, Michael Howard and Peter Paret trans. and eds. (Princeton, N.J.: 1976).

Corum, James S., *The Roots of Blitzkrieg: Hans von Seeckt and German Military Reform*, (Lawrence, Kan.: 1992).

Creveld, Martin van, *Fighting Power: German and U.S. Army Performance, 1939-1945*, (Westport, Conn.: 1982).

Dupuy, Trevor N., *A Genius for War: The German Army and the General Staff, 1807–1945*, (Englewood Cliffs, N.J.: 1977.)

Förster, Jürgen, "The Dynamics of Volksgemeinschaft: Effectiveness of the German Military Establishment in the Second World War," in *Military Effectiveness, Volume III, The Second World War*, Allan R. Millet and Williamson Murray, eds., (London: 1988).

Görlitz, Walter, *The German General Staff, 1657–1945*, (London: 1953).

Griffith, Paddy, *Forward into Battle: Fighting Tactics From Waterloo to the Near Future*, (Novato, Calif.: 1990).

Guderian, Heinz, *Achtung—Panzer!* (London: 1992).

Guderian, Heinz, *Panzer Leader*, (London: 1952).

Gudmundsson, Bruce I. *Stormtroop Tactics: Innovation in the German Army, 1914-1918*, (Westport, Conn.: 1989).

Halder, Franz: *Generaloberst Halder Kriegstagebuch*, (Stuttgart: 1957).

Hartness, Harlan N., "Report No. 15,260, Report on the German General Staff School, Staff Methods, and Tactical Doctrine," National Archives and Record Administration, Record Group 165, Box 1113, (3 May 1937) (the *Hartness Report*).

Hughes, Daniel J., ed., *Moltke on the Art of War: Selected Writings*, (Novato, Calif.: 1993).

Kesselring, Albert, *A Soldier's Record,* (New York: 1953).

Leeb, Wilhelm von, *Die Abwehr*, (Berlin: 1938).

Liddell Hart, Basil H., *The Other Side of the Hill*, (London: 1951).

Liddell Hart, Basil H., ed., *The Rommel Papers*, (London: 1953).

Lupfer, Timothy, *The Dynamics of Doctrine: The Changes in German Tactical Doctrine During the First World Wa*r, (Leavenworth, Kan.: 1981).

Macksey, Kenneth, *The Tank Pioneers*, (London: 1981).

Manstein, Erich von, *Lost Victories*, (London: 1958).

Megargee, Geoffrey P., *Inside Hitler's High Command*, (Lawrence, Kan.: 2000).

Mellenthin, F.W. von, *Panzer Battles: A Study in the Employment of Armor in the Second World War,* (Norman, Okla.: 1956).

Murray, Williamson, "Leading the Troops: A German Manual of 1933," *Marine Corps Gazette,* (September 1999), pp. 95–97.

Naveh, Shimon, *In Pursuit of Military Excellence: The Evolution of Operational Theory,* (London: 1997).

Newton, Steve H., *German Battle Tactics on the Eastern Front*, (Atglen, Pa.: 1994).

Rommel, Erwin, *Attacks*, (Vienna, Va.: 1979).

Rosinski, Herbert, *The German Army*, (Washington: 1944).

Simpkin, Richard, *Race to the Swift: Thoughts on Twenty-first Century Warfare*, (London: 1985).

United States Army, *Field Manual 100-5, Operations*, (Washington, D.C.: 1986, 1993).

United States War Department, *Field Manual 100-5, Field Service Regulations: Operations,* (Washington, D.C.: 1941, 1944).

United States War Department, *Technical Manual-E 30-451, Handbook on German Military Forces,* (Washington, D.C.: 1945).

Wallach, Jeduha L., *The Dogma of the Battle of Annihilation: The Theories of Clausewitz and Schlieffen and Their Impact on the German Conduct of Two World Wars,* (Westport, Conn.: 1986).

Warlimont, Walter, *Inside Hitler's Headquarters 1939–45,* (London: 1964).

Wedemeyer, Albert C., "Report No. 15,999, German General Staff School," National Archives and Record Administration, Record Group 165, Box 1113, (4 August 1938) (the *Wedemeyer Report*).

Westphal, Siegfried, *The German Army in the West,* (London: 1951).

Zabecki, David T., *Steel Wind: Colonel Georg Bruchmüller and the Birth of Modern Artillery,* (Westport, Conn.: 1994).

INDEX

The numbers in this index refer to the paragraph numbers within the text.